TRANSFORMATION
&REVELATION

UK DESIGN
FOR PERFORMANCE
2007–2011

Published in Great Britain by
The Society of British Theatre Designers
Theatre Design Dept
Rose Bruford College of Theatre & Performance
Burnt Oak Lane
Sidcup
DA15 9DF

Registered Charity No. 800638

Text copyright © 2011

ISBN 978−0−9529309−5−2 (1)

British Library Cataloguing in Publication Data:
a catalogue record of this book is available from
the British Library.

Design and typography by Stephan Hammes

Edited by Greer Crawley

Co-edited by Peter Farley and Sophie Jump

Produced by Blattler ltd

Photographs and Illustrations are by the
contributing designers unless otherwise stated.

Information in this catalogue has been provided
by contributing designers and is published in
good faith.

Thanks are due to the following for their
inspiration and practical help:

Stephan Hammes – catalogue designer
Daniel Blattler – production management
Neil Attrell – typesetting
David Brown – reprographics
Sean Crowley – exhibition designer, Cardiff
Holly McCarthy – assistant exhibition designer,
	Cardiff
Michael Spencer – schools exhibition designer
Kay Denyer – exhibition administrator
Ian Evans – technical director
Carolyn Davies – education officer
Alice Cabanas – marketing manager
Patricia Grasham – PQ and V&A exhibition
	co-designer with Peter Farley
Nick Moran – student exhibit
Alex Turnpenny – student exhibit
Dawn Prentice – Sadler's Wells
Leila Ransley – Sadler's Wells
Colin Maxwell – Royal Opera House
David Pritchard – Royal Opera House
Nick Hunt – Rose Bruford College of Theatre
	& Performance
Barbara Eifler, Sally Palmer and Kim Hart at the
	Stage Management Association
The Theatres Trust
Kate Bailey
Ros Morley
Martin Morley
Peter Ruthven Hall
Kate Burnett
The committee of the Society of British
	Theatre Designers
The many technicians, staff and students at
	the Royal Welsh College of Music & Drama
	who worked on the Cardiff exhibition

Transformation & Revelation draws on the
resources and membership of the following
organisations, which include theatre designers,
technicians and architects:

The Society of British Theatre Designers
The Association of Lighting Designers
Equity
The Association of Courses in Theatre Design
The Society of Theatre Consultants

The Society of British Theatre Designers
is deeply grateful to all the sponsors, from
private individuals to large organisations, who
have made this exhibition, its catalogue and
programme of educational events possible.

Sincere thanks are due to:

Rose Bruford College of Theatre & Performance
Royal Welsh College of Music & Drama
Wimbledon College of Art
Buckinghamshire New University
V&A Museum
Linbury Trust
White Light
ShowTex
Arts Council Wales
Welsh Assembly

Transformation & Revelation is dedicated to the
memories of Stefanos Lazaridis (1942–2010)
and Patrick Robertson (1922–2009).

*The Society of British Theatre
Designers was founded in 1975
by John Bury, with Ralph Koltai,
Nicholas Georgiadis and Timothy
O'Brien. It started life with the object
of deciding on the most appropriate
union to negotiate for designers. Since
then it has developed and diversified
and now has a wide membership.
It aims to enhance the standing of
British theatre design at home and
abroad in many different ways. One of
these is to organise, every four years,
an exhibition of theatre design which,
in part, represents Britain at the
International Quadrennial in Prague.
It also arranges seminars and forums
for discussion and development of
professional practice. The Society
puts designers in touch with one
another and with those working in
theatre in other countries.*

**The Society of
British Theatre Designers**
Theatre Design Dept
Rose Bruford College of
Theatre & Performance
Burnt Oak Lane
Sidcup
DA15 9DF
admin@theatredesign.org.uk
www.theatredesign.org.uk

As joint Honorary Secretaries of the SBTD since 2008 we are immensely proud of the progress achieved by the Society since its inception in 1975. Over the years the Society has been fortunate to have been led by a succession of dedicated Honorary Secretaries and Committee members who have all worked determinedly to explore, further and promote the role of the performance designer within the arts.

When the baton was handed to us in 2008 we had many aims, but we were particularly keen for the society to act as a hub for the sharing of information between designers who typically work in isolation from other designers. The new website, launched in 2009, enhances the image of the SBTD and its membership, providing each professional member a full gallery page, biography and contact facility. The website is also the only database of UK designers and, as such, acts as a first point of contact for the surrounding professions both nationally and internationally. In addition to the quarterly journal, the *Blue Pages*, members receive regular E-updates highlighting relevant information, opportunities for employment and engagement with industry related research and professional development. Membership has now reached a level not seen before and exhibition places were very much in demand resulting in the largest national exhibition ever!

The emphasis in this 2011 national exhibition, *Transformation & Revelation* is very much on exploration and the processes engaged in by designers as collaborative theatre makers, and we hope that you will share in our admiration and appreciation for the remarkable diversity displayed in imaginative thought and creative skill.

Looking back over the 35 years, performance design has evolved rapidly and often unpredictably. Now, at the beginning of this second decade of the 21st century, the performance designer, in partnership with our theatre-maker colleagues, looks forward to conceiving and challenging expectations in the new visions yet to be seen in live performance.

*Sophie Jump and Iona McLeish
Joint Honorary Secretaries, SBTD*

THE LINBURY PRIZE

For Stage Design

The Linbury Trust is pleased, once again, to be able to support the Society of British Theatre Designers in a Prague Quadrennial year. The Trust wishes the SBTD and all its exhibitors every success, not only in Prague, but also in the related exhibitions elsewhere in the UK, both before and after the Quadrennial itself.

The Linbury Trust was established in 1973 by Lord Sainsbury of Preston Candover, KG (John Sainsbury), and his wife Anya, Lady Sainsbury, CBE, the former ballerina Anya Linden. The trustees of the Linbury Trust make grants to charitable organisations and causes across a broad range of categories, including the arts; education; environment and heritage; medical; social welfare and developing countries. Linbury is particularly associated with support for the arts.

The Linbury Trust has supported theatre design in the UK for many years, not only through its direct support for the SBTD, but, most significantly, through its sponsorship of the Linbury Prize for Stage Design. This biennial prize, the most important of its kind in the UK, brings together the cream of emerging designers with professional theatre, dance and opera companies. Each of the four winners of each biennial competition receives a cash prize together with a professional commission to design a production for a major company. Companies that have collaborated with the prize in recent years include Birmingham Opera, Headlong, Random Dance, Theatre Royal Northampton, and the Young Vic.

More information on the Linbury Prize for Stage Design can be found at http://www.nationaltheatre.org.uk/46857/home/linbury-prize.html

THE
LINBURY
TRUST

Contents

Preface
SOPHIE JUMP

George Souglides: Kumudha transformed,
John Adams' *A Flowering Tree*,
Harris Theatre, Chicago, USA, 2008.
Photographer: Brian Dickie

One of the struggles faced in our line of work is labelling. Do we call ourselves theatre designers or scenographers? Is it craft or art? Can I call myself a theatre designer if I don't design performances that take place in a theatre? Am I a designer if I organise the performance space and its use but don't design anything that is physically placed in that space? Am I a scenographer if I design only one aspect of the performance?

No matter what we choose to call ourselves, there are many different kinds of designer and we work in many different kinds of environments, but we all have some basic concerns in common; the audience/performer relationship, where a performance can happen, suggesting themes, atmosphere, character, time scale, location and period, and proscribing and allowing movement. This is done through the organisation/ manipulation of, or creation of, space, costume, props, light and sound.

All aspects that go into performance need to be understood and explored by designers; they need to think like directors, writers, performers and audience. They need to be creative yet practical, able to both work in a team and to create and communicate ideas that inspire others.

Designing a production is a complex process. In most cases designers create models and technical drawings, costume drawings and storyboards, but not always. Sometimes the process is more direct, trying things out, making and adjusting as the rehearsals progress. Quite often it is a mixture of both. But in every case the drawings, objects, models, lists and references which are created, no matter how polished and complete or how scruffy and fragmented, are working tools intended to describe and communicate the world which the production will inhabit and convey, how to transform the performers and the space in order to reveal the meaning of the performance. They are also a fascinating glimpse into the mind of the designer!

However, getting designers to recognise the interest that others have for these 'working tools' can be difficult, and it seems this is not a new phenomenon. The following is from the catalogue introduction to a 1934 exhibition of theatre design called *Theatre Art*:

'It was almost staggering to find artists completely indifferent to the need of exhibiting their work. Much of it I had to dig out of cupboards and old portfolios. It was difficult to get many of the designers to go to the expense of mounting these loose leaves. Framing in most cases was out of the question. Picasso told me he couldn't be bothered to look for the designs of *Le Tricorne*.' (Lee Simonson)

The designers in this catalogue have taken time to consider the work they have produced over the previous four years, to root around in cupboards and portfolios, to choose the images and repair the models, to write about them in this catalogue and to exhibit them alongside costumes and other objects. By committing themselves to this process they have given themselves and us the opportunity to reflect on their work.

Curator's Perspective
PETER FARLEY

Richard Hudson, *Rushes – Fragments of a Lost Story*
Royal Opera House, 2008.
Photography: Royal Opera House.

Apart from a few notable exceptions – usually well-known painters, sculptors, architects or fashion designers – the theatre-going public are rarely aware of the identity of the designer or, indeed, the full extent of his or her role in the creation of a work of theatre. Seldom referred to by theatre critics, the design, when it is mentioned, is often attributed to the director. The Society of British Theatre Designers has sought to redress this balance by staging a national exhibition of Design for Performance every four years. This exhibition was initially motivated by the cycle of the Prague Quadrennial (PQ) – the international exhibition of design for performance attended by over 50 countries. Designers are selected from the national exhibition to represent the United Kingdom at PQ. The Society has over 400 members that range from highly successful, well-established designers to new designers just embarking on their careers. The national exhibition is open for participation to all members.

When curating an open exhibition of this sort, it is important to provide a theme which is flexible enough to include the increasingly wide range of theatre genres from drama, dance, opera and musical theatre to site-specific, experiential and immersive performance and, at the same time, specific enough to create a journey through a wide range of work, with text and questions that stimulate a dialogue with the work on display. Among the questions I wanted to ask were: How do designers create visual narrative? How do they use the transformation of structures and costumes to take us on a visual journey? What is the dialogue between the designers and their collaborators involved in this progression? I concluded that, working from the premise that the function of design is not merely to illustrate the performed text, music or movement, but to provide a further layer of visual narrative, it is not only the job of the director but also that of the designer to make us ask: "What am I going to see next? What will be revealed?' It is through this process of constant visual and aural transformation and revelation that we experience a work of theatre. Hence the title: *Transformation & Revelation.*

Furthermore, I wanted to ask: What is the function of an exhibition of design for performance? Is it trying to somehow recreate the productions on display through models, drawings, photographs and objects? Surely this is not possible, as a work of theatre only exists in the moment it is being experienced by the spectator and requires not only the design but every other component of its live, multi-layered self – text, sound, light, performers and audience – to complete the scenographic experience. So, I ask again, what are we trying to exhibit? What are we trying to reveal?

To answer this question I started to think again about the theatre designer as a 'backstage' person – literally (the power) 'behind the scenes' in every sense. I would venture that one reason for this is the notion of the 'magic of theatre' – that moment when 'the curtain goes up' (or used to go up) and the scene is revealed. The idea that what we as designers want to reveal at that moment is a visual fait accompli – an unveiling which is then given life by carefully visualised performers moving through time in constant transformation. It must look effortless.

Ben Stones, *An Enemy of the People*,
Sheffield Crucible, 2010.

artists need to exhibit their work in order to move on to the next phase, a designer needs a 'first night' in order to do the same. Once the creation is shared with or given away to the audience it is time to move onto the next project, which will act as a vehicle to carry forward the designer's visual preoccupations, and it is these which define their 'style' at various points in their career. A good example in this exhibition is Richard Hudson's design for Kim Brandstrup's ballet *Rushes*, where Hudson is further exploring the use of aluminium beaded curtains as a transformative device in much the same way as gauzes have been traditionally used using light to reveal or conceal a space beyond, except in this instance the innovation is that the performers can actually move through the 'gauze'. This is one of a multitude of visual explorations that Hudson has continuously developed from one production to another, whether opera, dance, drama or musical theatre.

Bearing in mind that nothing exhibited is the final product – the final product is the live performance – but merely a means to communicate the visual possibilities of it, models and drawings that, in many cases, are beautiful in their own right, are, nevertheless, made for a specific purpose and are not an end in themselves but a means of communication. It is easy to be seduced by a perfectly-made scale model or a beautiful drawing, and it could be said that part of their function is indeed to seduce directors and performers into embracing an idea and also to inspire costume makers and set builders. However, a perfectly-made scale model, such as Ben Stones' sombre designs for Ibsen's *An Enemy of the People*, or Paul Brown's striking staging of *Die Gezeichneten*, requires accurate and inspired interpretation by prop makers, set builders and painters, in collaboration with the designer, to give the objects, structures and surfaces specific qualities that are in keeping with the designer's style and intention, thereby accurately communicating the atmosphere of the production.

No one must know how it got there. It must just appear. This led to the thought that it would, perhaps, be interesting to exhibit not only the final designs but also, where possible, preparatory drawings and other work that demonstrate the designers' journey through ideas and working process, the transformation of concepts into reality – to start to allow the spectator a glimpse of who a designer actually is and how he or she thinks.

Like any artist, creativity is a continuous process that is occasionally punctuated by the product, which, in the theatre designer's case, is the production, and it is this that forms the vital focus and catharsis necessary to stop for a moment, reflect – and then continue the work. Just as fine

Paul Brown, *Die Gezeichneten*,
Teatro Massimo di Palermo, 2010.

Marie-Jeanne Lecca, *Agrippina*,
Operhaus, Zürich, 2009.
Photographer: Suzanne Schwietz.

Similarly, between the two-dimensional character drawing and the actual realisation of the character on stage, comes a further phase of the design process – that of interpretation. This development is very clearly revealed in Marie-Jeanne Lecca's costume drawings and production photographs for Handel's *Agrippina* for Zurich, where one can clearly see how the design of the black dress has been interpreted, not simply as black ruffled dress, but in a way that embodies the energy and verve of the drawing itself, and therefore an aspect of the character of Agrippina also. The collaboration between designer, costume maker and supervisor is crucial in helping the performer to make the character come alive.

Because of the large number of exhibitors and the enormous range of work, an overall concept of the transformation from light to dark has been used in the design of the catalogue. It was felt that there should be no specific division into themed sections or genres. This decision was made because it was considered that categorisation of types of work and definitions of specialisms were becoming more and more indistinct in contemporary professional theatre design practice and, for the purposes of this exhibition, we wanted the work to be about the theatre artist as an individual rather than being categorised as, say, a designer for dance or opera or drama.

I have cited just three or four examples of the many excellent ways in which the theme of *Transformation & Revelation* has been used by the designers in this exhibition to reveal the myriad strands of visual and aural thought that combine and interact to generate the scenographic experience. In this way, it is hoped that we would be able to bring the designer for performance out from behind the scenes and reveal his or her vision as an essential collaborator and contributor in the creation of a work of theatre and also to show that design is not simply about clothes and scenery but is primarily concerned with the careful layering and interpretation of inspired visual ideas.

when everything is working well, something mysterious happens... that isn't just the sum of the component parts. It can spring from the obviously fantastical and from the most minutely described realism... But something happens, and everything is transformed. We could use a scientific term like emergence for this process, or we could use an older word and call it sorcery... that strange and inexplicable thing is what the theatre is for.

Philip Pullman[1]

1   Pullman. P. 'Let's Pretend'. *The Guardian*. 24 November 2004.

Transformations
(from being in this way to being in that)
is one of categories of primary feats
of magic listed in S H Sharpe's book
Neomagic, *first published in 1932.*

Others include:

Productions
(from not being to being),

Disappearances
(from being to not being),

Transpositions
(from being here to being there), and

Natural Science Laws Disobeyed
(antigravity, magical animation,
magical control, matter through matter,
multiposition, restoration, invulnerability,
and rapid germination).[2]

Contemporary design for performance is full of dissolves and fades, appearances and disappearances, apparitions and conversions. Transformation scenes, Pepper's Ghosts, the mirrors, traps and other stage mechanics are being reinvented and redeployed in analogue and digital form to bring about the revelation of body, space, sound, light, objects. Translucent gauzes, painted silks, digital screens and wallpaper are among the scenographic materials of transformation and revelation.

The architect Peter Zumthor, in *Sounding Body*, specified the formula for spatial and atmospheric transformation as:

> energy > theatricality (*mise en scene*) > materials
mutually charging each other > text projection > stage direction
> drinking and eating[3]

It is an equation that links the practices of the theatre designer, alchemist and cook.

2   Sharpe, S H (1932), *Neomagic*. London: George Johnson, p.41.

3   Zumthor, P (2000), *Klangkörperbuch*. Basel: Birkhäuser, p.18.

Theatre design like cooking is a form of alchemy and the correspondence seems to have been intuitively recognised by many of these designers in their adoption of culinary metaphors. There are references to domestic and industrial fridges, food diaries, cake stands, tinned tomatoes, onions, knives, meat and peas.

Observing images of cut tomatoes… thinking of kitchen knives (**VERENA LEO**).

This culinary inspiration seems more than coincidental and suggests a natural empathy between the alchemists of the theatre and the kitchen. The designer's studio like the alchemist's laboratory and the kitchen is a place of sensation, experiment and experiences.

There is a process that occurs, much like peeling an onion (**SIMON BANHAM**).

Time, temperatures, odours and imaginings are part of the reality of cooking and design for performance. Matter is moulded, shrunk and shaped; substances are revealed. Material is aggressively acted upon: manipulated and manoeuvred, torn, shredded, cut, strung, pulled, thrown, battered. Through the alchemists' activities and actions, the stage becomes *scenically charged* (**JOHN PAWSON**), a canvas on which materials and *movement is spilt, flung, dripped and scraped* (**KIMIE NAKANO**).

Hydraulics, pixels and lumens, canvas, gauze, decibels, paint, plywood, rope, fluorescence, sodium, tungsten, chemicals, glues are the sceno–graphic equivalents of the alchemists' minerals and salts.

A tiny spark became a flame (**MICHAEL PAVELKA**), causing changes in states, combustion, explosion. On this *the chaotic stage* (**SARAH BACON**) there are *scenic collisions* (**SIMON KENNY**). Elements are *added, tested and subtracted* (**LARA FURNISS**). Structures and surfaces evolve. The properties of matter and mathematics are explored. Formulae are applied: the Fibonacci series, physical geometry, $E=mc^2$.

Peter Mumford, *E=mc²*, Birmingham Hippodrome Theatre, 2009.

The alchemists perfect the matter on which they work through transmutation. Through the processes of distillation and sublimation, experiment and experience, an exchange takes place: things materialise, vapourise, liquidise, solidify. Mixing together whatever is at hand, the methodology is improvisational. From the immaterial, the combinatorics, the 'try this' and the 'what ifs', the measurements and metaphorical ingredients, the designers invent or evoke the substances of their enchantments.

It was layered and dense, with its many references conveyed to the audience through video and live projection, an electro-acoustic soundscape, voice-over, slides, x-rays, pyrotechnics, tinned tomatoes, a horse's head and many other props (**SARAH BACON**).

The evidence of alchemical transformation is pervasive amongst our designers. Worlds are shrunk to the size of fish tanks (**CHLOE LAMFORD**) and Bakelite radios (**PAUL BARRETT**) and suitcase museums (**FIONA WATT**). Actors assume a variety of disguises and undergo numerous transformations to become stage animals and vice versa. *A goldfish played the part of the crowd and the performing horse was played, appropriately, by a lab rat* (**FRED MELLER**). A character is transformed *into the sofa itself '* (**RYSZARD ANDRZEJEWSKI**).

These designers investigate materials and processes to achieve a range of ends. **SHIZUKA HARIU** finds that *a new hybrid material from aluminium and cotton gave roughness and deepness on the stage.* Materials are selected carefully, with consideration for their performativity and resonance. *The concept came directly from a helmet and a field of peas* (**LARA FURNISS**). When the material imagination is creatively employed, poetic objects are created and the choices of props, set dressing, furniture or clothes, costume, hair and make-up are revelatory.

As well as having to align the right elements for magical transformation to take place, the alchemist must find the right words. Alchemy is also a rhetorical practice: words are the agents of magic. Speaking of the magical power of words, the philosopher Pierre Bourdieu has argued that 'the mystery of performative magic resolves itself in the alchemy of representation'.[4] Through rhetorical invention, sense perceptions are converted into phantasmic images. Magic, with its emphasis on imagination and fantasy, is intrinsic to both language and the theatre.

4 Bourdieu, P, and Thompson, J B (1991), *Language and Symbolic Power.* Cambridge, MA: Harvard University Press, p.106.

As Collins and Nisbet observe, "Language becomes 'an event' in a tapestry of devised moments, inseparable from the total scenographic frame. The visual and kinetic elements of production become indivisible, there are no hierarchies, words operate as symbols and images are spoken".[5]

It is for this reason that we have chosen to take our inspiration from the designers' texts as well as the images. Instead of contextual essays, we are letting the designers' words and images create a visual and textual rhythm to the catalogue. To suggest connections and relationships, but allow for over reading and re-interpretation.

A theme for an open exhibition presents a challenge not only for the exhibitors but for the curator and editor. A theme needs to be broad enough that connections and relationships can be perceived, but not so broad that it loses any meaning. The assumption is that there will be some relevant pre-existing links between the submitted work – shared concepts and common methodologies. While *Transformation & Revelation* suggests a preoccupation, it accommodates a diverse response. It was intended to provide a point of departure, not a directive to arrive at a definitive statement about UK design for performance.

Following on from the example of **PAMELA HOWARD**, who continues to explore with great insight the meaning of scenography,[6] and from **DONATELLA BARBIERI**'s research project 'Designs for the Performer', our desire is to 'expose, divulge and celebrate the voice of the designer'.[7]

Instead of attempting the near impossible task of representing a production solely through the evidence of photographs, this catalogue provides the chance to explore the process of making performance through the designer's own words.

Every aspect of the submission process, from the selection of the images for exhibition, to the writing of the accompanying text, is part of a creative process and can tell us something about that person's work. A photograph and a brief description can, of course, never tell the whole story, but they can act as a way into the designer's imagination. We can learn something about how they design, where ideas come from, why decisions are taken. The 200 entry forms revealed a wonderful range of voices.

5   Collins, J, and Nisbet, A (2010), *Theatre and Performance Design: a Reader in Scenography*. London: Routledge, p.143.

6   Howard, P (2009), *What is Scenography?* London: Routledge.

7   Barbieri, D, 'Designs for the Performer', a research project funded by the AHRB (now AHRC) and by London College of Fashion, which ran from 2002 and included a series of interviews, masterclasses and exhibitions, e.g. 2D>3D, PQ2003 and the Fashion Space Gallery, London.

The designers' words demonstrate that originality and energy in the theatre comes through openness to a wide variety of creative impulses; that ideas about what theatre design is should be constantly challenged, re-examined and explored. There is a self-conscious awareness of the scenographic debate and its dialogic practices, and at the same time a demonstrable pride in the traditions of theatre design and a delight in theatricality; the transformation of reality and revelation of artifice.

These designers make a unique contribution to the understanding of space, character and time. They have the ability to reference the body; to work with it spatially; to understand its discipline and demands. They show the imagination to address and respond to narrative; to solve problems and work under pressure; to collaborate and to inspire.

Other professions have recognised and envied their skills and opportunities. Despite the centrality of theatricality in contemporary art and design practices, too often theatre designers have remained silent, relinquishing the limelight to their more vocal collaborators and transdisciplinary rivals. This, however, is an opportunity for them to speak. When we don't have discourse, we only have images. Designers need to articulate their position.

Theatre design has traditionally been represented by sketches, storyboards, model and/or production photographs. It is hoped that these documents will reveal the design development and represent the intentions of the designer. However, the trajectories of design are never straightforward. The working of the visual imagination suggests that it is a complex process that manifests itself in a number of startling and challenging ways. The question arises of how well this non-linear process can be illustrated. Many designers choose not to use the conventions of models and sketches – working instead through collaboration, experimentation and improvisation *in situ*. Their procedures may take the form of time lines, choreographic notations, flow charts, diagrams and Post-it notes.

These 'diagrammatic' renderings could represent patterns of movement, the objects involved in a particular action, or the action itself. Although they may not seem like what is conventionally perceived as theatre design, there are things that make them like theatre design, i.e. they are interpretive, exploratory, reflective and revelatory.

The two-dimensional movement notations… translated the physical space transcribed by the movement of the dancer into drawing. (**POSTWORKS**).

There is a playfulness and profundity about some of the observations that reveal as much about the designer as the accompanying images. Their words, like their designs, are intelligent, subtle, inspired. Ideas are overlaid, interleaved, intertwined, edited, transcribed, collaged, painted, drawn, pencilled, erased, traced, overwritten, overpainted and Tipp-Ex'd.

We collected, swapped and amalgamated stories and matched them to diverse images, often drawing in each other's sketch books until their origins became untraceable (**MICHAEL PAVELKA**).

From the noise, dust, scratches created in paint, watercolour, graphite or ink, a personal language emerges. **IONA MCLEISH** describes *exploring the visual possibilities of language and meaning, reality and illusion* while **MIRIAM NABARRO** speaks of a *visual language which would allow the political power of the text to be illuminated.*

The designers' words and images demonstrate inventiveness, persistence, originality and bloody-minded determination. The scenographic discourse is expanded through imaginative exploration. There is *a yearning to personally transform… and pick up a pencil… and talk through lines of graphite* (**SEAN CROWLEY**).

A variety of forms of visual communication have been adopted, including Photoshop and graphic techniques. The theatrical language of Photoshop acknowledges its growing use as a creative tool whose potential is a source of both despair and fascination. Images are rendered, textured, brushed, sponged, drawn, inked, chalked, pencilled, animated.

The drawing and model are seen as sites for improvisation and play as well as precision and resolution. These are the designers' written instructions for interpretation and further making. Their words as well as their images reveal their processes and transform our perceptions about the practices of 'theatre design'.

The process starts with a conversation of ideas... ruminations on a bicycle (**SIMON CORDER**).

In our editorial discussions, we decided that the catalogue should have its own theatricality and scenography. Like the books of the alchemists it became a 'site of experimentation'. The designer and editors wanted to create a relationship between the book and the spaces, performances and designs it represents. The structure for the catalogue, therefore, is phrasal and stylised. It is an articulation of images and ideas; the patination of the page made up of pauses, phrases, lines, marks, gestures. The subject is enfolded into the design of the catalogue itself. This project is about contingent rearrangements instead of categories. We make no claim to be comprehensive but wish to reflect the range of divergent but valid practices. We choose like our designers to look for new possibilities in these traces of performance.

These miniaturised objects hold the autobiographical in the material of their making. They hold the potential for new spatial propositions, spaces that are to be inhabited from those that once were. (**ALDONA CUNNINGHAM AND JOANNA PARKER**).

'To do this, according to philosopher Michel Serres, we needed to turn our attention to 'stammerings, mispronunciations, dysphonics and cacophonies... background noise, jamming, statics, cutoffs, hysteresis and various interruptions.[8] Like Serres we are interested in communication, translation and the spaces in between – the media – the alchemical substance through which messages travel. The transmission is volatile and the messages can be decoded and re-encoded in unexpected ways.

a new space is created in between, in their imagination, full of surprising juxtapositions and synchronicities (**SOPHIE JUMP**).

New thoughts and associations can be produced through the alchemy of imagination. Magic is the science of metamorphosis and transformation. It provides the capacity for change and adaption.

Celebrating the processes of translation and transformation, the work expands on the inherent slippages that occur as we move from one language, physical state, space or discipline to another (**POSTWORKS**).

These designers are making original and exciting contributions to our contemporary visual language. In their work and words, the exhibitors eloquently illustrate the transformative power of scenography; the revelatory qualities of light, colour and design to transform bodies, spaces and political agendas.

This catalogue is more than a directory of designers, or a document of a period of UK theatre design. It is a representation of the original contribution that theatre designers are making to our contemporary visual language and culture.

Jamie Vartan, *La Traviata*, Malmö Opera, 2008.
Photographer: Dennis Trulsson.

8   Serres, M, 'Platonic Dialogue' (1968), in Serres, M, *Hermes: Literature, Science, Philosophy*, ed. J V Harai and D V Bell. Baltimore: Johns Hopkins Press, p.65.

Submissions
MEMBERS OF THE SBTD

'HERE IS THE PLACE TO SHOW THAT ALL BARGAINS MADE TO PROTECT POWER, HIERARCHY AND WEALTH WILL BE BETRAYED'

TIMOTHY O'BRIEN   P.140

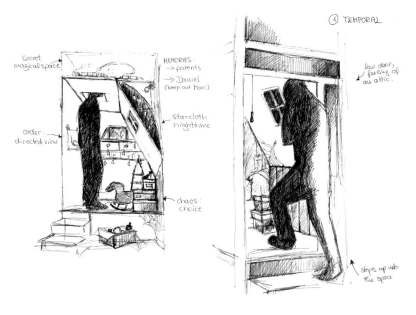

① TEMPORAL

MARIE BLUNCK   SET & COSTUME DESIGNER

SMALL WORLDS
Richard Warburton and Matthew David Scott, 2008

World Museum, Liverpool, August 2008

This interactive installation, devised by Slung Low, combines live and recorded performance to tell the story of Mark, a teenager with Asperger's syndrome, who sees the world differently. Each audience member is given some headphones, and helps Mark on a quest to find his brother's marbles. One by one, they travel through five boxes, each representing a room in the house, some real, some imaginary. In this first collaboration with Slung Low, we wanted to redefine how a young audience (12–18 years) see theatre, keeping them interested and focussed while having a good time. Each box gives an opportunity to reveal other worlds through techniques such as digital video found behind a hatch, or the live shadow of Mark's brother. Pushing imagination, the audience is invited to literally poke their head into the attic, revealing a miniature world they later re-encounter in full scale. Partially like a film design, and partially a surreal view of a house during mourning, each specific detail is to be examined and possesses a symbolic meaning. In the final kitchen space, you meet the mother (played by Sally Kent), and are confronted with the moving and intimate finale, and the resolution of the quest.

Theatre Company: Slung Low
Director: Alan Lane
Other creative collaborator: Fuse Theatre Company, Liverpool
Photographer: Simon Warner

SIMON BANHAM   SET & COSTUME DESIGNER

MAKE BELIEVE
Devised 2009

Contact Theatre, Manchester, and touring, October 2009

This piece investigates the nature of belief, posing questions about when we decide to believe. How do we decide what is true? And how do we separate the 'real' from the 'made up' in a piece of theatre? The scenographic input concentrates on this last question as a frame for investigating all others. The construction of the space referenced the traditional format of theatrical presentation, enabling acts of pretending whilst simultaneously deconstructing and revealing the artifice and therefore the reality of the event in its given (and varied) locations. Scenographically I attempted to physically replicate and reshape a theatrical space to parallel the gap that exists, within the live event, between the reality of the performer and the invented person they're pretending to be. This is a visual reading and the construction happens in the mind. Consistent with all my work for Quarantine there is a meta-theatrical frame that illuminates the ordinary and mundane, but I believe there is a process that occurs, much like peeling an onion, whereby the audience journey, through various reactions to and perceptions of the scenography, and with each step it becomes less evident (but nonetheless influential) until the 'truth' of the piece is arrived at – meeting a stranger, debating an idea, a moment of intimacy and personal sharing.

Theatre Company: Quarantine
Director: Richard Gregory
Choreographer: Johanne Timm
Lighting Designer: Mike Brookes
Sound Designer: Greg Akehurst
Other creative collaborator: Sonia Hughes

Pierina Legnani

CARL DAVIES SET & COSTUME DESIGNER

THE CALLING OF MAISY DAY
John Binias (libretto), Brian Irvine (music), Tim Rhys-Evans (music director), 2007

Weston Studio, Wales Millennium Centre, Cardiff, July 2008

The Calling of Maisy Day is a darkly comic opera set in a 21st-century call centre which is staffed by a coven of vampires who thrive on the blood of bitter office politics. The neutral palate and clean surfaces are a backdrop for the vampires' obsessive-compulsive behaviour and quest for style and success. The vampires' lack of real personality is reflected in bold, post-modern costumes, seemingly individual yet completely uniform alongside each other. The team leader, Maisy Day, hovers unconsciously somewhere between the 'heaven' of reality and the 'hell' of the call centre floor below. Blood pumps around the building's pipes like veins, dispensed from the water machine to hydrate the workers. A ceiling projection screen ticks with clocks and heart monitors, adding to the oppressive atmosphere whilst also acting as a porthole into Maisy's thoughts and visions.

Theatre Company: Welsh National Youth Opera
Director: Nik Ashton
Choreographer: Nik Ashton
Lighting Designer: Tim Lutkin
Photographer: Kirsten McTernan

ROMA PATEL SET & COSTUME DESIGNER

KNOCK AGAINST MY HEART
Oladipo Agboluaje, 2008

Clore Theatre, Unicorn Theatre, London, touring to studio theatres and schools, September 2008

A new play inspired by *The Tempest*, set in Rio's favelas, this bilingual production was a collaboration with Brazil's theatre company Nós Do Morro. The images from my sketchbook reveal some of my early design sketches and ideas. My involvement with this project began during its early development, so there were many changes along the way. However, the theme of Brazilian opposing cultures was always constant, and that became my starting point. The set, depicting a miniature favela on a hillside, doubles as a seat and small performance platform, with its irregular self-constructed houses becoming steps when required. This was backed by the outline of Sugar Loaf Mountain in bent cane; a circular floorcloth suggests landscape and a river. On the opposite side, order and 'refinement': a white-painted wooden balcony with the part-outline of a fretwork doorway suggests Prospero's plantation house, harking back to colonial days, in direct contrast to the chaotic construction of the favela. The characters all had an animal associated with them, and their movement and costume reflected this. In the case of Prospero, a chair was transformed to reflect the wings of an eagle.

Theatre Company: Theatre Centre and Nós Do Morro
Director: Michael Judge
Lighting Designer: Prema Mehta
Music: Stephen Hudson and Manuel Pinheiro
Dramaturgy: Carl Miller
Production/CSM: Alice-Jane Lingwood

THEATREPLAN   CONSULTANTS

MICHAEL CROFT THEATRE
Edward Alleyn Building, Alleyn's School, Dulwich, London
November 2008

Peter Ruthven Hall: With a theatrical tradition that is traceable to Elizabethan times, Alleyn's School planned a new venue that could be transformed into much more than a theatre, thereby demonstrating a continuing commitment to the arts for current and prospective parents. Adaptable theatres are becoming increasingly important resources for schools and colleges, not only to meet the demands of modern drama teaching, but also to host a variety of productions and performance formats. The initial concept for the future Michael Croft Theatre (named after the previous Head of English who founded the National Youth Theatre in 1956) was to provide 'an adaptable theatre with sufficient volume for use as a concert hall'. We believed that a versatile relationship between the audience and the performers was key to the flexibility of the space. The courtyard-style space was designed with three levels of fixed seating and a moveable central stalls area. The shallow rake gives a good sightline, but also integrates a means to provide a variety of acting arrangements. By moving the seating and resetting adjustable platforms, the theatre can be transformed from a proscenium end stage into a thrust stage as well as theatre-in-the-round, allowing teachers and pupils to freely experiment within diverse theatrical environments.

Client: Alleyn's School, Dulwich
Architect: van Heyningen & Haward
Theatre Consultants: Theatreplan LLP
Acoustic Consultants: Arup Acoustics
Structural Engineers: Price & Myers
Mechanical & Electrical Engineers: Max Fordham & Partners
Cost Consultants: Gardiner & Theobald LLP
Photography: Nick Kane/Theatreplan

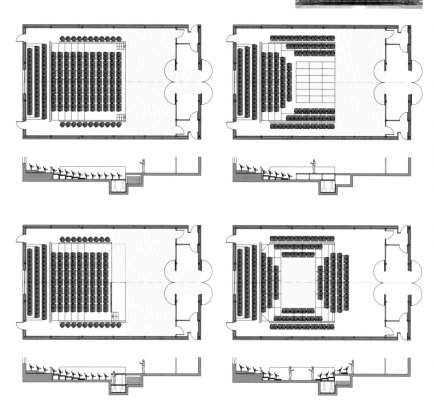

GABRIELLA CSANYI-WILLS   SET & COSTUME DESIGNER

DIE FLEDERMAUS
Johann Strauss II, 1874
A touring production, January 2009

The design process was, as ever, a reaction to the music, the libretto and, above all, director Jeff Clarke's ideas. We transformed the original frothy, funny 19th-century story into an even funnier, but more edgy, modern production. The design concept was based in surrealist and abstract art forms, giving the audience a more modern feel, the absurdity of it all and an underlying tension. Act I is all animal prints and hanging furniture, *nouveau riche* bordering on the vulgar. Act II, the Ball scene, is transformed into a Hallowe'en party. It is black and red, with appropriate skulls and glitter. Finally, in Act III, Eisenstein goes to rehab instead of a prison, as in the original. The 'surgery' is more edgy, with aggressive black and white designs on five screens that could then be used to great comic effect as well as suggesting 'other clients' and giving depth to the acting space. Creating conflicting juxtapositions revealed visual tensions that highlighted the comedy, as well as hinting at the emotional and, more often than not, animal instincts that lay underneath. The audience's imagination is a powerful tool that I enjoy trying to tap into, hence my minimalist approach.

Theatre Company: Opera Della Luna
Director: Jeff Clarke
Choreographer: Jenny Arnold
Lighting Designer: Guy Dickens

JOANNA SCOTCHER   SET & COSTUME DESIGNER

THE RAILWAY CHILDREN
Mike Kenny, 2010

The abandoned Eurostar Terminal at Waterloo International, July 2008

We were compelled by the idea of journeys. Not only the emotional journey of the characters, but equally by the very physical experience of travel that lies at the heart of the steam age. The joy of this process was the freedom to look at this disused station anew, but with creative eyes, recapturing the excitement of the passengers who once hurtled along these rail tracks and translating those journeys into a vehicle to carry our own narrative. As if waiting for a train themselves, the audience were positioned either side of the track. Within the two traverse-fixed wooden platforms, the scenes unfolded through the highly choreographed movements of the rolling trucks, which were continuously shunted and pulled through the entire length of the theatre. Using the paraphernalia of the railway era, laundry crates became tables and leather trunks became chairs. In this fashion, the climax of the landslide was invoked with a mountain of parcels, cases and crates, piled high on a goods wagon, that broke free of their lashings and cascaded over the tracks. From a cavernous, empty terminal space we were able to breathe life back into the environment, recreating the intimate, steamy world of the Edwardian rural station.

Theatre Company: collaboration with York Theatre Royal
Production Company: Centreline
Director: Damian Cruden
Choreographer: Chris Madden
Lighting Designer: Richard G Jones
Sound Designer: Craig Vear
Photographer: Simon Annand

SIGNE BECKMANN   SET & COSTUME DESIGNER

KING UBU
Lotte Faarup and Sven Ørnø, 2007, an adaptation of Alfred Jarry's *Ubu Rex*, 1896

Takkelloftet (Copenhagen Opera House) and touring, November 2007

The director and I wanted to portray the transformation of Ubu from a simple but greedy man to a violent tyrant. He is a man without any moral scruples, who recklessly bulldozes forward, feeling nothing but brutish satisfaction at the power he has gained. We wanted it to be absurd, chaotic, ugly, brutal, filthy, mad and funny. We drew inspiration from the crude language of the play and from a number of sculptures by Haugen Sørensen. One in particular struck a chord. It depicted an enormous pig, with the accompanying text: "Like the pig, we have soiled ourselves; like the pig we are lying in our own excrement. But pigs also have a great innocence. This conflicting caricature of a human being therefore appears both pathetic and smug, and you don't know whether to laugh or cry". In this way, as with all my recent work, I've tried to capture the essence of the play, and find a simple, thought-provoking, visual analogue.

Theatre Company: Corona la Balance
Director: Lotte Faarup
Lighting Designer: Jeppe Lawaetz

PIPPA NISSEN   SET & COSTUME DESIGNER

ELEPHANT AND CASTLE
Mira Calix and Tansy Davies, Blake Morrison, 2007

Aldeburgh Music, Snape Maltings, Suffolk, June 2007

A series of installations was set in both the landscape and buildings of Snape Maltings, with an audience that moved around them for different scenes. There were a total of seven installations, including a house set within a listed dilapidated ruin; a screen within the reed beds; a photographic fantasy of the Elephant and Castle shopping centre attached to the outside of the building; a lit billboard in the gardens; a theatre set of the shopping centre within the auditorium; and a lorry parked in the landscape with a band inside. The story of Hansel and Gretel was played out as films, projected onto different surfaces, while musicians walked through the landscape.

Theatre Company: Aldeburgh Music
Director: Tim Hopkins
Lighting Designer: Zerlina Hughes
Musical Director: Julian Warburton
Film: Pippa Nissen and Tim Hopkins
Photographer: David Lambert

LIZ ASCROFT   SET & COSTUME DESIGNER

BLITHE SPIRIT
Noel Coward, 2009

Royal Exchange Theatre, Manchester, December 2010

The challenge with *Blithe Spirit* is achieving and realising the ghost of Elvira and, later, Ruth. We set the play in the 30s so that our Elvira 'came back' from a time when a new type of woman had arrived on the scene. A woman with red lips who applied her make-up in public, smoked cigarettes, drank, danced, rebelled against convention, had free love and birth control, voted, had her hair cut short, showed her arms and her knees, took risks and was reckless. This seemed to fit with her ex-husband Charles' descriptions of her. "I remember how fascinating she was, and how maddening – I remember how badly she played all games and how cross she got when she didn't win – I remember her gay charm when she had achieved her own way over something and her extreme acidity

when she didn't – I remember her physical attractiveness which was tremendous, and her spiritual integrity which was nil…" "I remember how morally untidy she was…" "She certainly had a great talent for living – ". Therefore our Elvira was costumed in a beaded, fringed flapper frock which meant, even as a ghost, she was very much alive and full of movement. We used some antique glass beads, whose aged patina became the palette of dead people; the sound she made was pretty special too.

Theatre Company: Royal Exchange Theatre, Manchester
Director: Sarah Frankcom
Lighting Designer: Vince Herbert
Sound Designer: Steve Brown

LARA FURNISS   SET & COSTUME DESIGNER

PEOPLE WITHOUT HISTORY
Richard Maxwell, 2009

Performing Garage, New York, USA, March 2009

The brief was to create a touring set that could be carried on a plane as check-in luggage, and the focus was transformation: create one element to transform into multiple elements. The play links Shakespeare's Henry IV parts 1 and 2, starts in 1403 at the end of the Battle of Shrewsbury, then morphs into a love story in no specific time period with multiple locations. The concept came directly from a visit to the battlefield site: a helmet and a field of peas. A series of translucent panoramic screens on

castors echoes the structure of the pea field. Translucency conjures up layers in the landscape and layers of history. Continual movement of the screens allows for continual transformation of the space and emphasises an extract from the text "And under my eyes, the ground rolls by". Shifting colour palettes and the integration of projection onto the screens add more layers of transformation. The design was developed in rehearsals, as was the script. This created a fluid design process where all aspects of the performance influenced and informed each other.

Elements were added, tested and subtracted, and, as director Brian Mendes describes, "Nothing was precious, yet everything was important".

Theatre Company: New York City Players
Director: Brian Mendes
Lighting Designer: Margaret Mann
Other creative collaborator: Tom King
Photographer: Michael Schmelling

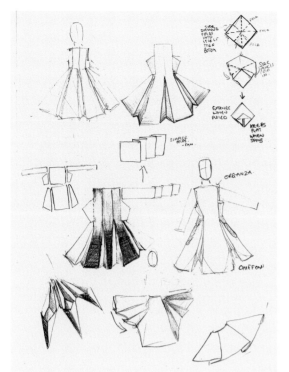

KATE LANE COSTUME DESIGNER

SUFI:ZEN
Shrikanth Sriram

Queen Elizabeth Hall, Southbank Centre, London, April 2010

Sufi:Zen was conceived as a discussion between Zen meditation and the rapturous motion of Sufi dervishes. It drew a cultural landscape from Persia to Japan. As the costume designer I was challenged to materialise, through costumes, a meeting point between cultures in order to create a discussion between two very different types of dance. After our discussions I became interested by the equation involving the simplicity of meditation and the fevered curves of the whirling. I wanted to create costumes able to reveal and materialise the tension between these two. In order to respect the different aspirations of Zen and Sufi I decided to create a costume that could operate a simple metamorphosis through movement. Following the Japanese tradition of origami, I started folding paper, exploring how the smallest form can expand and create a new shape. A shape made of simple lines could operate its own transformation during the choreography. I am currently interested in the way a costume not only acts as a narrative element for a show, but also the extent to which this costume has the ability to alter the physical feeling of the performer, conditioning the movement of the performer.

Theatre Company: Akademi
Choreographer: Gauri Sharma Tripathi
Lighting Designer: Adam Povey
Sound Designer: Gauri Sharma Tripathi
Other creative collaborators: Jonathan Lunn and Mavin Khoo
Photographer: Robert Piko

ALDONA CUNNINGHAM & JOANNA PARKER
SCENOGRAPHERS

TO BE INHABITED SPACES
An interactive installation

Theatre Materials Conference, Central School of Speech & Drama, London, April 2008

"He will say that objects are today recognised as something with which to play. And we will reply this is not why we like them here, but the real reason is that we have not displaced them for a violin simply because of this reasoning. We have displaced them because we have replaced them."
Gertrude Stein (1922), *Objects Lie on a Table – A Play*

Model pieces excavate the inscribed history of past productions and the designers that made them. These miniaturised objects hold the autobiographical in the material of their making. They hold the potential for new spatial propositions, spaces that are to be inhabited from those that once were. This improvisational play with the model allows for a form of engagement that is non-verbal, rapid and illogical. The resultant images leave a semi autobiographical trail and create an unintentional physical score. The installation takes participants on a journey through a series of dynamic improvisations animating these 'found' scale objects and figures. These immersive encounters allow for the physical presence of the designer to figure out new collaborative approaches with materials freed from past productions. Not to comment, or to fix, but to wander in a space of non understanding.

Photographer: Joanna Parker

DONATELLA BARBIERI   SET & COSTUME DESIGNER

COSTUME AS ART: ENCOUNTERS IN THE ARCHIVE
Conceived and produced by Donatella Barbieri,
with film-maker Netia Jones

V&A Theatre & Performance Archive

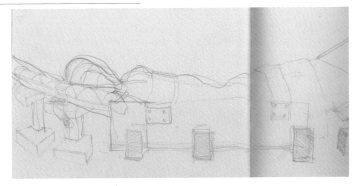

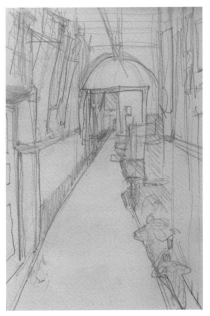

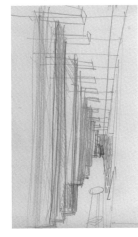

This short film makes the research process the work itself, and places the V&A Theatre & Performance Archive both as its central character and as its scenographic space. It is the harbour of carefully stored-away memories, hidden in thousands of solidly crafted boxes which, once opened, unravel stories, secrets and images that feed the creative imagination, projecting new meanings and creative possibilities into the future. This is a project conceived in collaboration with LCF Research Department and the Victoria & Albert Museum to offer insight into the costumed body through the interaction between specific costume elements and images, selected by six creative practitioners, whose disparate areas of research embody a range of perspectives, revealing the metaphoric complexity of the visual body in performance. The body, present through its vestiges, yet conspicuous by its absence, offers in the space it creates a moment of perception that invites an imaginative leap in the encounter with the viewer. Holding its own physical memory of performance, the intimate encounter with this absent/imagined/remembered performing body/object exposes its particular uniqueness. The drawings included are part of the research documentation, which fed into the development of the ideas for the film.

Film-maker: Netia Jones
Photography: images are scans of research drawings

FIONA WATT   SCENOGRAPHER

I AM THE CITY
The Company, 2009

Chatham Historic Dockyard, 2009–10

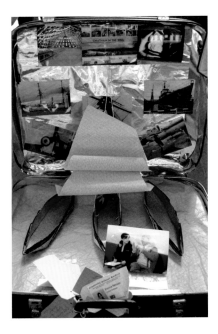

I Am The City culminated a two year cultural exchange project for Créativité sans Frontières, an intergenerational community company built simultaneously in Medway and Dunkerque to acknowledge dockyard closure in both communities in the 1980s, and to celebrate moving forward. That a community performer could create a story about the place they were from and take it anywhere they wanted to simply by putting one foot in front of the other became a motivating factor, positively counteracting some direct experiences of homelessness and transience within the group. Drawing on the traditions of travelling salesmen, hawkers and street traders, and inspired by Marcel Duchamp's *Bôite-en-valise*, we wanted to generate stories for performance by the simplest, most portable means possible. Through the making of suitcase museums, these miniature narratives in oral and model form became the core of our walking performance. Interacting with site, public space, the regeneration, heritage and museum sectors, the piece continues to evolve and grow at this point of intersection, inviting audiences to view and respond to the same object as prop, artefact, exhibit and installation.

Theatre Company: Créativité sans Frontières
Creative Producer (UK): Fiona Watt
Creative Producers (FR): Claude Vanderschueren and Regis Bertein
Other creative collaborators: Rachel Taylor and Maryvonne Playe
Photographer: Cliona Reilly

Theatre Company: **Cut to the Chase**
Director: **Jen Heyes**
Lighting Designer: **Phil Saunders**
Flamenco guitarist and composer: **Juan Martin**

OLIVIA DU MONCEAU   SET & COSTUME DESIGNER

BLOOD WEDDING
Frederico Garcia Lorca, 1933, in a version by
Ted Hughes, 1996

Liverpool Playhouse, November 2008

The design responded to an Andulucian trip with
the director in the summer of 2008. This fascinating
experience enabled first hand research of Lorca's legacy,
the Granadian landscape and the Spanish culture. Many
details influenced the design; the home of the bride
was based on the images of the pots and pans that
adorn the preserved caves of Sacromonte. The simple
design utilised a huge, blood-stained canvas, which was
flown into various positions to echo the Sierra Nevada
mountains. While transporting us effortlessly through
the play's various settings, it assisted in reflecting the
mood and the central themes. The wood floor was treated
like dried, cracked, barren earth, edged with mounds of
rotting oranges. The challenge was to take all the research
information and concentrate it into a few essential images.

HARRIET DE WINTON   SET & COSTUME DESIGNER

A MIDSUMMER NIGHT'S DREAM
William Shakespeare, 1594–6

Tobacco Factory, Bristol, February 2010

The research for this production spanned centuries of
culture, myth and legend. From this I pieced together
relevant fragments to create costumes designed to
disorientate the audience: familiar Elizabethan silhouettes
created with contemporary garments and fabrics. Each
world of the play is defined by this focused use of fabric:
romantic lace and velvet for the court, homespun yarns
of the 'rude' mechanics and insect-like armour cladding
the bodies of the monochrome, bespectacled fairies all
combine to give the desired effect. It was important to
preserve the history and legend associated with the story
and to maintain the disorientation of a timeless, dream-
like state throughout, using contemporary references.
Titania's costume was largely inspired by pop culture's
current obsession with the military, fusing the strength
and imposing presence of uniform, whilst utilising the
streamlined shell that armour creates to complement the
female form, and heighten Titania's power and sexuality.
This armoured torso was placed on top of a stunning
floral gown, the only injection of colour in the nocturnal
fairy kingdom.

Theatre Company: **Shakespeare at the Tobacco Factory**
Director: **Andrew Hilton**
Choreographer: **Kay Oliver**
Lighting Designer: **Tim Streader**
Sound Designer: **Liz Purnell**
Photographer: **Graham Burke**

PAUL BROWN   SET & COSTUME DESIGNER

DIE GEZEICHNETEN
Franz Schreker, 1911

Teatro Massimo di Palermo, April 2010

Act I: Alviano Salvago sits and plans his Edenic world – the island of Elysium. He is too deformed to experience beauty at first hand. The crates destined for the island are being packed with exquisite art works, but never far away is the unsettling knowledge that the local virgins are going missing.

Act II: In Duke Adorno's palace the playboy nobility hold court. They strut their power and wealth inside an artificial picture frame. Meanwhile, the artist, Carlotta, paints the ugly Alviano with a suffocated rose and Adorno's crushed sports car in the background.

Act III: We reach Elysium. The island is saturated with colour. An orgy develops as the two-dimensional scenery is replaced by a much more sensual use of colour: the white canvas floor and walls are splattered with paint. The populus daub and smear the paint over the set and themselves in Bacchanalian ecstasy. Finally, as the action sinks into depravity, the vital colours start to blend and merge to become a primal brown.

Theatre Company: Teatro Massimo di Palermo
Director: Graham Vick
Choreographer: Ron Howell
Lighting Designer: Giuseppe Di Orio
Sound Designer: Ron Howell

ANTONY GORMLEY   SCENOGRAPHER

SUTRA
Sadler's Wells, London, 2008

Larbi and I were asked (through the agency of Hisashi Itoh) by Shi yong Xin, the Abbot of Shaolin monastery, to reimagine the public display of the kung-fu discipline of Xan Chan Buddhism. I was looking for a way to objectify the life of a monk. A monk renounces the world in order to find liberty or possibility. The idea of containment or seclusion versus infinite extension was the principal behind the making of the boxes.

The boxes are 60 × 60 × 180 cm, and the idea was to find a size that would fit monks of varying ages, physiques and heights, and that this modular box could then be used as a building block for a variety of architectures.

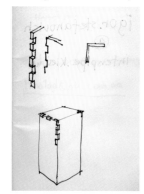

When assembled, the boxes make a wide range of structures, lateral and vertical. When flat, with their open ends up, they become a pond or paddy field; when placed the other way up, a platform; when placed on their sides and pushed together they become a hidden labyrinth; when placed on their ends, pillars or the blocks of a variety of architectures – houses, temples, pyramids, ziggurats or mountain. They can make walls or shelves. They can be the chambers of a cemetery. I never imagined that the box would become so versatile. I had thought that we might only choose one or two basic configurations. It was Larbi's genius to completely integrate the boxes into the movement.

Larbi was able to play the metaphoric implications almost infinitely; both on the tomb/womb/bath and on the sentry/box/cupboard/refugee boat lines of association. The boxes became body extensions, literally a second body: sometimes offering shelter from the gaze of the audience and sometimes to be dragged, as if dragging one's inevitable death. I wanted the boxes to be what they were; simply-made boxes for the body. We made them out of shuttering ply, used for casting concrete architecture. They had a pragmatic, utility feel which allowed them a kitchen-to-coffin flexibility.

Some basic principles have emerged in working with Larbi and Akram. Firstly, intimacy between performers and connection with the audience had to come from the action itself, not from some imposed structure or, worse still, a spotlight. Everything ought to be visible at all times: the openness of the stage and the openness of the experience should be maintained. Concentration had to be jointly owned both sides of the proscenium. Light on skin is the affective visual medium in dance. The floor has to be a connective surface providing an abstract context with the gauze walls, the rear gauze allowing both integration of the musicians as well as allowing the music to be their presence.

The unselfconscious energy, discipline and commitment of the dancers and Larbi's extended intelligence, inquiry and celebration made the emptiness of the boxes active, meaningful, alive.

Theatre Company: Sidi Larbi Cherkaoui/Sadler's Wells London
Choreographer: Sidi Larbi Cherkaoui
Music: Szymon Brzóska

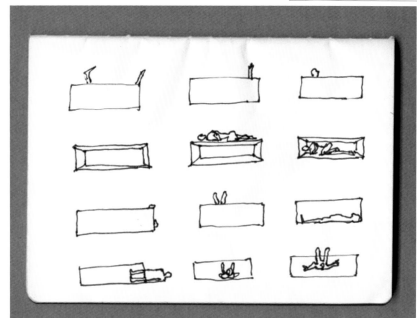

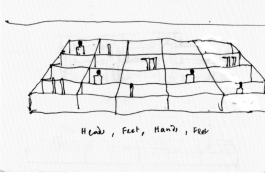

Head , Feet , Hands , Feet

KELLI DES JARLAIS SET & COSTUME DESIGNER

TITUS ANDRONICUS
William Shakespeare, 1590s

Glasgow Botanical Gardens, July 2010

Titus Andronicus takes place in an environment already transformed. The Romans have imposed themselves upon the natural world through their building. Now the power of Rome is fading, and nature is taking back control. As a site-specific piece, the sense of a temple or palace ruins, set within nature, creates the playing space. The characters act increasingly like beasts, wearing away the men, society and structure previously in place. Titus realises that his beloved Rome has changed, and does everything he can to combat it. During the rehearsal process, characters are explored through movement by the full ensemble. This allows each performer to develop the character's physicality, and the observation of this influences the specifics of their costumes. The design develops through quick sketches over photographs of the performers as the moment evolves and through discussion of the themes presented through the movement.

Theatre Company: Bard in the Botanics
Director: Marc Silberschatz

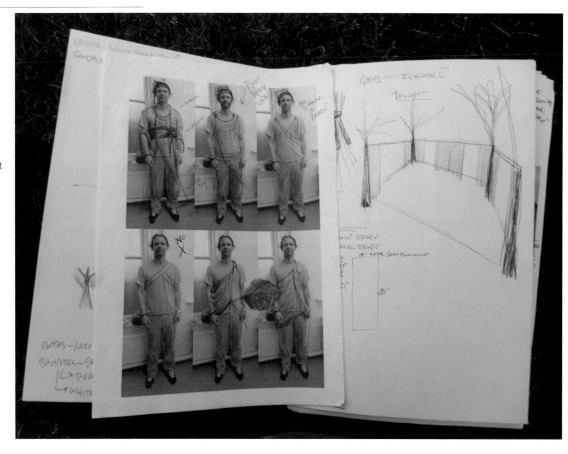

STEVE DENTON SET & COSTUME DESIGNER

SONGS FOR SILENCED VOICES
Dic Edwards (libretto) and Patrick Dineen (composer), 2009

Disused shop doorway in St John's Shopping Centre, Liverpool, December 2009

This project was created from a series of drama workshops working with homeless people in Liverpool. The challenge was to find characters that were timeless and suggested a personal history, but avoided the clichés associated with the general perception of people living on the streets. The resulting 10 minute opera was performed in the doorway of an empty shop in a busy shopping centre. The space had to be transformed simply using the kind of found objects homeless people could identify with: cardboard boxes, newspaper and an old pram. The three characters were simply Man, a soldier from an unidentified war and time, Woman, a woman of indeterminate age and background, and Musician, who could easily have been any street busker. Stories were revealed when they sang their songs.

Theatre Company: Collective Encounters
Director: Sarah Thornton

LEFT LUGGAGE THEATRE

ALVEUS
Devised by the Company, 2009

Segedunum Roman Fort & Baths, Wallsend,
June 2009

Left Luggage Theatre began its Segedunum adventure in
March 2009, delving into Wallsend's proud history and
reflecting on the everyday and extraordinary in this town
so influenced by the magnificent Tyne. Wallsend is a town
full of echoes of its past, but on the brink of a new future.
We worked with older people to explore their memories
of the place and the stories that are important to them.
We then collaborated with young people from Theatre
Tantara on *alveus: veris*, the practical research phase of
the project. We took a light touch in transforming the space
for performance, as it had a brimming resonance in the
quality of light, acoustics, smells and the sparse, sanctified
maze of rooms.
Left Luggage brought the threads of this collaboration
with skilled performers from the North East and across
the UK to create *alveus: solstice*. We sought to reveal the
space as a living being, full of the stories of Wallsend,
and a site in which we posed the question: are we on the
edge of great vision without even realising it? *Alveus* was
supported by the National Lottery through Arts Council
England, North Tyneside Council, Tyne & Wear Museums
and The Empty Space.

Theatre Company: Left Luggage Theatre
Co-directors & Designers: Alison Garner, Anna Harding, Kimberley Turner and
Verity Quinn
Dramaturg: Laura Lindow
Ensemble: Paula Penman, Alex Elliott, Matthew Blake, David Storey,
Anna Harding, Verity Quinn, Alison Garner and Kimberley Turner
Photographer: Vicki Smith

ASHLEY SHAIRP   SET & COSTUME DESIGNER

'TIS PITY SHE'S A WHORE
John Ford, 1633

Everyman, Liverpool, September 2010

This production will open the final ever season at the
Liverpool Everyman before it is demolished in 2011 to
make way for a brand new theatre. At the time of writing
the design is still evolving, and this white card model has
been used to communicate our ideas to the theatre staff.
The director and I are trying to create a fluid space in
which the story can be told in a rapid, cinematic way, but I
am also very interested in creating an environment which
acknowledges and references the theatre's previous life as
a chapel. The plan is to paint various sections of the theatre walls a light colour (as yet undecided), drawing attention to architectural details which are usually concealed.
We will create a huge wall which continues these features
and looks like a natural extension of the building. This
transformation will hopefully exploit the exhilarating width
of the space and create a dynamic new room in which the
revelations of this potent story can unfold afresh. The set
will be used for an Everyman Youth Theatre show after the
run of this play. I have suggested they transform, deface
and attack the structure, making it their own.

Theatre Company: Liverpool Everyman & Playhouse
Director: Chris Meads
Lighting Designer: Ben Pacey
Sound Designer: Matt Angove
Photographer: Sam Heath

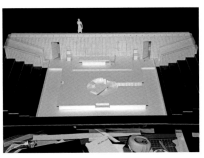

YOLANDA SONNABEND & MATT DEELY SET & COSTUME DESIGNERS

BEETHOVEN'S SYMPHONY NO.9
Ludwig van Beethoven, 1824

Akasaka Act Theatre, Tokyo, September 2008

Matt Deely: The choreographer, Tetsuya Kumakawa, wanted a spectacular setting to reflect the powerful, uplifting tones of the music. The orchestra was positioned on a raised platform upstage. This allowed the dancers to perform closer to the audience. The ballet is in four movements: the first expresses fire, the angry earth, magma, man; the second, water, life, woman; the third, garden of Eden, love, man and woman; and the fourth, the universe, spirituality, God and hope.

Theatre Company: K-Ballet Company, Tokyo
Director/Choreographer: Tetsuya Kumakawa
Lighting Designer: Hisashi Adachi
Other creative collaborator: Theatre Orchestra Tokyo

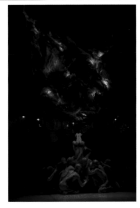

RACHAEL A SMITH SET DESIGNER

THE AMERICAN CLOCK
Arthur Miller, 1980

Redgrave Theatre, Bristol, June 2008

The American Clock is written as a collection of personal encounters with the Great Depression, while focusing in part on one family's declining wealth. The play is structured as a series of vignettes, spanning many different locations and characters, visiting the majority of them only once. The challenge was to create a versatile set able to represent each different location with symbolic clarity and distinction, allowing the space to expand and contract appropriately while being able to move between each transformation fluidly. I developed a set that would work like a combination lock: the billboard was split into three pieces which could fly in or out independently or together, underneath which were three trucks that moved back and forth. Each setting was represented by a specific arrangement of both billboard and truck. The trucks were dressed with piles of miscellaneous furniture, from which pieces could be pulled out to construct a scene, while the stage was stripped back to the bare walls, revealing the workings of the theatre to the audience. The tactile set allowed the cast to perform the transitions themselves, making the directional movement and physical narrative of preparing the scene integral parts of the scene itself.

Director: Roger Haines
Costume Designer: Madeleine Cole
Lighting Designer: Chris Goode

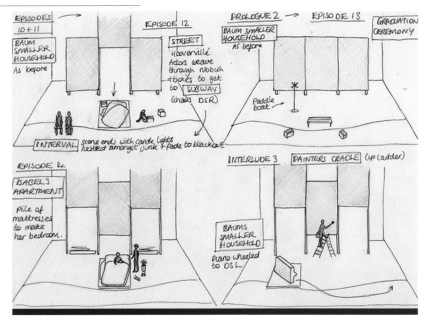

Banners for balconies.

VERITY QUINN   SET & COSTUME DESIGNER

HOMING IN
Luke Carver Goss (composer) and Ian McMillan (writer), 2010

Concourse, Sage Gateshead, May 2010

Homing In was commissioned for the Words and Music Festival at The Sage Gateshead, and brought together over 100 musicians from the region, plus a Greek-style chorus and Ian McMillan as ringleader-poet. This was a site-specific performance in the vast public concourse area in the Sage, with the Tyne and its bridges forming the backdrop to the piece. The concourse was a cavernous arena, with balconies disappearing into the rafters. Working closely with Debbie Little (director) and Tim Bennett (choreographer) we created a ragtag chorus of travelling pigeon racers and storytellers who arrived and transformed this vast space into a celebration of North East tradition and ritual. I gave them candy stripe banners and reams of bunting to transform the space into a huge pigeon cree that was filled with poetry, song and the sound of a hundred beating wings. "*Homing In* is a huge celebration, in music and words, of the idea of Home: making a home, leaving home, coming home. The piece uses the idea of the homing pigeon, liberated from the cree, flying far from the North East but unerringly returning home in all weathers. Just like the rest of us..." Ian McMillan.

Theatre Company: Sage Gateshead
Director: Debbie Little
Choreographer: Tim Bennett
Costume Assistant: Kate Eccles
Photographer: Kate Eccles

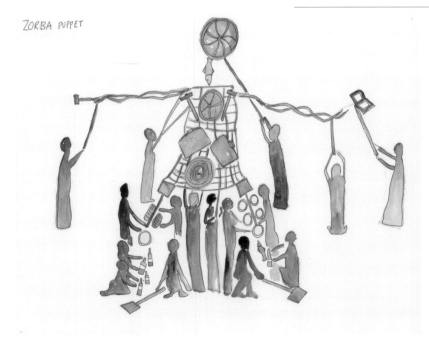

ZORBA PUPPET

BECKY HURST   SET & COSTUME DESIGNER

THE GREEK
Devised by Cartoon de Salvo and students from the Central School of Speech & Drama, 2009

Minack Theatre, Cornwall, June 2009

Cartoon de Salvo devised *The Greek* in collaboration with students from the Central School of Speech and Drama. We opted to use The Minack as a site-specific performance space, thus adopting the stunning and unique setting as the heart of our show, directly inspiring the story that we devised to perform there. A playful design language was adopted, using simple props and objects which all had inherent story value. These were then utilised to create different visual pictures. Initial ideas involved using the cast to conjure enormous puppets, instantaneously transforming everyday objects into magical characters. These early design sketches show ideas on how to create an enormous Zorba puppet from objects such as wine bottles, pickaxes, shovels and ropes – the stuff of life, work and the land. Zorba's lover Madame Hortense is created from more delicate objects – fine fabrics, lampshades, soft furnishings, bold colours and the world of the boudoir. These puppets were designed to be conjured magically from the everyday. They were to exist just for a moment, before the objects were recaptured and put to their daily use – as if they had only existed fleetingly in the audience's imagination.

Theatre Company: a co-production between Cartoon de Salvo and the Central School of Speech & Drama
Director: Alex Murdoch
Associate Director: Brian Logan
Assistant Set & Costume Designer: Sara White
Craft Tutor: Mike Bell
Choreographer: Lenia Tsigeridou
Musical Director: Zara Nunn
Sound Designer: David Sharrock

SIMON KENNY SET DESIGNER

WOYZECK
Georg Büchner, 1837

Central School of Speech & Drama, London, July 2007

The key to this production was locating the perspective and ambiguity of the narrative voice, from whose point of view we were experiencing the story at any given moment; and should we be objectively watching events unfold or empathise with any of the characters? Using the fragmented, enigmatic text as a starting point, three very different worlds were developed, reflecting differing perspectives from which the story could be seen. A romantically beautiful and violent natural landscape referred to the real surroundings as viewed from within the story; a hyper-real world of crumbling utilitarian architecture described the environment from a more objective viewpoint; while a highly abstract world of shadow, reflections and moving facades told something of Woyzeck's and Marie's internalised descents towards psychosis. It was the interplay of these worlds – the movement between locations, the scenic collisions, visual overlaps and juxtapositions – that drove the production. By overlaying these scenographic ideas in this way, the transformation of the physical scene mirrored the psychological and dramatic arc of the characters: essentially the moving scenery became an additional performer. The scenic choreography, evolution and reconfiguration over the course of this production – and much of my recent work – was key both in formalising the structure of the piece and in enhancing the narrative.

Director:
Geoffrey Colman
Lighting Designer:
Dan Hill
Sound Designers:
Jonas Roebuck and Jamie Flockton
Photographer:
Patrick Baldwin

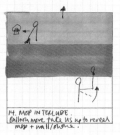

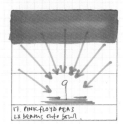

CHRISTOPHER GILES COSTUME DESIGNER

THE OPERA SHOW
Multiple composers, 2008

Kilworth House Theatre, Leicestershire, US and European tour, September 2008

For this unusual and very exciting project I was required to design visually striking and distinctive period costumes for Part 1 of the evening (Parts 2 and 3 being set in different eras). Starting with basic sketches of 18th-century garments, they then developed through punk, circus and fashion inspiration while maintaining a hint of Baroque style. I realised the transformation of a time period recreated for the 21st century, and the revelation of quirky and colourful costumes from detailed illustrations.

Theatre Company: Kilworth House Theatre
Director: Mitch Sebastien
Set Designer: Sean Cavanagh
Lighting Designer: Chris Ellis
Sound Designer: Mitch Sebastien
Photographer: Christopher Giles

MONSTER BALL
Lady Gaga, 2009

World tour, November 2009

Lady Gaga might be described as a contemporary queen of transformation. This was the first incarnation of her Monster Ball tour. It toured to theatres in north America during late 2009 and early 2010. It was transformed by her design team, Haus of Gaga, on a daily basis throughout the tour and then replaced by a completely new version in European arenas in spring 2010. The initial idea was a pure white perspective box with no visible light sources: it was a reaction against the constellation of black truss and myriad light units that is more usual in pop tours. During the weeks since conceiving the design, Gaga's aesthetic evolved steadily into something darker and more anarchic: the floor was painted gradually darker during rehearsals. By the end of the tour it was black. The lights crept stealthily into view. Her first comment on seeing the pure white box in rehearsal was "Great – now puke on it". I added a trussfull of junk which appeared to be ridden by a giant projected Gaga during a costume change transition.

Theatre Company: **Haus of Gaga**
Director: **Lady Gaga**
Costume Designer: **Zaldy Goco**
Choreographer: **Laurie Ann Gibson**
Lighting Designer: **Willie Williams**
Video Designer: **Nick Knight**

FAUST
Charles Gounod, 1859

Semperoper Dresden, May 2010

The design refers to 19th-century optical illusions that paved the way towards the illusion of the moving image: film – the ultimate illusion of the eternal life that is promised to Faust. Each section takes an instrument from Faust's studies and magnifies it: so Acts I and II exist in a giant zoetrope, Act III in a forest of prisms, Acts IV and V within a crowd of revolving mirrors. A fundamental function of the design is to enable revelation of performers in the heart of the space. The revolving slotted zoetrope reveals an entire chorus as a regimented row and then delivers them as a crowded mass to the centre of the stage. A chorus of 60 are revealed instantaneously across the full width of the stage via hidden zoetrope slots upstage of the installation of revolving mirrors. The installation in each act is used as an instrument to transform the lighting of the space. The zoetrope slices and spins the light as Mephisto races Faust through a whirlwind tour of 19th-century society; the prisms refract and rotate the light as the stories of Faust and Marguerite are interwoven; the revolving mirrors reflect and fragment the light around Marguerite's persecution and finally turn their reflected light upon her with an intensity that results in her final immolation.

Theatre Company: **Semperoper Dresden**
Director: **Keith Warner**
Costume Designer: **Julia Muier**
Lighting Designer: **Wolfgang Goebbel**
Associate Designer: **Bronia Housman**

SOPHIE JUMP DIRECTOR, SET & COSTUME DESIGNER

ATALANTA
Devised by the Company, 2010

Ashmolean Museum, Oxford, July 2010

Atalanta takes you on a 15 minute walk through the
Ashmolean Museum, guided by a voice in your earphones
as well as video footage on an iPod screen that matches
your pathway. Part of the pleasure is to sync the image
on the screen with the real environment in front of you.
A story unfolds based on the Greek myth of the runner
Atalanta and the continuing challenges that face women
in sport. The walk was designed to be experienced on its
own or, during performance times, with live performers
in the space, and to be downloaded from iTunes. After
15 years of seven sisters group exploring ways to lead
audiences through a site we came upon this technique
that blends site-specific performance and hand-held video
technologies. Screens usually demand all our attention,
but in this case the audience is forced to compare real
with filmed, and somehow a new space is created in
between, in their imagination, full of surprising juxtapositions and synchronicities, engaging them with the space in
a new and unexpected way.

Theatre Company: seven sisters group
Directors: Susanne Thomas and Sophie Jump
Writer: Richard Hurford
Video Artist: Davy McGuire
Performer: Kristin McGuire
Composer: Craig Vear
Photographer: Davy McGuire

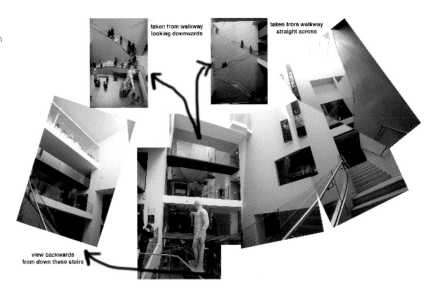

NICOLA EVE DOBROWOLSKI SET & COSTUME DESIGNER

DAMAGES
Steve Thompson, 2004

Old Red Lion Theatre, London, July 2009

This design is structured around the theme of a 'red
top' newspaper, clearly dividing the space into personal
'columns' of space. The characters, within the protection
of their own space, safely voiced their opinions, while
challenging others at heated moments by literally crossing
the lines. A corridor of communal space splits the stage,
providing a powerful entrance for the actors as they
head straight for the audience. The blank newspaper is a
battling ground for the characters to work out what the
public should read the next day. The costumes are plain,
with a flash of colour for each character, mimicking the
print of newspaper text.

Theatre Company: Lucid Muse
Director: Benet Catty
Lighting Designer: Benet Catty
Sound Designer: Simon Perkin
Photographer: Nicola Eve Dobrowolski

"Like the
we have
ourselve
the pig
lying in
excreme
pigs also
great in

pig,
soiled
s: like
ve are
our own
nt. But
have a,”
nocence

SIGNE BECKMANN, QUOTING HAUGEN SØRENSEN P.26

GERTRUDE.
played by Francesca Ryan

CHRIS GYLEE SET & COSTUME DESIGNER

HAMLET
William Shakespeare, 1599–1601

Tobacco Factory, Bristol, March 2008

The designs that excite me the most are those that unlock the potential of a space according to the needs of the story. For *Hamlet*, our original intention had been to use the Tobacco Factory exactly as we found it, with three simple wooden pews in an otherwise bare, in-the-round performance area – the characters, how they interacted and what they wore would tell us where we were. But over the years every surface had been painted with layer after layer of black, leaving only a void that swallowed light. It took us a week to strip it down to the hard industrial surfaces beneath, revealing quarry tiles, timber floorboards and concrete. The transformation of the venue created the Elsinore we'd imagined. The authenticity of the physical space allowed the events as they unfolded to be utterly real.

Theatre Company: Shakespeare at the Tobacco Factory
Director: Jonathan Miller
Lighting Designer: Tim Streader
Sound Designer: Elizabeth Purnell
Photographer: Graham Burke

EMMA CHILD SET DESIGNER

THE WIZARD OF OZ
L Frank Baum, 1939

Wycombe Swan Town Hall, February 2010

I wanted the audience to understand that all of the worlds created in our production of *The Wizard of Oz* were directly from Dorothy's own vivid imagination. To do this we set about transforming the foyer space of the theatre into Dorothy's house, to show the audience the sparseness of her grim reality. Objects from her everyday life were revealed in the installation. We see the Tin Man's axe and the Witch in a story book by her bed; the workers on the farm are working hard and mingle with the audience as they see a 'Home Sweet Home' cross-stitch picture. We can begin to understand why she wanted to imagine a more colourful and exciting world. By walking the audience through this space before they even sit down we offer them the opportunity to make up their own stories before the rest of the musical is even revealed. The set itself acted as a canvas that allowed the lighting to transform it into the different worlds Dorothy creates. With no flying systems and limited build time, we brought colour in with light.

Theatre Company: Wycombe Swan Youth Theatre
Director: Matthew Dye
Costume Designer: Liz Charleston
Choreographer: Dennis Victory
Lighting Designer: Sebastian Petit
Sound Designer: Kyle Sepede
Producer: Joy Griffiths
Assistant Designers: Rebecca Brower and Louise Mullan
Chief Construction: Tom Gibberd
Photographers: Neale Blackburn, Rebecca Brower and Emma Child

FIONA-MARIE CHIVERS   SET & COSTUME DESIGNER

THE NIGHT TIME WHISPERERS
Lynsey Dearlove and Steven Warbeck, 2010

Corn Exhange, Newbury, October 2010

This collaboration is part of a continuing adventure.
Working closely with the director, Belinda, I explored ways
of developing a sophisticated yet childlike visual language
inspired by the simple narrative. We have worked on
a number of projects together and are investigating
new ways to combine the performance and workshop
experience for young audiences and parents, incorporating
voice, movement, puppetry and music, through collaboration with musicians and performers, to create works which
aim to develop and challenge young audiences. The Night
Time Whispers are a collection of gruesomely sympathetic
characters which lead our protagonist through a series
of eye-opening dream journeys. I began by creating
drawings of these fictional characters which would later
manifest themselves as puppets through the dancers'
costumes. These drawings provided a visual text which,
along with Steven Warbeck's score and Sarah Homer's
powerful live interpretation of the music, would inspire and
inform the choreography.

Theatre Company: Bound2B
Director: Belinda Lee Chapman
Choreographer: Christopher Marney
Other creative collaborator: Christopher Marney

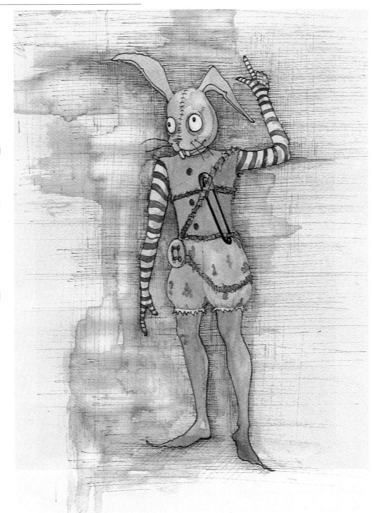

KELLY JAGO   SET & COSTUME DESIGNER

LOOKING FOR THE RAINBOW
Nick Wood, 2009

UK tour to children's centres and theatre spaces, May 2010

In formulating this design my focus was to achieve easy
transformation between the initial domestic home setting
and a variety of evolving worlds experienced by Mum and
Kirsty as they go in search of the Rainbow. My design
enables the characters to simply implement a series of
dramatic revelations, thus changing and adapting their
surroundings while continuing on their journey. They move
from a washing-filled living room, through a dark cave,
riverbank, fairground, forest and, eventually, the safest
place in the world, home. Designing for a young audience (up to three years), I planned simple, bold features,
bright colours and easily identified imagery, which help
them follow the story clearly. I focused around something
they would recognise – washing clothes – and created
a treasure hunt with T-shirt prizes at each stage, each
one a different colour of the rainbow. Once the hunt
was complete and each shirt stored safely in Mum's
washbag, she pegs the bundle to the line, which unrolls,
magically revealing the colourful rainbow. Reflecting on
this design, I feel that my focus on what would appeal
to young children, combined with the simple series of
transformations, enabled the success that was realised
with this production.

Theatre Company: Big Window Theatre Company
Director: Penny Breakwell
Musical Director: Daniel Willis
Photographer: Kelly Jago

FLORENCE HENDRIKS   SET & COSTUME DESIGNER

THE TEMPEST
William Shakespeare, 1611

Rhodes Art Complex, Bishop's Stortford, June 2010

In this production I was inspired by the mystical and outlandish elements of *The Tempest*. I created different locations within one set, the island and the sea, allowing an interactive relationship between the set and the actors. This approach seemed to encourage a stronger, more dynamic performance from the cast.

Theatre Company: Bishop's Stortford Youth Theatre Company
Director: Paul Bamlett
Lighting Designer: Max Hudd

DAVID HARRIS   SET & COSTUME DESIGNER

CITY
Hiru Dance, 2010

MU Theatre, Budapest, and touring to the Teatro Civico, Sassari, Sziget Festival, Budapest, and iDans04, Istanbul, May 2010

In this city, everybody is in a rush; workmen, shopkeepers, politicians… nothing is constant. The city is in a constant helix from one state to another. Here we see the environment change from anonymous towers into a jumble of meaningless advertisements as the dancers follow a system of dictated commands. I worked closely with the choreographers using cut up Post-it notes on paper and the model to configure specific scenes.

Theatre Company: Hiru Dance
Directors: Igor Urzelai and Moreno Solinas
Choreographers: Igor Urzelai and Moreno Solinas
Lighting Designer: Kata Dezsi
Sound Designer: Alberto Ruiz Soler
Photographer: Anikó Rácz

MIRANDA MELVILLE   SET & COSTUME DESIGNER

A FEW LITTLE DROPS
Devised by the Company, 2007

Outdoor performance touring Wales, June 2007

Water: what does it mean to us? What do we mean to
it? This devised project set out to arrive, circus-like, in a
new open-air place, transforming the environment. The
installation was to be a mysterious and intriguing object in
itself, some disturbing container for an audience to journey
within. Participants should be free to circulate as they
chose through the spaces and simultaneous action. We
worked through ideas of tsunami and an interactive eco
house, including video and audio – the circulation of water
linking everything. Ultimately, the three forms of Water,
Vapour and Ice became the defining ideas behind the
starkly contrasting and challenging structures. Audiences
were intimately entwined with performers, experiencing
sweat, liquid, inflatable space and decay.

Theatre Company: Volcano Theatre Company
Directors: Paul Davies and Fern Smith
Lighting Designer: Mark Parry
Sound Designer: Robbie Stamp

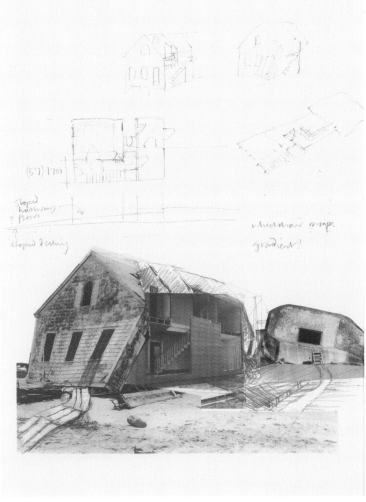

PETER HARRISON   LIGHTING DESIGNER

THE DOUBTFUL GUEST
Shôn Dale-Jones, 2008, inspired by the book by
Edward Gorey

Watford Palace Theatre, March 2008

The starting point for this project were the 16 pencil
drawings from Edward Gorey's book. These became the
staged tableaux and dramatic episodes that formed the
Bishop family's re-telling of their experiences. Working
with simple sketches, film references and colour examples,
we developed the lighting to become an additional tool
for the family to use in presenting their story. We built
a series of bold and stylised locations that created the
family house, using a hint of Victorian melodrama and the
darkness and gothic humor from Gorey's original work.

Theatre Company: Hoipolloi
Director: Shôn Dale-Jones
Set & Costume Designer: Stefanie Muller
Other creative collaborator: Alexander Rudd
Photographer: Geraint Lewis

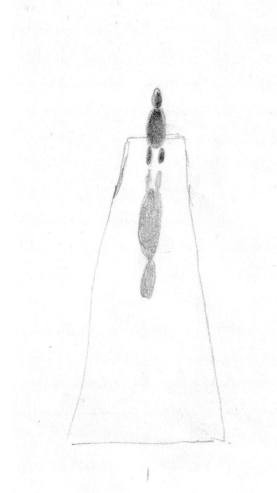

HELEN FOWNES-DAVIES SET & COSTUME DESIGNER

THOSE MAGNIFICENT MEN
Brian Mitchell and Joseph Nixon, 2010

Touring, February 2010

This was the story of Alcock and Brown's first non-stop transatlantic crossing told by two jobbing actors who, in their enthusiasm to perfect their show, build before the audience's eyes a reproduction Vickers Vimy biplane. As a team we needed to see how far we could effectively create a strong visual aesthetic, but also look as though it has been created by the actors themselves. The lighting played an integral part, particularly the shift in atmosphere from the recounting of the storytelling in Act I to imaging we were in flight through Act II. It was a critical image to get right, creating the magical sense of two men in flight in a hand-built set somewhere in a village hall. What has been most significant to me as the designer is establishing how each component part of the design came to be, what its history is and why it is there.

Theatre Company: New Perspectives Theatre Company
Director: Daniel Buckroyd
Lighting Designer: Mark Dymock
Sound Designer: Tom Lishman
Photographer: Robert Day

ANNE CURRY SET DESIGNER

THE BIRTHDAY PARTY
Harold Pinter, 1958

Ron Barber Studio Theatre, Crescent Theatre, Birmingham, October 2010

I have chosen a preliminary series of drawings for the characters Meg, Lulu, Goldberg and Stanley (Act II) from my design process work for Harold Pinter's play The Birthday Party. Act II represents the birthday party of the title, where the ambiguous dramatic tensions of Act I intensify, causing the transformation of narrative and characters. The narrative structure changes, becoming surreal. Actors transform their physical appearance: characters' body language, dialogue and actions intensify, combining to produce complex revelations about their emotional and psychological states. Act II illustrates sudden and illuminating disclosure, which does not take the form of a single major theatrical set change. Instead, there are multiple sudden and illuminating disclosures among the characters in the volatile atmosphere of this birthday party. Preliminary sketches reflect my continued conceptual preoccupation with figurative drawing and the exploration of character interpretation, with emphasis on the design of hair and make-up. The performance area is an intimate studio space; the venue intensifies the power of hair and make-up as a major contributor to characterisation and the costume design process.

Theatre Company: Crescent Theatre
Director: Liam Tombs
Costume Designers: Stewart Snape and Anne Curry
Hair & Make-up Design: Anne Curry

JOHAN ENGELS   SET & COSTUME DESIGNER

ARTAXERXES
Thomas Arne, 1762

Linbury Studio, Royal Opera House, Covent Garden, London,
November 2009

When Martin Duncan asked me to design *Artaxerxes*, we
both felt that as the Linbury Studio is such an intimate
space, we would try and create an extraordinary space:
a very exotic Persian-influenced space, that is also
reminiscent of the Elizabethan Globe. As we were dealing
with royal Persian characters, Martin saw them as exotic
birds within this simple blue space. Looking again at
Persian paintings, Kabuki costumes and, at the same
time, the exoticism of 18th-century taste, I created vividly
coloured costumes with incredible detail which would,
of course, be seen from inches away in the auditorium.
I donated two old Japanese wedding kimonos from my
own fabric collection to the production, which we used
for Christopher Ainsley and Elizabeth Watts. In the end it
was a very creative collaborative effort from all concerned
that brought this to fruition. The incredible wardrobe of the
ROH created the costumes.

Theatre Company: Royal Opera House
Director: Martin Duncan
Choreographer: Michael Popper
Lighting Designer: Nick Michaletos

RICHARD FOXTON   SET & COSTUME DESIGNER

LOOT
Joe Orton, 1966

Hull Truck Theatre, April 2010

In approaching the design of this I was conscious of the
need to adapt the theatre space to modify the relationship
between the auditorium and stage, giving the set the
correct proportions and focusing in on the actors. This
was achieved by moving the line of the proscenium
arch, adapting the side seating banks and lowering the
proscenium, allowing the stage to feel closer to the seating
and the performers to have the right physical presence in
the space.

Theatre Company: Hull Truck
Director: Gareth Tudor Price
Lighting Designer: Graham Kirk

KATHERINA RADEVA   SET & COSTUME DESIGNER

GLASS MOUNTAIN
Anna Reynolds, 2009

Trestle Arts Base, St Albans, and touring, September 2009

Emily Gray and I knew that we had to deal with two very different worlds in the show: the world of the Polish myth on which *Glass Mountain* is based, and the world of the contemporary coach traveller. The show switched between the different worlds constantly, so we knew that whatever it was that we put on stage had to be fully utilised, had to be fully flexible, to be easily removable and easily moved as part of the choreographed action. The world of the myth dealt with heights, hence the princes stuck on top of the mountain; but we were touring, and touring to some very small and some mid-scale venues, so the height in itself was a challenge. In the end I decided to create a mountain range from ladders with different heights, assuring that the sense of height existed in every venue. The world of the bus I reduced to the bare minimum: chairs. The entire design of the show was produced through devising, collaboration and constant changes during the rehearsal period.

Theatre Company: **Trestle Theatre Company**
Director: **Emily Gray**
Lighting Designer: **Matt Haskins**
Sound Designer: **Loz Kaye**

LIS EVANS   SET & COSTUME DESIGNER

CANTERBURY TALES
Mike Poulton, 2005

New Vic Theatre, Newcastle-under-Lyme,
and national tour, February 2010

A production of Chaucer's *Tales* that involves a cast of 16 actor-musicians playing over 80 characters, touring to 11 theatre spaces, including in-the-round, proscenium and traverse, required a flexible and inventive approach. The scenic elements needed to be versatile and fully adaptable. This resulted in a set of movable elements in kit form which could be arranged according to the venue. This tied in with the travel aspect of Chaucer's pilgrimage, as well as the tour. The set comprised 55 wooden pallet structures, which incorporated flaps and traps and location points for flags, banners and crucifixes. These could be stacked and used vertically and horizontally to create the various elements of each scene. There was a central tower with a platform, hanging points and a winch, and eight tall window panels (for use in proscenium). In addition, a number of barrels, poles, ladders and crates, some farming tools and a gallows tree, which, with a few bundles of cloth, were used in various ways by an inventive company to create additional characters and animals and the world of the play. Each actor had a basic medieval costume over which were worn a variety of hats, cloaks, wimples and veils, waistcoats and masks, layered to create their numerous characters.

Theatre Company: **New Vic Theatre with Northern Broadsides**
Director: **Conrad Nelson**
Choreographer: **Matthew Bugg**
Lighting Designer: **Richard G Jones**
Assistant Director: **Andy Cryer**
Musical Director: **Rebekah Hughes**

DAVID COLLIS   SET & COSTUME DESIGNER

WIND IN THE WILLOWS
Richard Williams, 2010

Haymarket, Basingstoke, December 2010

Having already designed the play twice before, and not wishing to replicate past ideas, this time I eventually opted for a series of large, fretted, foliate portals which were constantly on the move, thus creating various transformations of locale and atmosphere. When it came to designing the costumes, I actively avoided any overt reference to the animal world, evoking and amplifying their character through their clothes.

Theatre Company: Haymarket, Basingstoke
Director: Richard Williams
Lighting Designer: Stephen Holroyd
Sound Designer: Paul Howse
Photographer: David Cutts

DAVID COCKAYNE   SET & COSTUME DESIGNER

THE MERMAID OF ZENNOR
David Frost, 2010

Hall for Cornwall, Truro, March 2010

The piece is based on the traditional story of the Mermaid of Zennor, and moves continuously between the sea and the land. Initial work involved working closely with the composer and choreographer to evolve the scenario and the music, then extending into choreography and design. Numerous designs included a very deep cloth, moving to create sea or sky; a huge flown arch that could suggest both of those, and the shoreline; and moving mirrors reflecting the dancers, making them seem to float. These were generally rejected as too expensive, too difficult to make work in the time available, potentially dangerous, or all three. At one point, a large fan made of torn fabric rested on the stage, under the sea, also pulled up to form a wind-torn tree. In discussion with the lighting designer we felt it was too static, and we suspended a piece of paper in the model. We decided to work from that, and a flown gauze evolved that could hang in various ways, and collapse onto the stage, based on the work of Prunella Clough, a painter who has been a great influence on my work, both as a designer and as a painter.

Theatre Company: Duchy Ballet
Choreographer: Lucy Graham
Lighting Designer: Clare O'Donoghue

HAYLEY GRINDLE   SET DESIGNER

BEN HUR
Hattie Naylor (author) and Conor Mitchell (composer)
Main Stage, Theatre Royal Bath, October 2010

Through the design of *Ben Hur* I wanted to create a sense of dramatic, epic adventure, but also for every scene to visually engage and be memorable, not just the chariot race. *Ben Hur* can be perceived as complex due to the numerous locations and the movement between them. The set design needed to describe in subtle terms to the audience where the action was taking place. While working through the model, the signposts to achieving this became clear, i.e. through signature structures, props. Each differently located scene should hold its own sense of surprise and revelation; standing independently, but working to put down the foundation blocks for the visual peak. The movement within the architectures and structures transform the space. The space, height and pillars contribute to the sense of epic and allow the space to be transformed. Working in collaboration with costume designer Karen McKeown the performers embellished the set design. The cast became a fluid ensemble of wavelets of sea passing over their heads a raft and, in true epic form, becoming the chariot race via a choreographed piece inspired by the Roman testudo, i.e. using the shield formations of the Roman military.

Theatre Company: **Theatre Royal Bath**
Director: **Lee Lyford**
Costume Designer: **Karen McKeown**
Lighting Designer: **Su Dean**
Sound Designer: **Paul Dodgson**

KEVIN KNIGHT   SET & COSTUME DESIGNER

PASTORALE
Géérard Pesson, 2007

Staatsoper, Stuttgart

Without a completed score or libretto it is difficult to begin the work on any new opera. As part of my process, and as a key member of the creative team, I generated a series of collaged images alongside the storyboarding as the narrative developed. This helped in focusing our creative ambitions and enabled me to communicate clearly within the group.

Director: **Paul Curran**

SHIZUKA HARIU   SET DESIGNER

SACRED MONSTERS
Akram Khan, 2006

Sadler's Wells, London (premiered 2006 and 2008)
and world tour, 2006–10 (first premier September 2006,
second premier June 2007)

In *Sacred Monsters* the two iconic dancers Akram Khan
and Sylvie Guillem explore childhood memories and voices
by experimenting with their strong base of classical and
traditional dance. *Sacred Monsters* has been performed
at Sadler's Wells, London, and in theatres worldwide
between 2006 and 2010. The set design was based on
the idea of contradiction and harmony between the two
dancers' cultures. Shizuka Hariu analysed their dance
movements, and developed especially the concept of
gravity. In the design process, Fibonacci's mathematical
order provided two large-scale, harmonious curved
surfaces in order to emphasise their dynamic, wave-like
choreography. A new hybrid material of aluminium and
cotton gave roughness and depth on the stage. The set
design was adapted to the amphitheatre version for *Les
Nuits de Forvière* in Lyon, Barcelona and Athens in 2007.
The idea was transformed to the two curved surfaces
standing on the stage, offering a comfortable performance
area for both dancers and musicians. Finally, a contemporary sacred location lands softly in the Roman-style
amphitheatre. Hariu often designs the scenography
for contemporary dance performances; therefore her
design has been developing the idea of the metaphorical
transformation between movement and space.

Theatre Company: Akram Khan Company
Director/Choreographer: Akram Khan
Costume Designer: Kei Ito
Choreographers: Lin Hwai Min and Gauri Sharma Tripathi
Lighting Designer: Mikki Kunttu
Sound Designer: Philip Sheppard
Other creative collaborators: Sylvie Guillem and Akram Khan
Photographer: Shin Hagiwara

NAOMI DAWSON   SET & COSTUME DESIGNER

THE GODS WEEP
Dennis Kelly, 2010

Hampstead Theatre, London, March 2010

The play divides into three acts. The first takes place in
a recognisable world: a multinational corporate office,
in and around the boardroom. The second suddenly
plunges into a metaphorical space, a parallel world where
boardroom has become battlefield; civil war has erupted
amongst the colleagues. The third is an extension of
two and transforms into a post-apocalyptic wilderness.
The biggest challenge was how to make sense of the
huge leap between one and two, to make it clear that we
were in a parallel world rather than a naturalistic one. We
decided to solve this through a succession of revelations
and interventions within the space, rather than the removal
or addition of anything. The staircase moved position to
reveal a sense of destruction; grilles were blown out of
position, creating new entrances. The tree, which had
previously been an internal tree in an office atrium with
display lighting, became an external tree and the planter
on which it stood used as a hillside. The boardroom table
lowered into the floor, becoming an almost sacrificial stone
slab, and floor slates removed to reveal mud. A sense of
the boardroom prevailed, but where it was previously
symmetrical, cold and clinical, it became almost instantaneously its polar opposite, filled with mud, blood, disorder
and chaos.

Theatre Company: Royal Shakespeare Company, New Writing
Director: Maria Aberg
Choreographer: Ayse Tashkiran
Lighting Designer: David Holmes
Sound Designer: Carolyn Downing
Video Design: Ian Galloway and Finn Ross
Photographer: Keith Pattison

FOTINI DIMOU   COSTUME DESIGNER

CREDITORS
August Strindberg, in a new version by David Greig, 2008

**Donmar Warehouse, London, and Harvey Theatre, New York,
October 2008**

The character of Tekla is a free spirit, a woman aware and
comfortable with her femininity but still vulnerable and
unsure of herself. Trying to understand and describe a
character like her on stage was a fascinating process and
we (designer/director Alan Rickman and actress Anna
Chancellor) arrived at the final design of her costume after
time in the rehearsal room as well as the fitting room.
The way Tekla moves in her full 19th-century corseted
outfit was key to our decisions about the shape of her
dress, and it took some funny fittings when Anna had
to roll around the floor before the final stitches were put
into her dress. The colour, the steel grey central panel of
her dress, was meant to be like her armour. Buttoned up
and sharp, but lined in a deep red fabric barely visible
around her neck line and on the inside of her cuffs, meant
as a subtle hint of frivolity and femininity. Most of these
small but psychologically important details came from
several discussions between us and through our collective
instincts. It was a wonderful journey and a rare collaboration between all of us.

Theatre Company: Donmar Warehouse
Director: Alan Rickman
Set Designer: Ben Stones
Lighting Designer: Howard Harrsion
Sound Designer: Adam Cork
Photographer: Hugo Glendinning

BOB CROWLEY   SET DESIGNER

THE YEAR OF MAGICAL THINKING
Joan Didion, 2008

Lyttelton Theatre, National Theatre, London, March 2007

The design consisted of six paintings on silk, charting the character's journey to the heart of grief. Six landscapes of grief.

Theatre Company: National Theatre
Producer: Scott Rudin
Director: David Hare
Costume Designer: Ann Roth
Lighting Designer: Jean Kalman
Sound Designer: Paul Arditti
Other creative collaborator: Vanessa Redgrave

LOUISE ANN WILSON   SET & COSTUME DESIGNER

STILL LIFE
Louise Ann Wilson and Nigel Stewart, 2008

Far Arnside, at the border between Lancashire and Cumbria on Morecambe Bay, Lancashire, September 2008

Still Life was concerned with processes of composition and decomposition, and the relationship between the human and other-than-human world. It explored attempts we make through art and science to frame (compose, perceive) the natural world, but also how those attempts are disturbed and transformed by forces of nature beyond the frame. Small audience groups were led by a guide from clifftop to sandy shore, over limestone rock and salt-marsh grass. Installations made from objects discovered *in situ* provided trails for the audience to follow. These included fallen apples, pottery fragments, feathers, plastic bottles, flowers and blackberries. Along these trails, spectators encountered digital recordings, verbal descriptions, cardboard frames placed over natural and man-made objects, and photographs of objects no longer present (such as a dead gull and the sea at high tide). But, equally, the audience discovered a story concerning a woman from the past who they witnessed out on the sands, and a weathered washed-up man from the present they beheld dancing on rocks.

Theatre Company: co-produced by Louise Ann Wilson Company and Sap Dance
Directors: Louise Ann Wilson and Nigel Stewart
Choreographer: Nigel Stewart
Guide: Derek Tarr
Photographer: Nicola Tarr

HOLLY MCCARTHY SET & COSTUME DESIGNER

FROST/NIXON
Peter Morgan, translated into German by Michael Raab, 2006

German premiere: Hamburger Kammerspiele, Hamburg, Germany, September 2009

The whole design really stemmed from a desire and a need to portray very real people and real emotions, summed up in one line of the play: "because that was before I really understood the reductive power of the close-up". Using the live close-up was the key to taking the audience's focus out of the realms of merely watching a piece of theatre, getting them to completely engage with the full power of the text. When approaching the design for *Frost/Nixon* I had, initially, avoided reading up about the recent successful West End stage show and the monstrously successful recent feature film, in order to have a wholly honest and personal response to the text. This was really important because I knew that this, combined with the fact that I knew very little about the Watergate scandal beforehand, gave me a huge insight into the problems we would face transforming and telling this story to a brand new German audience. The design had to hinge on those final moments of the Frost/Nixon interviews, on our need to see every second of Nixon's progression from power to vulnerability.

Theatre Company: Hamburger Kammerspiele
Director: Michael Bogdanov
Lighting Designer: Lars Thies
Sound Designers: Gerlad Timmann and Niclas Breslein
Photography: German press

ROBIN DON SET & COSTUME DESIGNER

THE EMPEROR JONES
Eugene O'Neill, 1920

Olivier Theatre, National Theatre, London, August 2008

Written 90 years ago, *The Emperor Jones* was the first American play to present a racially integrated cast to a Broadway audience and feature a black actor in its leading role. O'Neill insisted that black actor Charles Gilpin play Brutus Jones, and a precedent was set that would galvanise the movement to integrate black Americans into the artistic process. Set on a West Indian island, the Emperor, superbly played here by Paterson Joseph, is on the run. His faux palace of gilded colonial corrugated iron is brutally transformed into a vision of a disintegrating shanty town, overflowing with anguished souls. Jones becomes the hunted and the dispossessed. It's one of the scariest transformations I've ever seen. At one point it seems as though Jones will be crushed under the vast, descending metallic structure. This NT production was nominated for the Evening Standard 2008 Design Award. Although the director had an extremely successful production of the play at the tiny Gate Theatre in Notting Hill with designer Richard Hudson a year earlier, she gave me free rein to create a new concept for the vast stage of the Olivier Theatre with a cast of 58.

Theatre Company: National Theatre
Director: Thea Sharrock
Lighting Designer: Nail Austin
Sound Designer: Gregory Clarke
Choreographer: Fin Walker
Music: Sister Bliss
Photographer: RCD

MARIE-JEANNE LECCA   COSTUME DESIGNER

AGRIPPINA
Georg Friedrich Händel, 1709

Opernhaus Zürich, May 2009

Agrippina is a one-woman show; even if not continuously present on stage, she is there through her plots and scheming. She relentlessly keeps revealing an inexhaustible versatility and ability to react to ever-changing circumstances by reshaping her ambitions and machinations. What was interesting for me was that, even though the core of the character does not transform in the least during the piece, she performs for an 'audience' and, as a true stage animal, she gives the impression of transformation, and reveals herself to her 'audience' in different guises, ranging from mother and widow, through to predator and maneater.

Theatre Company: Opernhaus Zürich
Director: David Pountney
Set Designer: Johan Engels
Choreographer: Beate Vollack
Lighting Designer: Jürgen Hoffman
Conductor: Marc Minkowski
Photographer: Suzanne Schwiertz

ANNE MINORS PERFORMANCE CONSULTANTS

THE BISHOP CENTRE, GODOLPHIN & LATYMER SCHOOL,
HAMMERSMITH, 2009
Client: Godolphin and Latymer School

The challenge for us lay in sensitively inserting the performance infrastructure into the Grade II*-listed church so the volume and original detail of the space could still be read, yet allowing the space to be acoustically closed down for young voices. Inspired by liturgical movement between the altar at the east end, the font at the west and the gospel reading in the centre of the nave, we retained this synergy by designating the chancel and organ as the music performance area, the west end as the drama stage (with high wing space) and the centre nave for theatre in the round. With a few key changes – a well to the nave, balconies in the side aisles and retractable acoustic and black-out surfaces – early studies and models showed how the church could be transformed into a highly flexible space for drama, concerts, assemblies and examinations, creating a new kind of congregation space with dynamic energy. The integrated production lighting and sound system now enables the students to operate the performances and run backstage, which has attracted greater numbers of students to production work, giving those who were normally shy on stage a new passion for technical theatre.

Theatre Company: Godolphin & Latymer School
Conservation Architects: Burrell Foley Fischer
Theatre Consultants: Anne Minors Performance Consultants
Structural Engineers: Price & Myers
Building Services Engineers: Troup Bywaters & Anders
Project Managers: Gardiner & Theobald
Acousticians: Applied Acoustic Design

JOHN MacFARLANE   SET & COSTUME DESIGNER

CINDERELLA
Sergei Prokofief, 1940–4

Birmingham Hippodrome, November 2010

Theatre Company: **Birmingham Royal Ballet**
Director: **David Bintley**
Lighting Designer: **David Finn**

SEAN CROWLEY   SET & COSTUME DESIGNER

ELLING
Axel Hellstenius, 2001, from the novel by Ingvar Ambjørnsen

Kammerspiele, Hamburg, and German national tour,
Elling, April 2008; *Elling 2*, January 2010

Elling and *Elling 2* were expansive narratives of the
tortured and tragic, if extremely funny, re-introduction of a
psychiatric patient into the community in Oslo. The holding
frame combined apartment, hospital, and tiled walls merg-
ing into blue skies and white clouds, symbolic of Elling's
traumas and triumphs. The set was transformed through
the use of multiple digital projection images, moving
seamlessly between café, supermarket, hospital, bedroom
and numerous city-wide locations. Designing using the
computer doesn't, from my perspective, replace drawing
or modeling, but it does change the thinking process.
Although it offers speed and efficiency, it does remove the
tactile sensory experience, The real pleasure still is taking
those 3D models and transforming them, via 2D printouts,
into actual real 3D models, with which to invest care and
pride in releasing the scale model with attention to detail,
and then in producing the final 1:1 scale design. *Elling*
worked extremely well with an excellent cast and crew,
but it begins to mark a yearning to personally transform…
and pick up a pencil… and talk through lines of graphite.

Theatre Company: **Kammerspiele**
Director: **Michael Bogdanov**
Lighting Designer: **Lars Thiess**
Sound Designer: **Niclas Breslein**

MICHAEL PAVELKA   SET & COSTUME DESIGNER

OFF THE WALL
Dramatic narrative by the creative team of *Stan Won't Dance*,
with original music by John Barber, 2007

Royal Festival Hall, Hayward Gallery and South Bank
environment, London, July 2007

Off the Wall was a devised, futuristic spectacle to reopen
the transformed South Bank Centre. I worked closely
with Liam Steel and Rob Tannion to create a street fable
that incorporated a large choir, parcours, circus and
dance; well over 100 performers in all. The ambitious
site included the exteriors of the Hayward Gallery, Royal
Festival Hall and piazza, and adjacent offices. We collected, swapped and amalgamated stories and matched
them to diverse images, often drawing in each other's
sketch books until their origins became untraceable. Our
preoccupations were the gravity of a mechanised lifestyle
as epitomised by the brutal site, and contrasting release
of weightlessness. What surprised us was how dynamic
this collection of architectural forms was to work with,
using their height, opacity or transparency to transform
their appearance or overturn their everyday use. We
added geometric structures such as a skeletal grid and
geodesic globe, and linked the roofs with zip lines across
concrete canyons. Our challenge was to make maximum
visual impact using single or multiple bodies to create a
human story in an inhuman environment, whereby a single
voice became a choir, a tiny spark became a flame, and an
action became a formidable movement.

Theatre Company: **Stan Won't Dance**
Directors: **Liam Steel and Robert Tannion**
Choreographers: **Liam Steel and Robert Tannion**
Lighting Designer: **Huw Llewellyn**
Sound Designer: **Andy Pink**
Aerial Skills Consultant: **Alex Frith**

TOM PIPER   SET & COSTUME DESIGNER

AS YOU LIKE IT
William Shakespeare, 1596

Courtyard Theatre, Stratford-upon-Avon, April 2009

The journey from Court to Arden and exile to love was dramatised through the way the space was changed. We began in a very ordered, monochrome Elizabethan world, a simple rectangle of floor and wall in matching parquet, which was opened up to reveal a massed tangle of vine. Initially Touchstone burst through a door as human tumbleweed, covered in creepers, literally bringing the disorder of Arden to disrupt the simple beauty of the space. The banished lords pushed up traps in the floor to further break up the world. The atmosphere was harsh and wintery, in which everybody had to struggle to survive. In the second half, the period costumes were gradually peeled away to a more modern silhouette, as we moved into a carefree summer. The auditorium, foyer and even the street outside were hung with love poems to create an abstract forest that enveloped the audience. What had begun as a very ordered image of the past thrust into, but very distinct from, the public, became contemporary and immediate, with all the boundaries broken between stage space and onlookers. They genuinely shared the same room.

Theatre Company: Royal Shakespeare Company
Director: Michael Boyd
Choreographer: Struan Leslie
Lighting Designer: Wolfgang Goebbel
Costume Supervisor: Poppy Hall
Photographer: Elli Kurtz

MICHAEL SPENCER   SET & COSTUME DESIGNER

VARIATION, VERIFICATION AND VINDICATION
Michael Spencer, 2008–9

Foyer, Central Saint Martins College of Art & Design, London

In December 2009 the playwright David Hare summed up the recent period called the 'noughties' as "the decade of looking away", by which he meant that the digital tended to take precedence over the live. However important the conversation might be, the mobile has to be answered. Recently, in a packed London tube train, I was witness to the break-up of a relationship, as a man squeezed next to me conducted a long and painful conversation over a mobile phone. I was so close I could hear her responses, as could those around me. Our mere presence became spectatorship. Maybe he should have sent a text. This devised performance intended to reveal these changing relationships. In retrospect, it raised more questions than it answered. Its structure challenged the conventional time-based contract between spectator and performer, where audiences are delivered a completed narrative within a single event – normally 7.30 pm start (with interval). I attempted an interconnecting thematic over 38 live events – now further distilled into a 12 minute film. It questioned the idea of focused performance by being located in a transient space. I performed all 38 performances myself alone, transforming my own reality and that of my everyday surroundings.

Director: Michael Spencer
Photographers: Maaike Stoffaris (video), stills by members of the audience as part of the piece

TIM HATLEY SET & COSTUME DESIGNER

MONTY PYTHON'S SPAMALOT
Eric Idle and John du Prez, 2006

Palace Theatre, London, September 2006

The challenge with *Spamalot* was to find a way to transform original Python Eric Idle's script based on the well-loved film *Monty Python and The Holy Grail* and reveal it as a West End musical. Monty Python has such a strong visual aesthetic, led by the genius Terry Gilliam, and I wanted to embrace his 2D cut-and-paste world and put it into three dimensions on stage. I knew the scenes had to move forward swiftly, and the humour of the set and costumes had to be in line with the text, acting, music and direction – as if another member of the company. I explained this to the team by drawing storyboards for each section of the show, and making endless sketch models.

Director: Mike Nichols
Choreographer: Casey Nicholaw
Lighting Designer: Hugh Vanstone
Sound Designer: ACME Sound

SARAH BACON   SET & COSTUME DESIGNER

MEDEA/MEDEA
Dylan Tighe, 2009

Gate Theatre, London, June 2009

If there is transformation and revelation in any tale that is worth telling, then theatremakers constantly seek original ways to draw on the old tales, making these qualities resonate anew. Medea is the story of a woman, a cultural outsider, who murders her own children to avenge their father, the man who has left her for a younger and more politically useful woman. Our production was not a straight theatrical playing of Euripides' tragedy, but a devised interpretation of an existing film of the tale, second by second. It was a myth-busting meta-theatrical performance, as much about revealing the mechanics of theatre as reworking the story of Medea. It was layered and dense, with its many references to iconography, identity, symbolism and semiotics, conveyed to the audience through video and live projection, an electro-acoustic soundscape, voiceover, slides, x-rays, pyro-technics, tinned tomatoes, a horse's head and many other props. No traditional theatre lights were used. The space was painted white, denying the audience the comfort of invisible darkness. A black gauze curtain set between the performers and the audience was only removed for the curtain call, revealing the aftermath, the chaotic stage, transformed by performance.

Theatre Company: The Gate/Headlong
Director: Dylan Tighe
Lighting Designer: Chahine Yavroyan
Sound Designer: Sean Og
Other creative collaborator: Ian Galloway
Photographer: Bill Knightly

BEN STONES   SET DESIGNER

AN ENEMY OF THE PEOPLE
Henrik Ibsen, 1882, in a new translation by Christopher Hampton

Sheffield Crucible, January 2010

Christopher Hampton's translation of Ibsen's *En Folkefiende* is more cinematic than other versions. The plot deals with a doctor of a small Norwegian town that discovers that the water to the town spa is poisoned, and as it is the main source of growth for the town the officials attempt to cover it up. The challenge facing me and Daniel Evans was the transition between four different locations, all varying in scale. The final shape of the space was based on the discovery that Ibsen wrote scenes that expand and contract. The modest Norwegian home of Dr Stockmann transforms into the dark and empty printing press of *The People's Messenger*. In Act IV the stage is set for an epic town meeting, with the vast crowds of townsfolk at the dilapidated, grand home of Captain Horster, before finally transitioning to the small attic study at the family's home. The finish and look of the set came from a research trip that Daniel Evans, Antony Sher and I took to Norway, where we saw the effects the sea had had on the beautiful wooden architecture: a visual metaphor for a town that is gradually being poisoned by its source of wealth.

Theatre Company: Sheffield Theatres
Director: Daniel Evans
Lighting Designer: Tim Mitchell
Sound Designers: Ben and Max Ringham

FRED MELLER   SET & COSTUME DESIGNER

WOYZECK
Georg Büchner, 1836

Southwark Playhouse, London, March 2008

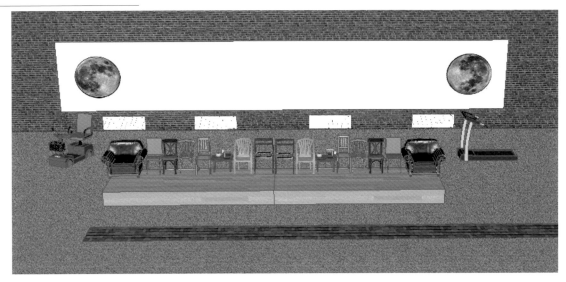

Woyzeck as an experiment in transformation. Büchner's unfinished play is reconfigured to exploit the interventions of forum theatre, where real lives are transformed through drama. The play is played a second time and the audience are invited to join in and make interventions, transforming the meaning and perception of sanity, murder and suicide. The Doctor experiments on Woyzeck, and the audience are made implicit in this. Half the audience were taken through a separate entrance and given white coats to wear. When the rest of the audience were seated, they entered and sat among them like a group of medical students. A critic had complained about the temperature of the space, which is located in railway arches. Since Cardboard Citizens have a reputation for site-specific promenade performances, we transformed these perceptions through overheating the space, placing radiators and thick carpeting everywhere. Design elements were discovered through the actions of the characters. The physicality defined the use of the space and objects: authenticity, rather than a false aesthetic. Woyzeck was constantly on the move on a running machine, but the inactive Captain inspected his troops using a mobility scooter. The fine line between sanity and madness was expressed by the mirror image of the design. A tight budget meant there were not enough actors to play the parts required, so the company brought in their pets. A goldfish played the part of the crowd and the performing horse was played appropriately by a lab rat. The grandmother's story transformed as a face in the moon.

Theatre Company: Cardboard Citizens Theatre Company
Director: Adrian Jackson
Lighting Designer: Ian Saunders
Sound Designer: David Baird
Photographer: Roy Luxford

DAVID BURROWS   THEATRE CONSULTANT

REFURBISHMENT AND TRANSFORMATION OF THE THEATRE AT WIMBLEDON COLLEGE OF ART
February 2009

Wimbledon College of Art Theatre, London, February 2009

During my last five years working at Wimbledon College of Art as Head of Theatre I led the project to refurbish the College theatre. Built in 1963, the theatre had become disheveled, problematic in the context of health and safety, and lacked a recognisable auditorium. Initial discussions with colleagues determined our likely future needs and I produced some SketchUp drawings as an architects' brief. I then led the lengthy process of compromise, specification and refinement until the project's completion. Collaboration with local architect Marcus Beale was especially rewarding as, being a performer himself, he was extremely sensitive and responsive to our ideas. An overarching inspiration for the ethos of the new space was Manchester's Royal Exchange Theatre, designed by Richard Negri, former Head of Department at Wimbledon. Negri's experiments at Wimbledon exploring audience configurations led directly to his concept for the Exchange. It seemed appropriate, then, to apply some of those ideas to our refurbishment, incorporating daylight from skylights (cf. Manchester's domes) above the auditorium (with remote-controlled blackout) and creating an ambience of freshness in a context of overall functionality. The theatre, transformed, formally opened on 5 February 2009 with a performance of fragments from Negri's own playlet *Everyman Revisited*.

Client: Wimbledon College of Art, University of the Arts, London
Architect: Marcus Beale Associates
Lighting Consultant: Dave Horn
Photographer: Gary Alexander

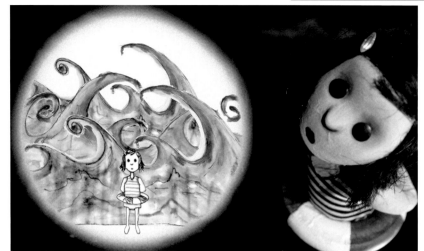

BEK PALMER   SET & COSTUME DESIGNER

MY MOTHER TOLD ME NOT TO STARE
Finegan Kruckemeyer and Martyn Harry, 2010

Touring production, February 2010

This opera for young audiences is about the disappearance of disobedient children from a warped, puritanical, fairytale town. A globe, encapsulating a village and an island structure in the set, reflected the isolation of this dark, troubled world. A central disc transformed scenes, becoming the moon, sun, or projection screen revealing alternative views of the town as if looking through a peep-hole onto snippets of animation and shadow puppetry. The tree holding the town bell, which rings whenever a child goes missing, becomes a memorial to the disappeared, as the mysterious narrator hangs (usually festive) baubles containing the spirits of the disappeared on it. For the final scenes, globes embedded around the set slowly illuminate to reveal the fate of the children, encapsulated in bubbles in the Fixing Kitchen, ready to have the badness boiled out of them and be reborn as new, innocent babies. Puppets were chosen to represent selected characters. Five cameos of the town's disobedient children are each represent by a different style of puppet appropriate to their own tale of a broken rule. The protagonist's parents, cobblers, became body puppets, using the performer's own lower body, transforming the character's physicality while leaving them erect to sing.

Theatre Company: Theatre Hullabaloo and Action Transport
Director: Nina Hajiyianni
Lighting Designer: Mike Francis
Photographer: Sylvia Selzer

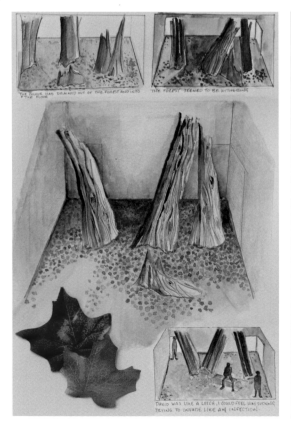

SHEREE TAMS   SET DESIGNER

GET AWAY
Greg MacArthur, 2007

Old Red Lion Theatre, London, 2007

Isolation and increments of horror were the subtext. We used this idea to formulate a place, a remote wood-land far away from the epidemic spreading across the world. The director David Dorrian and I decided to look at the Temagami region of northern Ontario, where we discovered the old growth white pine forest, with spirits living in the wood. We then discovered old growth pine 'stags' – dead pine trees. These giant, dead trees were large, eerie and big enough to conceal built-in cupboards where we could hide props and costumes. Actors hid behind the stags when they were not in a scene. We added evidence of the local First Nations community: dream catchers, directional signposts pinned to the trees, camping pots, an old Monopoly game and a tree stump for sitting.

Theatre Company: Second Glance Theatre
Director: David Dorrian
Set Designer: Sheree Tams
Costume Designer: Giulia Scrimieri
Lighting Designer: Joshua Tomalin

BECS ANDREWS   SET & COSTUME DESIGNER

MOMO
Michael Ende, 1973

Stadttheater Bern, October 2010

The story: Momo, a girl who lives in a ruined amphitheatre, gradually finds her world over-run by grey men who steal time from ordinary people and smoke it in their grey cigars, by making them work faster and faster so they turn grey themselves. She travels to the end of time, where she experiences the time-lily eternally blooming and dying and as her friends get corrupted she sees no option but to stop time and prevent the grey men from taking over completely. The challenge and pleasure in designing *Momo* is to tell such a complex narrative through dance and retain enough open space for large expressive movements. The colour-coding in the costumes and the contrast in the two 'real' locations – city and amphitheatre (which merge as the city takes over) – forms the backbone to the design. The abstract world of the end of time is created with a huge video projection of a timelapse lily and video projection of a digital clock speeding up, demonstrating the grey men's grasp tightening as the piece progresses.

Theatre Company: **Stadttheater Bern**
Director/Choreographer: **Didy Veldman**
Choreographer: **Didy Veldman**
Video Designer: **Becs Andrews**
Video Maker: **Hambi Haralambous**

KATE UNWIN   SET & COSTUME DESIGNER

THE AFRICAN COMPANY PRESENTS RICHARD III
Carlyle Brown, 1987

Greenwich Theatre, London, then touring, January 2009

The director began by emailing me a list of questions dissecting my initial reaction to the play. He used this to work up a vision based on research, history and life experience, which he then shared with me; the main emphasis being that this theatre company of black actors were performing Shakespeare in 1821, before slaves were set free, using storytelling to empower themselves and each other. It was also important that this play connected with, and was relevant to, oppressed people today. I was inspired by recent artistic reaction and response to slavery, as well as the disturbing historical facts and imagery. The set located them in a traditional theatre setting, but the backdrop was a curtain of chains and the wings were the ribs of a slave ship. The dark wood of the ribs and the floor at first appeared to be dusted with a shimmering gold, but under this the wood was soaked with a deep blood red. The costumes were a combination of historical details and structure, with modern black street style using layers of different textures and modern prints.

Theatre Company: **Collective Artistes**
Director: **Chuck Mike**
Lighting Designer: **Rachel Francis**
Sound Designer: **Greg Patmore**
Photographer: **Adam Tiernan Thomas**

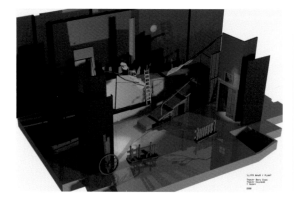

MARTIN MORLEY   SET DESIGNER

LLYFR MAWR Y PLANT
Gareth F Williams and Catrin Edwards (composer), 2008

Theatr Gwynedd, Bangor, and tour of medium-sized Welsh
theatres, November 2008

Following an initial discussion with Tony Llewelyn, the
director, and reading the synopsis of the musical version of
the Welsh classic *Llyfr Mawr y Plant* (no complete script at
this stage), I made a quick CAD model which established
the key elements: space and levels; not an anonymous
theatrical space, but one grounded in the locality from
which the original book sprang. Slate footpath with rusty
hand rail and characteristic slate fence. Sinister suspended
branches and rough slatted doors. Items culled from the
locality: real in themselves, but suggesting the location
rather than portraying it. The default textures of the
original computer model, slick and glossy, needed to be
developed into something more earthy and atmospheric,
but the original elements remained. We worked to create
an environment that would be all-pervading but filled with
secret doors and sliding rocks to enable the necessary
changes. We aimed to delight and surprise while drawing
out the darker undercurrents in the story. My design
philosophy is to listen to the text and director, together
with the creative team, and to produce a design that will
only truly work for that particular production. I have tried to
follow this path throughout my career.

Theatre Company: Theatr Bara Caws/Theatr Gwynedd/Galeri co-production
Director: Tony Llewelyn
Costume Designer: Aimi Hopkins
Choreographer: Cai Tomos
Lighting Designer: Iestyn Griffiths
Sound Designer: Sion H Gregory
Photographer: Martin Morley

PAUL BURGESS   DIRECTOR/DESIGNER

A PLACE AT THE TABLE
Devised by the Company, 2009

Camden People's Theatre, London, April 2009

This was a designer-led, devised project about the
conflicting narratives that shape Burundian history,
centring on the 1993 coup. The structure of the resulting
piece reflected exactly its creative process: the results of
research were presented, conflicting versions compared
and only then did the actors explore the effect this
sometimes harrowing material had on them. The design
was approached with an entirely open mind. My ideal
process as a director-designer is not to impose concepts
on source material but let them emerge. In this case, partly
as a result of creating the piece round a rehearsal room
table, our process led us to fill the theatre with as a big a
table as possible. The audience were invited to sit around
it alongside the cast. Through the performance the table
made a series of conceptual and physical transformations.
It was a UN conference, a kitchen, a radio station. It
became a stage and a giant drum. Things were buried or
dug up from soil hidden under its panels. Finally it became
a dining-room table for 36 people, as the audience were
given food and invited to stay after the show to eat and
chat with each other and the cast.

Theatre Company: Daedalus Theatre Company
Costume Designer: Lily Babirya
Choreographer: Cécile Feza Bushidi
Lighting Designer: Katharine Williams
Composer: Matthew Lee Knowles
Photographers: Mathieu Leborgne/Daedalus

JOHN BISHOP LIGHTING DESIGNER

SAMSON
George Frederic Handel, 1741

Buxton Opera House, Buxton, Derbyshire, July 2008

Early design discussions between Daniel Slater, Dan Potra and myself led to a clear and concise visual language that we would use to narrate the biblical story of Handel's oratorio *Samson*. Updating the period and location to present day Gaza would bring the strong parallels of biblical conflict and present-day conflict sharply in to focus for a modern-day audience so accustomed to images of war on our news screens. Transforming the plain, oatmeal-coloured, semi-translucent set into an interesting variety of modern locations became my over-riding challenge as the production period progressed, finally resulting in the revelation of the singers' physical forms, characters and inter-relationships in a coherent series of visually striking semi-realistic and imaginary settings which illustrated the passion of the oratorio as the story unfolded.

Theatre Company: **Buxton Festival**
Director: **Daniel Slater**
Set & Costume Designer: **Dan Potra**
Choreographer: **Nicole Tongue**
Conductor: **Harry Christophers**

MAYOU TRIKERIOTI SET & COSTUME DESIGNER

GHOSTS
Henrik Ibsen, 1881

Scholeion, Greek Festival, Athens, 2008

This production of Ibsen's *Ghosts* was done in a non-theatrical space: a set of empty storerooms, part of what used to be an old tinfoil factory. The fact that the design had to incorporate the seating, as well as the director's need to stress the themes of religion, chastity and faith in the play, led to a Protestant church-like arrangement. In line with church architecture as well as traverse theatre, the audience faced each other, sat in stalls like a congregation, but also as if they were the jury to an unnamed trial, observing "these monsters disguised as bourgeoisie". In a way deprived of their anonymity yet taken back into a sense of community and ritual, each group formed en masse the backdrop of extras for the other half of the audience, subtly assuming a different role and involving themselves artistically in the *mise en scène*. The floor was filled with gravel, which affected both walking and movement, and glass doors separated the audience space from the outside world, which was blessed with cathartic summer rain.

Theatre Company: **commissioned by the Greek Festival**
Director: **Ektoras Lygizos**
Choreographer: **Mariela Nestora**
Lighting Designer: **Max Penzel**
Sound Designer: **Haralambos Gogios**
Make-up: **Ioanna Lygizou**
Photographers: **Mayou Trikerioti and Evi Fylaktoy**

ABIGAIL HAMMOND   COSTUME DESIGNER

7734
Jasmin Vardimon, 2010

Trinity Laban, London, September 2010

In my experience of costuming contemporary dance, set design tends to be quite minimal. In *7734*, by Jasmin Vardimon, the space is inhabited by hundreds of items of clothing, at times covering the entire stage. This has created new challenges for me, and as these notes go to print we are in the last month of rehearsal and so refer to a process still in progress. Vardimon's work is dance theatre, and her preferred costume style is ordinary clothes. During rehearsals the dancers have worn garments from the set, useful in helping to establish character and integrate costume changes. However, this has meant that I joined a process slightly locked in an aesthetic of cheap, second hand clothing. Initially focussing on the Holocaust, the theme developed to encompass a broader exploration of mankind's recurring ability to destroy each other. This decision was crucial to my process, as it allowed me to reference a modern world and to identify the power figures through a graphic/abstract look. As the chore-ography is consolidating so I am gradually replacing the items of clothing from the set with designed items, adding concept and style, highlighting moments of uniformity and individuality throughout the journey.

Theatre Company: **Jasmin Vardimon Company**
Director/Choreographer: **Jasmin Vardimon**
Set Designer: **Guy Bar Amotz**
Lighting Designer: **Chahine Yavroyen**

FABRICE SERAFINO   SET & COSTUME DESIGNER

MEDEA
Jean Anouilh, 1946, translated by Suba Das

Theatre Royal Stratford East, London, June 2007

Set in west Africa, the piece reveals the final, violent night of a desperate refugee woman abandoned by her husband. Suba Das and I agreed on inviting the members of the audience right into Medea's world. We wanted to engage them in a physical way, as well as include them in the design, sharing the space with the performers and, by doing so, transforming the Theatre Royal's stage into a different kind of performing space. Inspirations from African artists helped us to create the world: Senam Okudzeto's artwork dealing with refugees' matters directed us to the 'Ghana Must Go' bags, El Anatsui's to recycled metalwork. Africa was suggested with red sand, piled into a corner, almost spilling onto the entire floor. The enclosure inside the Theatre Royal's brick walls and metallic fire curtain provided an omnipresent urban, oppressive feel. Seated on the bags, the audience was in the heart of the action, which was literally unravelling all around them, narrated by the nurse, in a direct and African storytelling mode.

Theatre Company: **Theatre Royal Stratford East**
Director: **Suba Das**
Choreographer: **Kenrick Sandy**
Lighting Designer: **Anthony Newton**
Photographers: **Johnny Munday, Fabrice Serafino and Anthony Newton**

MARK BAILEY   SET & COSTUME DESIGNER

A MIDSUMMER NIGHT'S DREAM
William Shakespeare, 1594–6

Anthony Hopkins Theatre, Clwyd Theatr Cymru, Mold,
Flintshire, February 2008

The director and I wished to take the audience on a
journey of the imagination, into a place where magic could
happen. From a stark Athens the space changed in view
of the audience as 100,000 leaves floated down, carpeting
the ground in green. Into this world came Puck and the
fairies, their costumes white on the front and leaf green on
the back allowing them to appear and disappear simply
by turning round. This production, as much as any I have
designed, illustrates my desire to simplify and clarify, using
bold statements that allow the audience's imaginations to
take flight.

Theatre Company: Clwyd Theatr Cymru
Director: Tim Baker
Choreographer: Rachel Catherall
Lighting Designer: Nick Beadle
Sound Designer: Matthew Williams
Composer: Dyfan Jones

NERISSA CARGILL THOMPSON   SET & COSTUME DESIGNER

CHARRED GRIZZLE
Devised from a concept by Tom Hogan, 2009

Street theatre touring festivals premiered at
Grassington Festival 2009, North Yorkshire, June 2009

Charred Grizzle mixes commedia dell'arte characters with
the comic nasty of the bouffon clown. What appears to be
just another bistro has a more sinister side. The ultimate
eating experience drives the chef and maitre d' to the
most extraordinary lengths to impress. Aqueous Humour
specialise in street theatre. We use masks to help create
visually striking characters to draw our audience in from
a distance; it is up to the performers to keep them there.
In this show, using masks also helped in the doubling
of the female character as it enabled the performer to
transform between wildly different characters very quickly.
Half-masks are used as, although the show is non-lan-
guage based, there is still a strong vocal element. I created
the designs in clay and then used papier mâché to make
the masks. I have experimented with other materials, but
always return to paper. It gives me the best balance of
definition, weight, ease of construction/maintenance and
cost. "The beauty of the mask does not lie in the mask or
the skill of the performer; it is the skill with which they are
brought together that creates real magic."
Tom Hogan, Artistic Director, Aqueous Humour.

Theatre Company: Aqueous Humour
Director: Colette Murray
Other creative collaborator: developed in partnership with Grassington
Festival '09 and Arts Council England
Photography: Nerissa Cargill Thompson and Aqueous Humour

RUSSELL CRAIG   SET & COSTUME DESIGNER

CINDERELLA
Phil Porter (author) and Martin Ward (composer), 2009

The Weston Theatre, Unicorn Theatre, London, December 2009

Cinderella lives on a floating retirement home for old magicians. The boat revolves transforming into the palace staircase. Male actors transform into female guests at the Butterfly Ball.

Theatre Company: Unicorn Ensemble
Director: Tony Graham
Lighting Designer: Oliver Fenwick

ELIZABETH WRIGHT   SET & COSTUME DESIGNER

SHINING CITY
Conor McPherson, 2004

Studio, Theatre by the Lake, Keswick, 2010

Within the context of Adobe Photoshop software, the term 'transform' describes a range of actions that can be used to create or manipulate digital images. The digital storyboard shows the process by which two photographs were combined and adapted to create a wall image for *Shining City*. In combination with lighting and sound, the grainy, abstract cityscape aimed to communicate a sense of the world beyond the immediate environment, a therapist's office, also evoking the shadow of Ian's past as a priest. The composite image was carefully constructed so that the two-dimensional print would intersect with three-dimensional scenic elements such as the suspended window fragment and the angle above the door.
On another level, this design represents the transformation of Theatre by the Lake's Studio, a traverse space, every two days into three different environments for *Silence* and *The Glass Menagerie*, as well as *Shining City* during the 2010 summer season of plays in repertoire.

Theatre Company: Theatre by the Lake
Director: Zoë Waterman
Lighting Designer: Jo Dawson
Sound Designer: Andrew J Lindsay
Photographers: Keith Pattison (image 1), Elizabeth Wright (image 2)

JOHN PAWSON ARCHITECT

CHROMA
John Pawson, 2006–7

Royal Opera House, Covent Garden, London, 2006

All architecture concerns itself with the way people will use and move through space, but these dynamic issues are obviously heightened on a dance stage. Part of the specific challenge lay in the way that, unusually for an architect, work of this nature splits how space will be physically experienced from how it will be seen. We wanted to make something which was comfortable for the dancers to use and visually comfortable for the audience. We started with three versions originally, each exploring a slightly different set of spatial conditions and colour options: black, white and grey. Models were constructed to give a sense of what the finished spaces would be like, and these models became the focus of a series of conversations between Wayne and the lighting designer, Lucy Carter. It quickly became clear that a particular version of the white void offered the richest creative possibilities, combining an authentic sense of architectural place with the spatially-charged canvas for the architecture of the human body. The finished set is only a slightly revised version of one of those first models. Although the physical structures are all fixed, light can transform the character of the space – manipulating, for example, our perception of the backplane, which can be made to appear to advance or recede. The idea of the controlled opening was part of the design from the beginning, to frame the void and to act as a means of reading the body operating in space. The significance of the precise dimensions of the aperture had key functional, as well as aesthetic, implications: the slightest manipulation of the frame had an impact on the sightlines from a range of locations within the body of the opera house. In the end, the task was to create the best possible container for movement and light – an environment where the eye is free to register the subtlest shifts in the musculature of the body and in the colour and character of the light. The result is, in one sense, a charged limbo. That the architecture required to create this manifestation of void is actually quite substantial is one not lost on the people responsible for its construction, one of whom commented that the set for a 20 minute ballet is an edifice on the scale of a full-scale production of *Carmen*.

Theatre Company: Royal Ballet
Director/Choreographer: Wayne McGregor
Costume Designer: Moritz Junge
Lighting Designer: Lucy Carter
Music: Joby Talbot and The White Stripes
Project Architect: Mark Treharne
Model: Hiro Takayanagi
Photography: Richard Davies

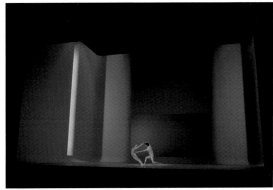

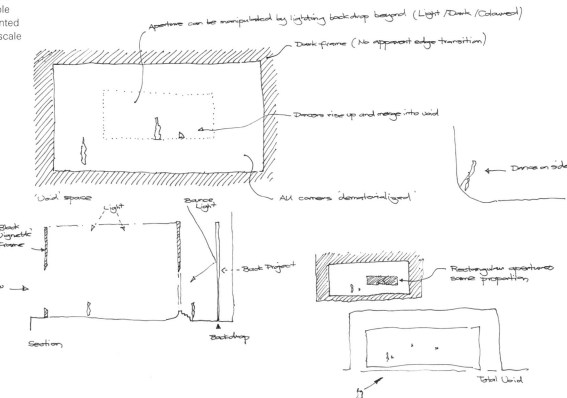

THOMASIN MARSHALL   SET & COSTUME DESIGNER

THE MISANTHROPE
Molière, 1666, adapted by Martin Crimp

The Drum, Theatre Royal Plymouth, April 2009

The world of *The Misanthrope* is one of materialist squalor and gossip! The play, at its heart, explores questions of meaning and perspective in a world where trash is treasure. Working with Young Company it was important to explore these themes and the related issues that are so significant, especially in the lives of young people. The set dramatises these ideas, as a solid material wealth rests, and is increasingly dependent, on a bed of rubbish as its foundation. The design highlights the juxtaposition of rubbish and glamour: a floor covered with gossip-filled newspapers, set within a room decorated with beautiful mock Baroque furniture. The city skyline at the back of the apartment is compiled of stacks of tabloid papers, as today's news is precariously built on yesterday's. Over the course of the first act, the presence of discarded litter increases dramatically. By the opening of Act II the room resembles a rubbish tip. The characters enter to join the Louis XIV-themed party, dressed in exuberant Baroque-style costumes made entirely from plastic bags! Amid a festival of glitzy trash and litter the characters reveal themselves in celebration for what they truly are, and their lack of value.

Theatre Company: **Young Company**
Director: **Andrew Dawson**
Lighting Designer: **John Purkis**
Sound Designer: **Richard Purkis**
Photographer: **Rob Ditcher at Photographik**

MATT DEELY & YOLANDA SONNABEND
SET & COSTUME DESIGNERS

BEETHOVEN'S SYMPHONY NO.9
Ludwig van Beethoven, 1824

Akasaka Act Theatre, Tokyo, September 2008

The choreographer, Tetsuya Kumakawa, wanted a spectacular setting to reflect the powerful, uplifting tones of the music. The orchestra were positioned on a raised platform upstage, allowing the dancers to perform closer to the audience.

Theatre Company: **K-Ballet Company, Tokyo**
Director/Choreographer: **Tetsuya Kumakawa**
Lighting Designer: **Hisashi Adachi**

AMANDA STOODLEY   SET & COSTUME DESIGNER

MAKING AN EXHIBITION OF OURSELVES (AT HOME)
Exchange Education, 2010

The Studio, Royal Exchange Theatre, Manchester,
January 2010

Home is the place where we are most likely to be ourselves, display ourselves and give ourselves away. Our homes express and reveal infinite possibilities, reflecting who we are, where we are in our lives and what we might be. The design examined the geography of home and particular characteristics of different rooms. We used recognisable signs and elements to exhibit a wide range of information about ourselves. I worked closely with Kay, Pete and the Exchange Education team to create a sense of home – an environment and atmosphere that felt familiar and authentic, but also theatrical and surreal. This was an interactive exhibition, in which visitors were invited to contribute, explore and become the performers in the transformed theatre space: 16 organisations and 593 individuals, including members of the general public, school pupils, community groups and Exchange Education projects' participants, contributed to the exhibition. A variety of containers and activities were provided, and work included the fridge of hidden sadness, the blanket of dreams, the cabinet of pain and relief, suitcase lives, food diaries, lists, notes, thoughts and secrets. I am fascinated by the effect of different theatre places and spaces on audience behaviour and perception, and also in the relationship between exhibition and theatre. This project enabled me to engage visitors extremely closely, by offering some home comforts and encouraging their natural curiosity to delve, discover and instinctively perform.

Theatre Company: Exchange Education – Royal Exchange Theatre
Director: Amanda Dalton
Lighting Designer: Kay Harding
Sound Designer: Pete Rice

ATLANTA DUFFY   SET & COSTUME DESIGNER

SEMI MONDE
Noël Coward, 1926

Guildhall School of Music & Drama, London, April 2008

Set variously in the foyer, lounge, terrace and bars of the Paris Ritz between 1924 and 1926, Coward's play charts an extravagant social merry-go-round of private lives, intertwining then unravelling in public places. The director's initial instincts and my research into the period led me to Edward Steichen's 1920s silver print *Heavy Roses*. On the cusp between voluptuous full bloom and decay, it seemed an apt metaphor for the lives and times of the play. In the end I worked another of his images into the curved wall of the set, and Emma Chapman's lighting not only reinforced the cyclical, claustrophobic qualities of both play and space, but also subtly transformed this Chinoiserie-like image to give it an unsettlingly living, creeping presence. Furniture, light, costume and choreography worked together to denote changes of scene with clarity and fluidity. Coward asks for a scene set against opulent display cases. Ours were concealed within the wall which, when lit, revealed bejewelled figures, not waving but drowning. As always, this designer's imaginings were enriched by the practical skill and imagination of her collaborators, both student and professional.

Director/Choreographer: Alistair McGowan
Choreographer: Wendy Allnutt
Lighting Designer: Emma Chapman
Photographer: Nobby Clark

'In recent times I have become more interested in how the real and authentic object thoughtfully placed in the appropriate context may reveal more than the self-consciously designed artificial object. **The resonance and power of the authentic** may be a more useful and meaningful visual metaphor'.

MIRIAM NABARRO SET & COSTUME DESIGNER

PALACE OF THE END
Judith Thompson, 2008

The Studio, Royal Exchange Theatre, Manchester, February 2009

Judith Thompson's *Palace of the End* is a trilogy of monologues exploring three facets of the war in Iraq through the voices of Lyndee England, the US marine behind the abusive photos in Abu Ghreib; David Kelly, British weapons inspector; and Nehrjas, an Iraqi widow who undergoes torture. In the scenography I wanted to reflect the power, purity of structure and simplicity of purpose of the writing. Working closely with director Greg Hersov, lighting designer Richard Owen and composer Clare Windsor, I searched for a visual language which would allow the political power of the text to be illuminated. Avoiding an illustrative approach, I was strongly influenced by the American light artist James Turrell. I approached the studio space at the Royal Exchange as a site-specific space, reconfiguring the audience entrance, opening up the doorway into a backstage corridor and building false archways to give the sense of diminishing perspective. At the furthest point I floated a $6 \times 7'$ lightbox fitted with neon, which could illuminate the lives of each character. I then created distinct 'worlds' for each character as floating islands in front of the neon box. Produced in Manchester as the UK premiere, this production then toured to Galway Festival and the Traverse Theatre in Edinburgh in 2009, where it received the Amnesty International Freedom of Expression Award 2009.

Theatre Company: The Studio, Royal Exchange Theatre
Director: Greg Hersov
Lighting Designer: Richard Owen
Sound Designer: Claire Windsor
Producer: Richard Morgan
Photographer: Miriam Nabarro

KEITH BAKER SET & COSTUME DESIGNER

UNDER MILK WOOD
Dylan Thomas, 1954

National tour, September 2007

After a successful rural tour we were given funding to remount this production and tour nationally. I was able to re-visit the design and clarify and simplify some of my ideas. Previously I had tried to match Thomas's unique 'domestic surrealism' with its scenic equivalent, but we discovered that the very strength of Thomas's radio play makes design largely redundant. His beautiful descriptions and evocative word-pictures outdid anything I could provide. Instead we settled on a cosy in-the-round sitting room with mismatched chairs, surrounded by washing lines with net curtains, household linens and less usual items such as maps and sheet music to evoke the public/private world of Llareggub; a world of gossip and secrets and prying neighbours. Illuminated model houses on glass cake-stands enabled us to view the village slumbering at the start and end of the performance. The major revision to the design was the addition of the illuminated floorboards, which create a ghostly corridor for the dead Messrs Ogmore and Pritchard to slowly crawl along, eternally nagged by their surviving wife. Costumes were a mix of under- and outer-wear, reflecting the public/private world of the characters and hinting at a 'village gone mad'.

Theatre Company: Oxfordshire Touring Theatre Company
Director: Brendan Murray
Lighting Designer: Mark Dymock
Sound Designer: Jon Nicholls
Photographer: David Fisher

HANSJÖRG SCHMIDT   LIGHTING DESIGNER

KURSK
Bryony Lavery, 2009

Young Vic, London, May 2009

This was a show of the senses. The audience needed to feel, see and hear two submarines: the British nuclear sub where the action is set, and the doomed Russian submarine *Kursk*. The challenge was to transform the Young Vic's Maria Theatre into a submarine and to reveal the inner workings of the boat and crew. The main interest for me lay in the significance of the boat's structure and the importance of systems in the submariners' lives. Every object has its place and is of great significance. So in our production all of the lights became part of the scenographic system, objects suspended within a controlled blackness that allowed other senses to take over. No theatre lights were used; instead bulkhead lamps, LED strips, illuminated control units and domestic lamps made this world feel real. The lighting enabled the audience, who were free to stand or sit anywhere in the space, to glimpse fragments and details in order to fully construct the reality of the submarine and the submariners' lives in their own imagination.

Theatre Company: Sound&Fury
Director: Sound&Fury (Mark Espiner, Tom Espiner, Dan Jones)
Set & Costume Designer: Jon Bausor
Sound Designer: Dan Jones
Photographer: Keith Pattison

CHARLIE CRIDLAN   SET & COSTUME DESIGNER

LA BOHÈME
Giacomo Pucchini, 1896

Wedmore Village Hall, July 2008

Wedmore Opera performed *La Bohème* in a traditional Victorian village hall – characteristically long and thin with a high, shallow, raised stage. Raking the audience, creating a 180 seat auditorium, meant fantastic sightlines for everyone and a previously unseen view of the space. I also raked the shallow stage away from the audience and a leaning garret window bisected the whole stage diagonally. I created a walkway into the hall, encircling the orchestra. The delicate railings and a milieu of posters hinting of Ataget's Paris blended the stage with the audience. The new space had an epic quality, an intimacy and a wonderful acoustic was created. Act II transformed Act I's garret, high above Paris. The window rose to stand vertically, becoming boutiques in a busy arcade on Christmas Eve with doors from which shopkeepers and café owners spilled. Wreaths adorned gas lamps flown in above the chorus thronging the stage, children vying for position around the toy seller. The compact stage enhanced the hustle of an arcade. The vertical glass wall stripped back and, with the addition of the tavern sign, gave us a bare, cold no-man's land for Act III, 'La Barriere'. The performance, directed by Marylin Johnstone and with the leadership of professional soloists and orchestra was, for me, a transformation in every sense of the word: village hall to world-class stage, as moving and beautiful as seen in national opera houses.

Theatre Company: Wedmore Opera
Director: Marylin Johnstone
Lighting Designer: Mike Rippon
Conductor: Carolyn Doorbar
Photographer: Tessa Podpadeck

NICK MORAN   LIGHTING DESIGNER

DILEMMA OF A GHOST
Ama Ata Aidoo, 1965

Africa Centre, Covent Garden, London, and UK tour, November 2007

This story begins with the long awaited return to his African family of a son educated in the USA – with his African-American bride. Although this production began as a tour, the concept was to stage the courtyard of a Ghanaian village home in the dilapidated 18th-century galleried space of Covent Garden's Africa Centre. The space acted as conscious underscore to a theme of the play: the continuing impact of the slave trade on the lives of African and African-American people, a trade that helped to make possible buildings like the one we were in. The play was collaboratively rehearsed in the Africa Centre before the tour, where there is no technical infrastructure. We had to improvise a transformation of the space from a disused club, with a limited budget. I brought a simple lighting system into the rehearsals to try out ideas with the director and cast, working with the space rather than trying to impose an infrastructure on it. We discovered some novel solutions, including bouncing light into the performance space via a large sheet of Rosco mirror foil and suspending a single PAR Can downlight from a beam 8 m above the stage without access to ladders.

Theatre Company: Border Crossings
Director: Michael Walling
Set Designer: Elsie Owusu
Costume Designer: Semma Iqbal
Live underscore & music: Osei Korankye
Assistant Lighting Designer: Dan Large

MARTYN BAINBRIDGE   SET & COSTUME DESIGNER

ARCADIA
Tom Stoppard, 1993

Clwyd Theatr Cymru, Mold, Flintshire, February 2007

Working with a great director on this exquisite play was a real treat. Sidley Park, in Derbyshire, a grand country house in the classical style, provides the focus for the action, which jumps between 1810 and the present day. The elegant interior remains unchanged, as does the large table, both of which have to act for both time periods. It is here that the actions of the early 19th-century inhabitants are revealed by the squabbling academics of the present day. Scientific, sexual, academic and Byronic revelations bring together the different periods of time. The gardens, subject to a 'make over' in the Romantic style, are not seen but constantly alluded to. The problem was how to create a great garden without actually seeing it. The curved line implies a horizon, or the gentle hills of the soon-to-be-transformed garden, with the horizontal curve of light changing as the action dictates. The throb of a Newcomen steam engine acts as a constant reminder of the great transformation which is engulfing not just the garden but the lives of the characters, and indeed the country, on the verge of great industrial change. Transformation and Revelation could indeed be the title of this play.

Theatre Company: Clwyd Theatr Cymru
Director: Terry Hands
Lighting Designer: Terry Hands
Sound Designer: Matthew Williams

MORGAN LARGE SET DESIGNER

CAT ON A HOT TIN ROOF
Tennessee Williams, 1955

Novello Theatre, London, March 2009

The design for this all-black production of Williams'
Cat on a Hot Tin Roof became a location where the other
inhabitants of the house could voyeuristically eavesdrop
on the conversations within, a porous room where the
oppressive heat of the Deep South could seep into the
bedroom and suffocate the characters, yet also a cage-like
structure trapping Maggie the cat within its walls.

Theatre Company: Front Row Productions
Director/Choreographer: Debbie Allen
Lighting Designer: David Holmes
Sound Designer: Richard Brooker
Assistant: Andrew Riley
Photographer: Nobby Clarke

JOHANNA TOWN LIGHTING DESIGNER

WAR AND PEACE
Sergei Prokofiev, 1942

Theatre Royal, Glasgow, January 2010

It has always been the job of a lighting designer to transform the visions of a director and set designer. This can
sometimes take the form of a very simple conversation
about the production, which the lighting designer then
interprets into their lighting design; or it may be a much
longer dialogue that includes reference material and a
clear pictorial model presentation. *War and Peace* was
such a production. Due to my late appointment as lighting
designer, the director and set designer had already
conceived a very clear visual palette for each scene.
They also had a well-planned journey through the music
and had individually collected some very bold reference
material. This vision would enable the audience to go on
an epic journey through the opera. It was obvious that, for
this production to work technically and fluidly, it was going
to be my job as lighting designer to transform each scene
and each location, and that all the reference material I had
been given was going to become my palette. I feel that
this production achieved its goal and, through the lighting,
the audience were taken on a truly epic journey that
continued to transform again and again in front of their
very eyes.

Theatre Company: Scottish Opera and Royal Scottish Academy of
Music & Drama
Director: Irina Brown
Set Designer: Chloe Lamford
Choreographer: Kally Lloyd Jones
Lighting Designer: Johanna Town
Photographer: Kenneth Dundas

IAN TEAGUE   SET & COSTUME DESIGNER

PRETEND FAMILIES
Clair Chapwell, 2007

Schools tour, February 2007

Thematically, this play dealt with issues of identity and belonging, loss, separation and the links between family members and friends. Although there were multiple locations, much of the story took place in a London park. I was interested in the idea of family trees and the Mexican tree of life. The imagery I presented at early meetings with the director and writer combined images of trees and family photos. I developed various strands of imagery, but nothing quite gelled until my son, on the journey home from school, picked up some red plastic-covered wire and said "this would make a good tree". He was right. I used the wire to make three model trees, which I photographed and started playing around with in Photoshop. I pasted in a collage of my own family photos as a background. Although the design of the trees evolved through a series of models, the concept and overall feel was established here. As the design developed the three trees remained, but a central tree took on some characteristics of a climbing frame. Eventually, the background collage became movable screens which revolved to give interior or home spaces for two of the characters.

Theatre Company: Spare Tyre
Director: Arti Prashar
Sound Designer: Tayo Akinbode

NETTIE SCRIVEN   SET & COSTUME DESIGNER

JOURNEY TO THE RIVER SEA
Eva Ibbotson, adapted by Carl Miller, 2006

Unicorn Theatre, London, 2006; revival 2007

Journey to the River Sea embraces the transformative power of journeys. Orphan Maia leaves behind the Victorian values of her London education, seeking a home and family with distant relatives living in the Amazon, only to find the same ignorance and prejudice reinforced within their colonial world. But friendship with Finn and indigenous people leads to a journey deep into the Amazonian forest, revealing glimpses of an alternative world. Friendship – rather than kinship ties – becomes the power to heal loss. As an ensemble we created fluid space, the performers transforming the visual landscape moment by moment through choreographed use of props, furniture and cloth. At one moment, a busy market place for dancing the capoeira; at another, the crossing of the Amazon river; another, the burning of the colonial house. Essential sculptural details sharpened the emotional undertow: Finn's solitary tree his lonely perch, an emblem of exhausted natural resources; soft, winding bends and twists of the river; verdant undergrowth pulsating beneath the colonial world. Each moment was revealed through filters of colour, shadowing Maia's physical and emotional journeys from a world of dominant whites, through grey blues, to the deepening hues of vibrant greens laced with red.

Theatre Company: Unicorn Theatre and Theatre Centre
Director: Rosamunde Hutt
Choreographer: Jeanefer Jean-Charles
Lighting Designer: Ceri James
Musical Director: Matthew Bailey
Photographer: Ben King

HAYLEY SPICER   SET & COSTUME DESIGNER

THE ROTTEN PLOT
Jude Emmett, 2007

Studio Theatre, Everyman Theatre, Cheltenham, January 2008

The Rotten Plot was about the transformation of an unloved, littered wasteland into a delightful community garden through the power of recycling! The aim was to create a touring production to go to schools and community centres to spread the recycling message to primary age children and their parents in a fun and 'unpreachy' way. The set was designed as a wasteland, with puppet holes and areas for the actors to quick-change into numerous characters. At the very end of the show, the puppets transformed the set through the use of a fabric quilt and a drop-down backdrop, to turn the set into a magical garden. The set had to be portable enough to tour to schools and also be visually appealing to young children, to enable them to interact with the set. As part of the production we devised a series of workshops with local schools, using drama and visual arts skills to create their own version of the show.

Theatre Company: Everyman Theatre Company
Director: Camille Cowe
Lighting Designer: Corin Hayes
Sound Designer: Corin Hayes

CLAIRE LYTH   SET & COSTUME DESIGNER

THE TALENTED MR RIPLEY
Adapted by Phyllis Nagy from the novel by Patricia Highsmith, 1998

Queen's Theatre, Hornchurch, March 2010

The writer suggests a set of "limitless open space and horizon". I felt a broken up surround of clouds that could be projected onto would provide the space, with moving storm clouds to dramatise the link scenes. I developed an op-art inspired floor of violent ripples with two 'eyes' watching, to create an unsettling atmosphere. The boat would be represented by a see-saw set into the rake, while a giant swinging compass upstage would follow the motion of the 'boat'. The entire play is essentially set in Ripley's head, and deals with his obsession about transforming himself into Richard Greenleaf. I chose to use projections of period travel posters to reveal the locations and split scenes, swiftly and subtly. I think the design particularly reflected the ongoing preoccupation I have always had with the importance of lighting and its ability to transform a space instantly. My more recent preoccupation has been how to make the surround/masking an integral part of, rather than an aside to, the set. I decided to echo the aggressive asymmetry of the rake with the cloud masking, instead of using conventionally placed legs.

Theatre Company: Queen's Theatre, Hornchurch
Director: Bob Carlton
Lighting Designer: Matt Eagland

PHIL R DANIELS   SET DESIGNER

GUYS AND DOLLS
Frank Loesser, 1950

Outdoor, Kilworth House Theatre, Leicestershire, June 2010

The set was designed to be self-standing and self-masking, as the performance space was a simple flat paved area in an open air theatre. We decided to set the piece on a non-naturalistic set, as both the director and I felt that this sat better in the open environment. The setting we settled on was that of a craps table. Dice and chips were moved around the setting to create furniture and more intimate environments. The mission was created from a discarded mission leaflet with the band being positioned behind, appearing in the space for a printed photo. The leaflet in real scale was also handed out to the audience members by the mission cast, creating a link between audiences and acting space and scale. The setting had also to contain all the theatrical devices we needed for the piece, as it had to transform the space into a fully functioning theatrical environment.

Theatre Company: Kilworth House Theatre
Director/Choreographer: Mitch Sebastian
Costume Designer: Charles Cusick Smith
Lighting Designer: Chriss Ellis
Sound Designer: Chris Whybrow

GUY O'DONNELL   SET & COSTUME DESIGNER

GLUSCABI
Loan Hefin, 2009

Small-scale tour, spring/summer 2010

Gluscabi is a small-scale touring production intended primarily for young children. The design and conceptualisation was informed by the primary Foundation phase in Wales. The Foundation phase focuses on learning through activity and the exterior environment. The set design was intended to mirror the external classroom spaces created in many primary schools to underpin these teaching strategies. A particular focus is placed upon the natural world and the environment. We attempted to mirror this in the set with the creation of a large tree, constructed from steel then woven into with differing varieties of willow. I think our aims were successful, as most of the schools during the production's tour have asked if they can keep the set!

Theatre Company: Theatr na n'Og
Director: Phylip Harries
Other creative collaborator: Beryl Richards (willow weaver)

ANDREW WOOD   SET & COSTUME DESIGNER

STORYTREE
Company/participant devised, 2007

Touring, March 2007

Storytree is an object, a series of spaces, a collection of practitioners and a range of participatory and performance events. It works with children and adults in schools, at festivals and in communities, to explore and celebrate the stories that bind us together. Every project is unique, using storytelling, story making and a range of performance styles to create and present new participatory works. To unlock the imaginations of all those who take part, to inspire them to listen, speak, create and collaborate, *Storytree* can be manipulated and transformed. From its branches hang sculptural fruits containing objects that reveal stories and engage the audience in participatory experiences. These points of inspiration are explored along with their worlds, characters and journeys, to create new works to be shared and returned to the tree to begin the cycle again. Work takes place within one of *Storytree*'s two distinctive geodesic domes or with its portable shadow booths. Each new piece will seek to respond to these environments, transforming them to accommodate the ideas that become performance reality. Through the projects a wide range of different artists breathe life into the space, transforming it into a host of other worlds for exploration and play.

Theatre Company: **Storytree**
Director/Choreographer: **Ian Douglas**
Theatre Practitioners: **Jeff Cook and Daniel Serridge**
Photography: **Company members**

ADELE KEELEY   COSTUME DESIGNER

MARY BARTON
Andrew Louden and Emma Reeves, 2007

The Studio, Bournemouth, December 2008

Interpreted from the 1848 classic novel by Elizabeth Gaskell, this period piece portrays the differences between the hardship of poverty and the lifestyle of the Victorian privileged. I always render my costume designs on the computer, but was very conscious that the images should convey the atmospheric feel of the production. Recording each stage of the rendering process enables me to step back and edit the design if required. The most exciting part of the process for me is the transformation from page to stage, and how the maker interprets and realises the drawn image into the actual costume.

Theatre Company: **AUCB Acting Company**
Director: **Ken Robertson**
Set Designer: **Rebecca Pride**
Costume Designer: **Adele Keeley**
Lighting Designer: **Peter Clifton**
Sound Designer: **John Camble**
Photographer: **Andrew Cope**

LOIS MASKELL   SET DESIGNER

ONE STEP FORWARD, ONE STEP BACK
dreamthinkspeak, 2008

Liverpool Anglican Cathedral, April–May 2008

Inspired by Dante's *Paradiso* and William Blake's poem 'Jerusalem', *One Step Forward, One Step Back* was a large-scale promenade piece that responded site-specifically to concealed spaces within the Liverpool Anglican Cathedral. The spectator was taken on a psycho-geographical journey. The design encouraged the viewer (or pilgrim) to glimpse motifs and clues, incorporating models, installation and film. These design elements pointed to the insidious pull of consumerism over spirituality, knowledge and notions of the individual (Adam and Eve seen shopping in a supermarket, and a team of Santas interrupted planning a guerrilla-style operation). Counterbalancing this was the main narrative theme of enlightenment (knowledge, power, redemption). Just as Beatrice is Dante's guiding light, the use of light, or its absence, guided the audience out of the darkness toward something like hope.

Theatre Company: dreamthinkspeak
Director: Tristan Sharps
Costume Designer: Olivia du Monceau
Lighting Designer: Adam Horton
Sound Designer: Katie Sweeney
Architectural models: Mark Fleming at Studioscope

MATT EDWARDS   SET & COSTUME DESIGNER

BEYOND MEASURE
Bridget Foreman, 2008

York Theatre Royal Studio, September 2008

Inspiration for the set and costumes began with collaborative discussions with the director, Juliet Forster. Initial ideas were then developed from the concepts of change, sexual awakening and confined frustration. This led to a number of avenues, including recording close-up textures of cathedral stonework that were eroded and organic. We also wanted to create an impression of shifting surfaces and a sense of being trapped without walls, possibly self-induced. The costumes are intrinsic to the space, and reflect the anguish, joy and narrative of the character. There is also an element of three running throughout the set and costume, to reflect the three men who attempt to influence Isabella. With the storyboard for the film projection I began to introduce elements of fantasy, desire, decay and the cycle of the seasons.

Theatre Company: Back and Forth Productions
Director: Juliet Forster
Choreographer: Ruth Tyson-Jones
Lighting Designer: Penny Gaize
Sound Designer: Craig Vear

MARK JONATHAN   LIGHTING DESIGNER

SALOME
Richard Strauss, 1905

Bayerische Staatsoper, Nationaltheater, Munich,
October 2007

The formulation of the design involved a number of
meetings with the creative team in Los Angeles, Vienna
and Munich. The set design had the capability of each
portal section sliding to stage left and right as well as
rising up and sinking on the theatre's elevators, providing
an unlimited variation for the many scenes in the opera.
Hans Schavernoch and I discussed at length what the surfaces of his set design should be, to have the luminescent
quality that he wanted. Meanwhile, how one managed
the lack of conventional space for lights was solved by a
combination of LED lights that travelled in the upstage side
of the set units, along with underfloor fluorescent lighting
and some big lighting sources that found their way onto
the stage when the set opened. Everything was tested in
advance and, in the German style, we mocked up the set
and lighting effects months before rehearsals began.

Theatre Company: Bayerische Staatsoper
Director: William Friedkin
Set Designer: Hans Schavernoch
Costume Designer: Petra Reinhardt
Choreographer: David Bridel
Conductor: Kent Nagano

JOHN RISEBERO   SET & COSTUME DESIGNER

THE LION, THE WITCH AND THE WARDROBE
C S Lewis, adapted by Adrian Mitchell, 1998

St Stephen's, Hampstead, March 2009

After 30 years of dereliction, the spectacular St Stephen's
re-opened as a performance venue in 2009 following a
major restoration project. Not only did the former church
provide a resonant setting for the religious analogies
in CS Lewis' classic story, but also here was a building
being given a second chance after decades of decay – a
neat parallel with Narnia's return to life after 100 years of
winter. Within the stunning Victorian shell of the building
we created a performance space from scratch. Staging,
seating, lighting and sound equipment were all brought
in – a major transformation project in itself. Adrian
Mitchell's magical adaptation presented us with a series
of atmospheric locations, ranging from the London Blitz, to
the wintery woodlands of Narnia, the White Witch's frozen
palace, and the awe-inspiring pageantry of Aslan's camp
at the Stone Table. A basic setting – a diamond-shaped
stage projecting out into the nave – is transformed using
the simplest of means from scene to scene, using the
unique architecture of the building wherever possible.
When we meet the great lion Aslan for the first time, the
back wall of the stage opens to reveal the apse beyond,
bathed in golden light.

Theatre Company: Antic Disposition
Directors: Ben Horslen and John Risebero
Musical Director: Christopher Peake

ANNA HOURRIERE   SET & COSTUME DESIGNER

PERSONAL ENEMY
John Osborne and Anthony Creighton, 1953

White Bear Theatre, Kennington, July 2010

Personal Enemy is a short play written by John Osborne and Anthony Creighton in 1953 and censored in 1955 by the Lord Chamberlain. It is set in Langley Springs, USA, in summer 1953. The play tells the drama of an average American family, victims of McCarthy's witch-hunt, the Korean war and the persecution of homosexuality. I created a set design half way between an American domestic interior of the 1950s and a war camp in Korea. A few items of furniture suggest a living room/kitchen area surrounded by earth and sandbags, and a backdrop gauze of a Korean landscape painting. During the performance, the TV repeats the image of the backdrop as a haunting image, subtly transforming into surreal visions and increasing the play's dramatic effect.

Theatre Company: Fall Out Theatre
Director/Choreographer: David Aula
Lighting Designer: James Baggaley
Sound Designer: Ed Lewis
Photographer: Damian Robertson

BECKY DAVIES   SET & COSTUME DESIGNER

SECOND SIGHT – OEDIPUS/ANTIGONE
D J Britton, 2010, from the Theban plays of Sophocles

Admin Offices, Sherman Theatre, Cardiff, February 2010

In anticipation of its renovation, the empty Sherman Theatre was to be utilised for its final production, *Oedipus/Antigone*, in a way which defied the building's conventions. Every inch of the theatre became potential performance space and so I developed a concept, inspired by *Oedipus*, for the Sherman Admin Offices. In this concept, the Seers had been ordered by Oedipus to embark upon an investigation into the death of the late King. Using a majority of objects and materials from the space itself, I created the Seers' own office environment. The performers acted out this futile and monotonous process resulting in inevitable hysteria and frenetic activity. This narrative was mirrored visually. They inhabited the filing cabinets like second homes; documents, Post-it notes and parcel tape became the wallpaper, police photographs formed the family tree, and a suspect was held across the corridor in a room lit by a single, flickering strip-light. What has become most apparent from working site-specifically is the potential of objects and their composition to create a narrative which transports the audience's imagination from the confines of the space's everyday, utilitarian use.

Theatre Company: Sherman Youth Theatre and Acting Out
Director/Choreographers: Phillip Mackenzie, Jason Camilleri, Becky Davies
Lighting Designer: Katy Stephenson
Photographer: Jo Ward

CHLOE LAMFORD SET & COSTUME DESIGNER

IT FELT EMPTY WHEN THE HEART WENT AT FIRST
BUT IT IS ALL RIGHT NOW
Lucy Kirkwood, 2009

Installation/promenade performance created at Studio K at
the Arcola Theatre, London, October 2009

I created an *Alice In Wonderland*-inspired promenade
design in order to explore the experiences and imaginings
of Dijana, a Croatian prostitute who is trafficked into this
country. Lucy Kirkwood's text was an amazing array of
visual ideas which, with director Lucy Morrison, we began
to weave together my design ideas, me sending Lucy
Kirkwood images, and her visiting the model box. The final
design became part of Lucy's text itself. The audience
followed the action around each of seven different spaces
created in the deserted factory that is Studio K at the
Arcola Theatre, a joyous process of sharing ideas. The
audience begins the journey in Dijana's dingy room, from
which she escapes via a vent in the wall into a bewildering
and disturbing journey. The audience follows her, seeing
her scramble through tunnels, seeing tiny worlds in fish
tanks, through dangling toys on chains and eerie sounds.
We meet her in a strange corridor, representing the
detention centre where she ends up. Here, during a scene,
she coughs up a little key that unlocks a tiny door, the sign
above reading '436 days ago'. We follow her again into her
past, where all her hopes and aspirations are garlanded
around us, manifested in objects – baby clothes, fake
flowers, cleaning products – the ephemera of the cheap
shops of the local area. The audience is sitting on the
white plastic goods that she had dreamed of for her life
with the man who forced her into prostitution.

Theatre Company: Clean Break
Director: Lucy Morrison
Lighting Designer: Anna Watson
Sound Designer: Becky Smith
Photographers: Chloe Lamford and Sheila Burnett

ADRIAN VAUX   SET DESIGNER

AUGUST: OSAGE COUNTY
Tracy Letts, 2008

Habima National Theatre, Israel, December 2008

I was keen to create a multi-level space in which it was possible for several scenes to be played at the same time – as was written. When I saw the tour of this production at the National Theatre in London this was not possible, since it was the version from Broadway set in a very small space.

Theatre Company: Habima
Director: Ilan Ronen
Costume Designer: Yelena Kelrich
Lighting Designer: Meir Alon

MAIRA VAZEOU   SET & COSTUME DESIGNER

FRESH MEAT
Dylan Costello, 2010

Courtyard Theatre, London, June 2010

Fresh Meat is about cannibalism, and a metaphor for the hunger of love when we crave it. What initially looks clean and sterile, slowly transforms into a chamber of torture. We created a very clinical lounge that was based on the idea of a meat freezer, where the lives of the characters are trapped and their destinies are frozen and unable to escape the prison they put themselves into. At the start the characters are outside of this, and when they jump through the doors they enter the sinister world of the drama. Freezer doors become cell doors; blinds become a bloodied canvas; meat hooks on the walls reveal the narrative's darker theme, while the cold lighting exposes the characters' inability to find warmth in their relationship. Working fans and the sound of a motor becoming louder create an uncomfortable setting.

Theatre Company: Act 1 Productions
Director: Manolis Emmanouel
Lighting Designer: Kristina Thanasoula
Sound Designer: Kate McCarthy

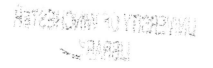

MADELEINE MILLAR SET & COSTUME DESIGNER

THE BARTERED BRIDE
Bedřich Smetana, 1866

Harlequin Theatre, Redhill, and Minack Theatre, Cornwall, July 2010

This production was presented in two very different venues: the Harlequin Theatre, Redhill, and the Minack Theatre, Cornwall – transformation. James Hurley and I worked very closely developing the concept for the production, looking at the history of Bohemia at the time the opera was written – a time of intense cultural transformation. The Austro-Hungarian Empire was loosening its grip on the area and a new Czech culture was emerging, through theatre, music and puppetry touring to the provinces. Our production is set in the 1880s/90s; a circus troupe (who arrive in Act III of Smetana's opera) is present from the very beginning in our presentation, and become a vehicle for cultural transformation onstage. They encourage the villagers to unwind and find themselves, eventually revealing a nod to traditional Czech costume in the women's clothing. The set starts with what could be the spokes of a giant wheel being raised, and the poles and ladders are decorated with roses growing on a broken bear cage from a circus troop long since gone. The double-headed eagle crest of the Austro-Hungarian Empire on top of a large set of gates eventually gets covered by the circus banner, and other banners hang from the ladders, subverting and transforming the dominant culture.

Theatre Company: **Surrey Opera**
Director: **James Hurley**

ELROY ASHMORE SET DESIGNER

LA TRAVIATA
Giuseppe Verdi, 1853

Icelandic Opera, Reykjavik, February 2008

We saw this production as an organic whole, taking many of the narrative ideas from the original Dumas novel *La Dame aux Camélias*. Much of the story line was shown during and as part of the scene changes which happened in full view of the audience. One scene would transform or morph seamlessly into another without any real set change as such. Windows became railings, a table became a ramp, and part of an Art Deco window became a swinging pendulum for the final scene counting out the last moments of Violetta's life. The production was set during the hedonistic roaring 20s in and around New York. Flora's party in Act II Scene III became a private film premiere of the silent film *Carmen*, which was shown during the Spanish dance music. At the end of this scene, one drunken man is reading a newspaper dated 1929; the party is over. This was to prove prophetic. A year on from this production it was to be the Icelandic banks that unfortunately would crash.

Theatre Company: **Icelandic Opera**
Director: **Jamie Hayes**
Costume Designer: **Filippía Elísdóttir**
Lighting Designer: **Björn Bergsteinn Guðmundsson**

Director/Choreographer: Marguerite Caruana Galizia
Lighting Designer: Natalie Lindiwe Jones
Performing Dancers: Alejandra Baño, Elizabeth Langdon Davis,
Harriet Latham and Katy Pendlebury

VERENA LEO   SET & COSTUME DESIGNER

QUARTET
Requiem by Michel Chion, 1973

Robin Howard Theatre, The Place, London, June 2008

QUaRteT was twice performed as two different versions.
For the first version, I joined the choreographer quite
late in the artistic process. My design was shaped by
the already existing movement that had been developed
through exploring quite abstract themes, and continued
cutting, pasting and reversing of the dance material.
Drawing was an essential part of understanding and
getting to know the choreography. I then started looking
into aspects of constructivism and observing images of
cut tomatoes used by the choreographer. There, thinking
of kitchen knives, I found a notion of violence, which
interested me. I started exploring domestic themes
and spaces. Adding hanging chairs and a kitchen table
suddenly put the four female dancers into a context that
gave the movement new meaning. Strengthened by the
lighting and without being overly realistic, the space
gained in depth and impact. The piece grew through the
feeling of wanting to burst, break out and expand space
in all directions. This was enforced by keeping one of the
stage doors open during the entire performance, thus
making it part of the stage setting. For the second version,
almost a year after, we integrated a white backdrop, as it
could not be removed for the performance. Consequently,
we introduced lighting more effectively as a way of
creating space. Two dismantled chairs were hanging, the
rest remained in the form of a sculpture. It was a case of
redefining the piece without losing what we initially aimed
for and, I think, being forced to reduce finally highlighted
the rather dark essence of the piece even more.

NANCY SURMAN   SET & COSTUME DESIGNER

THE DAUGHTER-IN-LAW
D H Lawrence, circa 1912, not performed until 1968

New Vic Theatre, Newcastle-under-Lyme, September 2009

Designer's notes: In The Daughter-in-Law, D H Lawrence
has left us both a full-blooded account of working class
life in a small mining community in Nottinghamshire at the
beginning of the 20th century, and the intimate story of
a marriage in crisis. The dark, brooding landscape of the
design is a blend of the familiar and the expressionistic; it is
inhospitable and hazardous, a physical counterpoint to the
psychological pitfalls of the play. The design was heavily
influenced by the paintings of the miner and artist Tom
McGuinness and his use of bright colours in dark, distorted
environments. So the space is transformed by two great pit
wheels suspended over the stage. They dominate the space
and loom over the protagonists, unacknowledged but ever-
present; a visual metaphor, both sculptural and symbolic.
Lighting Designer's note: My approach to lighting this
production in the round was to create an intense, highly-
contrasted lighting environment through which the
audience experienced the action. Due to the nature of the
space, each audience member saw my lighting design from
a different perspective. For instance, to some people strong
daylight meant that the action was heavily backlit, throwing
long shadows towards the audience. To others this same
key light was a strongly examining front light, as if looking
through a window into the action. Each scene had its own
distinct character. However, the aesthetic was consistent
throughout, and I relied on a strong source of light for each
scene. The last scene is lit almost entirely by oil lamp light.
The space was encircled with shallow, carefully-focused
point sources so that we could shift the emphasis on the
actors' faces so that at all times only one warm shaft of light
illuminated the action. The shadows were filled, not by a
rich, warm, reflected light, but by Tom McGuinness's grimy,
blue hues.

Theatre Company: New Vic Theatre
Director: Joanna Read
Lighting Designer: Mark Doubleday
Sound Designer: James Earls-Davis

RICHARD HUDSON   SET & COSTUME DESIGNER

RUSHES – FRAGMENTS OF A LOST STORY
Michael Berkeley, 2008, to music by Sergei Prokofiev

Royal Opera House, Covent Garden, London, April 2008

The choreographer wanted the space to be divided in
three. I chose to do this with fine curtains made of tiny
aluminium beads. These behaved like gauzes – solid when
lit from the front and transparent when back-lit. They have
the advantage of allowing the dancers to pass through.

Theatre Company: Royal Ballet
Director/Choreographer: Kim Brandstrup
Lighting Designer: Jean Kalman
Video: Dick Straker
Photography: Royal Opera House

VICTORIA JOHNSTONE   SET & COSTUME DESIGNER

ORIGIN OF THE SPECIES
Bryony Lavery, 2009

Studio 2, Arcola Theatre, London, October 2009

The main design challenge with this production was a
stage direction that required Molly, a retired archaeologist,
suddenly to dig up the body of a prehistoric woman from
somewhere in the set, having previously appeared to be
all alone in her sitting room in Yorkshire. The prehistoric
woman, who Molly names Victoria, then comes to life.
I felt that this element of deadpan surrealism was crucial to
the text and had to be reflected sensitively in the design.
My intention was to interweave naturalistic details in the
treatment of the room and its furniture with unsettling
elements like the floor of the cottage appearing to float
over an expanse of sand. I had a lot of fun embellishing
this with the set dressing, juxtaposing skulls with biscuit
tins on the mantlepiece. My response to the challenge
of how to reveal Victoria was to have the actor lay down
before the performance in a shallow opening in the floor
and then be covered in sand and a rug laid over her. Molly
then rolled back the rug and brushed the sand away. The
revelation of another performer appearing suddenly within
striking distance of the front row of the audience was very
transformative and unsettling.

Theatre Company: Primavera Productions
Director: Tom Littler
Lighting Designer: Christopher Nairne
Photographer: Robert Workman

CORDELIA CHISOLM   SET & COSTUME DESIGNER

ARIADNE AUF NAXOS
Richard Strauss, 1916

The New Athenaeum, Royal Scottish Academy of
Music & Drama, March 2009

Ariadne auf Naxos is an opera deeply concerned with
the theme of transformation; transformation from
preparation to performance, but also the transformation
and eventual transfiguration of Ariadne. Set in the house
of the richest man in Vienna (in our production the house
of a contemporary art patron), the prologue shows us
the pre-show preparation for an entertainment to be
performed in the opera. The corridor of toilets functioning
as dressing rooms is transformed (after a furious
20 minute interval in which the fantastic crew shovelled
four tonnes of sand – the physical implication of this
transformation) into a performance/gallery space in which
Ariadne's desert-island installation is constructed. Into this
'high-art' installation then crashes Zerbinetta's anarchic
burlesque troop, who further transform the space (with the
help of costumes, lighting and a change of musical style)
into a place where they can perform a series of cabaret
routines in a futile attempt to transform Ariadne's grief.
The final transformation of the opera comes with the
arrival of Bacchus, who does eventually manage to break
through Ariadne's inertia. As Ariadne changes, so too
does the island; it is transformed through soft pink lighting
(the white set allowing us great flexibility to change the
atmosphere and colour of the space) into the romantic
environment of her dreams. And then, finally, the space
breaks open and Ariadne and Bacchus walk out through
the back wall and off into the sunset together.

Theatre Company: Royal Scottish Academy of Music & Drama
Director: Ashley Dean
Lighting Designer: Johanna Town
Conductor: Tim Dean
Photographer: Johanna Town

GEORGE SOUGLIDES   SET & COSTUME DESIGNER

LA DAMNATION DE FAUST
Hector Berlioz, 1846

Lyric Opera of Chicago, February 2010

La Damnation de Faust is an enormous piece, an incredible journey through Faust's life with Mephistopheles as his guide, culminating in his decent to Hell. Unlike Goethe's Faust, he doesn't sign his soul to the devil until the very end. It is not a selfish act, but to save the woman he loved from execution. But Mephistopheles double-crosses him: Marguerite is executed and Faust led to his death. In our production, Faust is an obsessive mathematician in his small, white room suspended in space, surrounded by the world of his equations. The small room expands to the whole stage and transforms to the world of his memories of the past, and the future that leads him to Mephistopheles. The ceiling of white beams is actually a series of LED lightboxes that can move in every direction, depending on the emotional state of the characters and the piece.

Theatre Company: Lyric Opera of Chicago
Director: Stephen Langridge
Choreographer: Philippe Giraudeau
Lighting Designer: Wolfgang Göbbel
Choreographer: Philippe Giraudeau
Projections Designer: John Boesche
Photographer: Robert Kusel

JACQUELINE TROUSDALE   SET & COSTUME DESIGNER

SKELLIG
Adaptation by David Almond from his novel, 2008

National tour, 2008

Closely working with director Phil Clark, we developed design ideas around the central character, Michael, and his experiences of belief, fear, loss and, ultimately, flight. He is aware that the old man he finds in the garage is possibly "an extraordinary being". We looked at many artists, especially William Blake. Our stage level evolved as a space rooted in reality that transcends into the unknown. The state of the garage was the key to the world we were exploring. On the stage level, I created a collection of everyday earth-coloured objects packed neatly and orderly under a staircase, which in turn became an important part of each scene. This staircase section moved away to reveal Skellig in the garage and also served to isolate the central section. The earthbound objects gave way to silver-coloured junk taking flight: bicycle wheels, piping and light reflective pieces. As they ascend beyond a circular platform, part of a bicycle forms an arched window from which Skellig enters, and from this level the children experience the danger house, owls and flying, surrounded by stars. The highest objects gave additional lighting opportunities to illustrate the unworldliness of Skellig.

Theatre Company: Birmingham Stage Company
Director: Phil Clark
Lighting Designer: Jason Taylor
Sound Designer: Lewis Fowler
Composer: Jak Poore
Photographer: Ian Tilton

Skellig

JOHN BROOKING   SET & COSTUME DESIGNER

THE ENTERTAINER
John Osbourne, 1956

Lichfield Garrick Studio, Staffordshire, October 2009

The Entertainer was written specifically for a proscenium stage. I had to compress both the domestic and theatre scenes into one space and, along with Andrew Hall, the director, made the design and action a continuous whole.

Theatre Company: Lichfield Garrick Repertory
Director/Choreographer: Andrew Hall
Lighting Designer: John Martlew
Sound Designer: Peter Orton-Brown
Photographer: Paul Tristram

KEN HARRISON   SET & COSTUME DESIGNER

JANE EYRE
Charlotte Brontë, 1847, adapted by Polly Teale

Perth Theatre, March 2010

In Polly Teale's adaptation, Bertha Mason, locked away in the attic at Thornfield, gives physical expression to Jane's hidden emotions, and her rejection of the restricted life imposed upon her. In this production, a silvered gauze gave an added sense of her exclusion. In movement devised by Lisi Perry, Bertha, played by Vanessa Cook, climbs the ceiling of her attic room and slides down Rochester's bed curtains. Release comes through Thornfield's final destruction. Landings and stairs fall away, the collapsed pieces lying at sharp angles. As the attic floor tips over, Bertha is sent through the opened door into fiery smoke below.

Theatre Company: Perth Theatre
Director: Ian Grieve
Lighting Designer: Chahine Yavroyan
Movement Director: Lisi Perry
Music & Sound: Iain Johnstone and Jon Beales

DAVID HOWE   LIGHTING DESIGNER

EUGENE ONEGIN
Pyotr Ilyich Tchaikovsky, 1879

Theatre Royal, Glasgow, January 2008

My design process was led by the colours and textures
that Becs Andrews (set designer) had chosen. I felt that,
with a large chorus and the many principals in the opera,
we should allow the very personal drama to play out in
this bigger space and not 'drown' the stage with light
and confuse the images. Light needed to define space
and time within the slightly abstract setting. As the piece
progressed, the lighting became more and more angular:
single light sources gave the chorus form and shape,
while the use of side light lifted the protagonists from the
picture. The paint colours of the set were enhanced with
deep, saturated light, which gave them a greater depth
and, in the earlier scenes, discharge lighting produced
stronger daylight/moonlight shadows. The two scenes
shown are the opening of Act III (Ballroom), where colour
is strong and low-angle cross-light lifts and shapes
the Court dancing; and Act III Scene II, (the last scene),
which begins with two characters lit from a single source
off-stage, resulting in a shadow play against a wall, the
size of shadows changing as their argument ebbs and
flows. The final image of the opera was purely in silhouette, and left ambiguous as Onegin exits.

Theatre Company: Royal Scottish Academy of Music & Drama
and Scottish Opera
Director: Will Kerley
Set & Costume Designer: Becs Andrews
Photographer: Becs Andrews

JANE LINZ ROBERTS   SET & COSTUME DESIGNER

THE FLYING MACHINE
Phil Porter, 2007

Unicorn Theatre, London, May 2008

Designing Phil's extraordinary dark comedy involved
transforming the Unicorn's stage into the children's
ward of a crumbling eye hospital ruled by a tyrannical
nurse. For the first time, this new stage was opened out
using the full depth and removing the false proscenium.
I placed a rotunda, with an imagined sliding roof, upstage
under the strengthened area of the grid, where we could
fly our machine with its three passengers. During the
play, orderly precision – each bed set neatly by its pillar
and tap – transformed into a chaotic landscape of beds
and equipment strewn across the space while water
rained down from the sprinklers. Collaboration with
sound and lighting designers was vital to transforming
the design into a vivid world. An echoing soundscape
suggested the sinister world beyond, and bright white
light flooding down into the rotunda told us that the roof
was opening. Taking inspiration from Leonardo da Vinci
and Jean Tinguely, the flying machine was assembled
on stage, transforming ugly junk – zimmer frames, bed
frames, office chairs and a skeleton mannequin – into
a functioning machine with wings that flapped and a
propeller that turned. As the actors pedalled furiously, they
somehow breathed life into it.

Theatre Company: Unicorn Theatre
Director: Rosamunde Hutt
Choreographer: Lawrence Evans
Lighting Designer: Nick MacLiammoir
Sound Designer: Graeme Miller

SOPHIA LOVELL SMITH   SET & COSTUME DESIGNER

FLATHAMPTON
Daniel Jamieson, 2010

Royal & Derngate Theatre, Northampton, July 2010

Mission: transform the Derngate auditorium and stage into a town – a treat not to miss! The writer, director and I gradually began to select shops and places of activity that would offer children and adults interactive play with cooks, doctors, musicians, bank cashiers, stylists, reporters and many other Flathampton inhabitants. The set had not only to fill the Derngate but also begin life in 2D, a simple flat-pack set that looked good flat and gave the town's characters a strange 2D perspective. As life begins to change to a 3D world, this 2D town set needed to be simple to erect by the actors and children and become a 3D town, with shops, a bank and hospital; and at last The Flathampton Daily News had a really big story for the reporters (the children) to write up. It was an exciting challenge to transform space, offer an audience the role of physically revealing the changes and to participate in a town's development. Working with structure continues to engage me; it offers the chance to work with skilled makers and create shapes that can be both permanent and transitory, whether it is for a theatre, church, ship or an outdoor space.

Theatre Company: Royal & Derngate Theatre, Northampton
Director: Dani Parr
Lighting Designer: Tom Nickson
Photographer: Alex Soulsby

PAMELA HOWARD   SET DESIGNER

THE GREAT GAME
Richard Bean, Lee Blessing, David Edgar, David Greig, Amit Gupta, Ron Hutchinson, Stephen Jeffreys, Abi Morgan, Ben Ockrent, Simon Stephens, Colin Teevan, Joy Wilkinson, Siba Shakhil, Richard Norton-Taylor, 2009 (remounted 2010)

Berkeley Repertory Theatre, Minneapolis, and Skirball Centre, New York University, USA, April 2009

For *The Story of a Wall*, my starting point was the real-life story of the famous Afghan artist Ustad Mohammed Mashal, who painted a panorama of *500 Years of Afghanistan* on the wall of the bazaar in Herat. He was forced to watch as the Taliban whitewashed it out, deeming it to be idolatrous. Searching for a unifying theme for 12 half-hour plays spanning 1842–2009, and knowing we needed to stage 9/11 emblematically in Part 3, I thought this would be an apt metaphor for the whole trilogy. I created a new version of *500 Years of Afghanistan* as a wall painting against which all the plays could be staged with the simplest of props and furniture. The wall is transformed by the Taliban in Part 2, when it is violently whitewashed. In Part 3, which shows the death of Commander Masoud, the white wall becomes a screen against which the film of 9/11 is projected. The wall/ white screen falls down and is transformed into a field of opium poppies seen against a heavenly blue sky. Beauty and Death as grim partners. *The Story of a Wall* asks why people are so afraid of Art.

Theatre Company: Tricycle Theatre
Directors: Nicholas Kent and Indhu Rubasingham
Assistant Director: Rachel Grunwald
Costume Designer: Miriam Nabarro
Choreographer: Sydney Florence
Lighting Designers: James Farncombe and David Taylor, USA
Sound Designer: Tom Lishman
US Intern: Carl B Hamilton
AV artist: Ed Borgnis
Photographer: John Haynes

PAUL EDWARDS SET DESIGNER

HÄNSEL UND GRETEL
Engelbert Humperdinck, 1893

Holland Park, London, April 2008

Hänsel und Gretel was performed outside in Holland Park.
Most of the opera is set in a forest. Rather than compete
with nature, I designed one location – an over-sized
room – that shrunk the adult singers down to child size
and transformed in Hansel and Gretel's mind to become a
terrifying forest where the wallpaper came to life.

Theatre Company: Opera Holland Park
Director: Stephen Barlow
Choreographer: David Greenall
Lighting Designer: Peter Mumford

SAKINA KARIMJEE SET & COSTUME DESIGNER

HÄNSEL UND GRETEL
Engelbert Humperdinck, 1893

Sir Jack Lyons Theatre, Royal Academy of Music, London,
November 2008

Our version of *Hänsel und Gretel* started in the
contemporary credit-crunch world in which it was staged,
with Act I set in a grimy kitchen of piled up white goods
and overdue bills. The hyperreality of Act I transformed
into the strange, sinister forest of Act II. The kitchen broke
up and moved off, choreographed to the orchestra. A
lighting change revealed that what appeared as masking
was actually gauze panels with curved forms behind,
which became the trees of the forest. This stylised forest
was shadowy and looming, making Hänsel and Gretel
appear small and easily lost. Through the use of different
coloured light the forest constantly evolved, emphasising
changing atmosphere and the passage of time. The fairy
tale-like gingerbread house was an enticing, sugary child
trap. Hänsel entered the house and became imprisoned as
it rotated to reveal bars of a cage, lit up under the witch's
spell. The gingerbread house appeared through the mist in
the forest and was moved on castors by the witch herself
from inside. Unseen by Hänsel and Gretel, she sang out of
flaps in the door and shook her fists menacingly out of the
windows before making her entrance.

Theatre Company: Royal Academy of Music
Director: John Ramster
Lighting Designer: Jake Wiltshire
Photographers: Brian Doherty and Sakina Karimjee

IAN MacNEIL SET DESIGNER

TINTIN IN TIBET
David Grieg, 2007, adapted from Hergé

Playhouse Theatre, London, December 2007

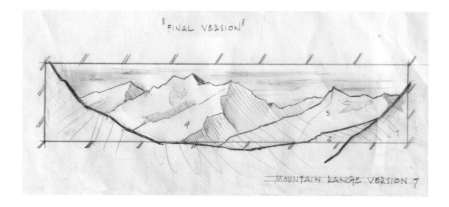

I grew up loving Tintin books for the characters, the line and the colour. Herge's line is so lyrical and expressive. His research is really thorough and all his choices so meaningful. The book *Tintin in Tibet* is a hymn to friendship and manages to attain a level of abstraction and spirituality, and is extraordinarily moving. In the end it is storytelling through a series of images, which actually made it quite easy to design for the stage.

Theatre Company: Young Vic
Director: Rufus Norris
Costume Designer: Joan Wade
Choreographer: Toby Sedgewick
Lighting Designer: Rick Fisher
Sound Designer: Paul Arditti
Music: Orlando Gough
Associate Designer: Jim Gaffney

"FINAL VERSION"

MOUNTAIN RANGE VERSION 7

BILLY ELLIOT
Lee Hall and Sir Elton John, 2005

Imperial Theatre, Broadway, November 2008

New Musicals are tough to design and a 'Book Musical' is, I think, harder to design than a 'Concept Musical'. I sort of grew up on Concept Musicals in the 70s and 80s and fed off them continuously. In a Concept Musical the design is encouraged to announce itself at regular intervals throughout the evening, and is, arguably, the audience's primary point of contact with the show. Certainly was for me. Frankly, often there just wasn't much else happening. But with *Billy Elliot* the story was everything and Dance was to be the primary means for expression. Bummer. It's a Book Musical in the 50s and 60s tradition in that it takes place in a series of Ordinary Locations and they are Realistic and there are Lots of them. For a designer this means subsume yourself and try to not ever get caught letting it be 'about the design'. As I say: Bummer. In the end, of course, if you persevere with a restriction you can actually make it interesting for yourself. Paul, the associate, and I absorbed the endless requirements of the direction and choreography and continuously bit our tongues before saying "but that will LOOK crap". Certainly whenever we DID say it we were made to feel unbelievably selfish and DID we understand just how DIFFICULT it was to make a new musical? I ended up thinking about Jocelyn Herbert more than I ever have before, and that made me stronger and better able to be nice. One of the luxuries of a hit is that as it gets remounted in different parts of the world you can change things each time. The scene in which Billy has his audition was radically redesigned in every continent, and I was only really happy with it the third time we did it – in New York. Simple, clear and real. Like a good Book Musical.

Theatre Company: Working Title
Director: Stephen Daldry
Costume Designer: Nicky Gillibrand
Choreographer: Peter Darling
Lighting Designer: Rick Fisher
Sound Designer: Paul Arditti
Associate Designer: Paul Atkinson
Photographer: Frank Herholdt

ALEX MARKER   SET DESIGNER

DEATH OF LONG PIG
Nigel Planer, 2009

Finborough Theatre, July 2009

I like to think that the Finborough is the design equivalent
of a close-up magic routine. The venue is situated
above a pub in a cleft between two forking roads, so
the audience are acutely aware of its relative size before
they walk through the front door. However, it is always
fun to confound people's expectations of the kind of
production they are about to see. Transformation of the
entire space is the key. When I first learnt that Nigel's
play, about Robert Louis Stephenson and Paul Gauguin,
was set in Samoa and Tahiti I knew the possibilities for
such a transformation could be very exciting. Part colonial
residence, part rushwork hut, surrounded by paint-covered
walls and carved Tiki figures, there is nowhere to hide and
the audience almost become part of the play. I have used
this approach many times at the Finborough, transforming
it into various locations, including a trench on the western
front, the Palace of Versailles, Brighton station and a South
African farmstead, to name a few. Each time, the aim is to
support the actor's belief in the world they inhabit and to
immerse the audience in the world of the play.

Theatre Company: JQ Productions in association with Neil McPherson
Director: Alex Summers
Costume Designer: Penn O'Gara
Lighting Designer: James Smith
Sound Designer: Andy Evans
Photographer: Stuart Allen

GARANCE MARNEUR   SET & COSTUME DESIGNER

ORPHANS
Dennis Kelly, 2009

Traverse Theatre, Edinburgh; The Door, Birmingham Repertory
Theatre; and Soho Theatre, London, July 2009

How safe do you feel in your own house? Are thick brick
walls, spiked fences and barbed wire enough to protect
you and your family? What happens when danger is not
only at your doorstep but within your home itself? Dennis
Kelly's dark, psychological thriller was mostly set in a
living room, but the fear of crimes in the streets was often
mentioned by the characters. We felt that the environment
and psychological process of the characters needed to
be portrayed through the design. Following the theme
and aesthetic of *film noir*, along with photographs and
research on how the architecture of a borough can expose
its inhabitants to insecurity and crimes, we decided to
set the play in a single room with high walls surrounded
by spiked fences and darkness. The walls played a key
role in the transformation of the set throughout the play.
At first, they appeared like solid walls covered with a
muted-tone flowered wallpaper and family portraits: a
rather friendly environment. As the tension escalated, car
headlights travelling at the back of the set made the walls
and floor translucent, revealing broken foundations and
spiked fences, gradually transforming the family home into
a prison.

Theatre Company: Birmingham Repertory Theatre Company in association
with Paines Plough
Director: Roxana Silbert
Lighting Designer: Chahine Yavroyan
Sound Designer: Matt McKenzie

TIMOTHY O'BRIEN   SET & COSTUME DESIGNER

DER RING DES NIBELUNGEN
Richard Wagner, 1876

Teatro Nacional de São Carlos, Lisbon, October 2009

The director, Graham Vick, and I were allowed to make the whole theatre the setting for our Ring cycle. We sought to escape the myth, hero worship and Marxism of its performance history. Our material is the study of human nature, which – despite our immortal longings for higher significance – is all we possess. We embraced the young Wagner's belief in the first theatre, that of the Greeks, presented in full light and plain view of the audience. The theatre of São Carlos, a phoenix risen from the rubble of the great earthquake of 1755, is the setting for the theft of the Rhinegold, the birth and death of Siegfried, and the passing of the Gods. The stage is lifted and extended to fill the auditorium. Seats drowned in the stalls are restored at the former stage end. The stage floor is equipped with lifts to deliver revelations. There is no sky. The action infiltrates the audience. Everyone is close. The words – essential to understanding – are not swallowed up by the music. Here is the place to show that all bargains made to protect power, hierarchy and wealth will be betrayed. Over 15 hours a transformation occurs in all of us, performers and spectators alike.

Theatre Company: Opera of São Carlos
Director: Graham Vick
Choreographers: Graham Vick and Ron Howell
Lighting Designers: Peter Kaczorowski (*Rheingold*); Giuseppe di Iorio (*Walküre*, *Siegfried* and *Götterdämmerung*)
Photographers: Timothy O'Brien and Alfredo Rocha

GARY McCANN   SET & COSTUME DESIGNER

NORMA
Vincenzo Bellini, 1831

National Opera of Moldova, Chisinau, February 2010

Bellini's setting of ancient Gaul under Roman occupation is updated to a modern day war zone: bullet holes punctuate the walls which frame the space, the sacred grove of the Druids is charred, skeletal forest, and the great head of the god Irminsul lies abandoned on the parched, blackened landscape. Costumes were inspired by science fiction illustrator Enki Bilal. The entire design process was conducted via digital means: costumes were Photoshopped collages, and the set designs originated as models generated in Cinema 4D.

Theatre Company: National Opera of Moldova
Director: Laurence Dale
Lighting Designer: Valerie Kukarskiy

RALPH KOLTAI   SET & COSTUME DESIGNER

AN ENGLISH TRAGEDY
Ronald Harwood, 2008

Watford Palace Theatre, 2008

The play concerned the British tailor John Amery, who broadcast to Britain from Germany in support of the Hitler regime during the Second World War. I formulated my design, in the form of a swastika as the acting area, with the capability to disintegrate in the course of the play.

Director: Di Trevis
Lighting Designer: Roger Frith
Music: Dominic Muldowney

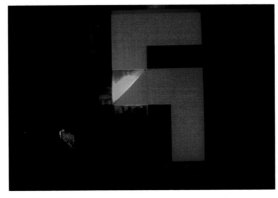

COLIN RICHMOND   SET & COSTUME DESIGNER

ANIMAL FARM
George Orwell, adapted by Peter Hall
Lyrics by Adrian Mitchell
Music by Richard Peaslee, 2008

Quarry Theatre, West Yorkshire Playhouse, October 2008

Every inch of the Quarry Theatre's vast stage was used in presenting *Animal Farm*, a cold, damp world of mud, ladders, sheds and farm machinery. The already thrust stage in Leeds spread its arms out to the audience, allowing our actors to access the auditorium, via the Juliet balconies, on three different levels. A huge series of windmill blades descended and turned towards the end of Act II; a long table with bloody carcasses trundled on, crammed full of old broken china and blood-filled gravy boats; a tractor chugged across, ridden by three pigs brandishing shot guns, hailing their triumphant victory over the humans. Over time, the pigs morphed into the humans and the humans into the pigs, making the final image all the more shocking and upsetting as they sat down to their fly-infested bloody feast. Female pigs in torn 1940s ball gowns and male pigs in muddied tuxes emblazoned with shiny brooches and rosettes looked as one, as each member of the table revealed their dirty, greedy face from behind snouts and masks. Costume never burdened the actors, but allowed complete freedom. Their animalistic qualities were explored more through performance rather than depending mostly on the visual, allowing us to recognise the human traits in each animal, drawing us further into their devastating story.

Theatre Company: West Yorkshire Playhouse
Director: Nikolai Foster
Choreographer: Gary Lloyd
Lighting Designer: Ian Scott
Sound Designer: Mic Pool
Musical Direction: Cathy Jayes
Photographer: Keith Patterson

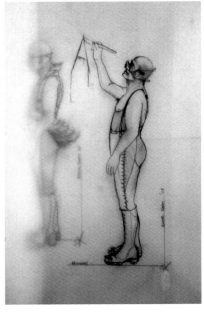

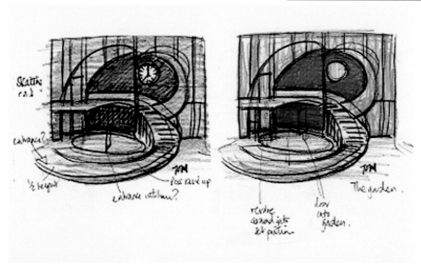

LAURA McEWEN SET DESIGNER

TOM'S MIDNIGHT GARDEN
David Wood, 2000

Nottingham Playhouse, June 2008

My collaboration with the director, Andrew Breakwell, began with a discussion on how to develop all the transformations implicit in the story within the available space. We both felt that a sweeping shape would work not only for the staircase in the house but could also represent a steep, grassy bank in the garden. The curves within the design continued into the floor through the revolve at the base. This was used to reflect the journeys in time in the story; as Tom goes back in time the disc revolves anti-clockwise, mirroring the hands of the clock. The transformation from house to the garden had to be simple, as it happens many times throughout the play. This was achieved by lighting through layers of black gauze to reveal a turquoise cyclorama and the rich blues and greens of William Morris wallpaper, a link to the leap in time back to Victorian England. The projected image of the clock face, such an integral part of Tom's stay in the house, then dissolved to reveal images of the moon or sun in the garden.

Theatre Company: Nottingham Playhouse
Director: Andrew Breakwell
Costume Designer: James Farncombe
Choreographer: Dan Willis
Lighting Designer: Drew Baumohl
Sound Designer: Kitty Winter

TAKIS SET & COSTUME DESIGNER

DITCH
Beth Steel, 2010

Old Vic Tunnels, 2010

We mounted *Ditch* in the cavernous tunnels underneath Waterloo Station to capture the epic quality and sense of scale in Beth's writing. In order to project a vision of the future I decided to look at the apocalyptic imaginings of Hieronymus Bosch for his colour palette and textures. In a similar vein to Pina Bausch (*The Rite of Spring*), I wanted to evoke a sense of a natural order, making both earth and water a central feature on stage. It was important for me to create a sense of the world that the characters inhabit before actually reaching the auditorium itself. Each member of the audience journeys through a series of installations capturing the demise of civilisation. I reinvented classical images of farm life with a modern slant, converting carcasses into neon-lit sculptures and deconstructing a large oak tree suspended in mid-air, its roots hanging above a conceptual pool of blood.

Theatre Company: Old Vic/HighTide
Director: Richard Twyman
Lighting Designer: Matt Prentice
Sound Designer: Christopher Shutt
Music: Tom Mills
Photographer: Matt Humphrey

RICK FISHER   LIGHTING DESIGNER

TURANDOT
Giacomo Puccini, 1925

English National Opera at London Coliseum,
October 2009

The director's and designer's bold decision to stage
Puccini's opera *Turandot* in a large, modern Chinese
restaurant demanded bold lighting choices to make the
Coliseum's vast stage work for intimate scenes, as well as
dramatic ones, dance sequences and big choral moments.
The strong red of the walls and floor in Acts I and II led
to strong lighting choices of colours and angles, bringing
variation to the set and allowing the whole space to be
visually interesting, yet dramatically appropriate. For Act
III, the setting dramatically changed to the cold, white
and reflective kitchen of the restaurant. Once again, the
lighting transformed and revealed the single large space
in ways appropriate for the following scenes: the solitary
tension and beauty of *Nessun Dorma*; the tense, yet
intimate confrontation between Calaf and Turandot; the
surreal entrance of the dancers through a large industrial
refrigerator; and the final moment where the entire ENO
chorus witness the triumph of love.

Theatre Company: English National Opera
Director: Rupert Goold
Set Designer: Miriam Buether
Costume Designer: Katrina Lindsay
Choreographer: Aletta Collins
Sound Designer: Lorna Heavey
Photographer: Marcus Tozni

PREMA MEHTA   COSTUME & LIGHTING DESIGNER

THE PENGUIN CAFÉ
Prema Mehta in collaboration with The London College
of Fashion
Inspired by *Still Life at the Penguin Café*, originally
choreographed by David Bintley and orchestrated by
Simon Jeffes

Cochrane Theatre, London, March 2008

The Penguin Café was a choreographed journey through
the seven continents of the world. Along the way, we
encounter endangered species across Asia, Australasia,
Africa, Antarctica, North America, South America and
Europe. With over 100 people involved in the project,
our collective aim was to create a visually stimulating
production. Costumes, wigs and make-up were created
by the highly acclaimed London College of Fashion.
During pre-production I worked alongside the director,
set designer and video designer to discuss our joint
vision for the production. My lighting design was also
influenced by the development of the costumes. The
style of lighting utilised throughout the performance was
inspired by the colour, detail, material and technical effects
of the costumes.

Director: Max Key
Set Designer: Jessica Curtis
Sound Designer: Matt Downing
Choreographer: Hanna Gillgreen
Video Designer: William Reynolds

CHARLES CUSICK SMITH   SET & COSTUME DESIGNER

THE LIFE OF STUFF
Simon Donald, 1992

Proscenium Theatre, Pitlochry Festival Theatre, August 2009

The setting is based in several areas of an abandoned warehouse in the Glasgow docklands, soon to be renovated to become Blisters night club and disco. Travelling between the main area, the basement and the roof of the building, two of the four on-stage lift shafts traversed onstage and closed down the acting area. The off-stage sliding doors meet centre stage to define the small, cramped area of the cellar. When the two sliders opened, the roof of the warehouse was revealed behind. On another occasion the interior of an office was revealed.

Theatre Company: Pitlochry Festival Theatre
Director: John Durnin
Lighting Designer: Wayne Dowdeswell
Sound Designer: Ronald J Mcconnell
Photographer: Phil R Daniels

ANNA EFREMOVA   SET DESIGNER

VE DAY CONCERT
Royal Albert Hall, London, 2010

A combination of chronicle, digital scenography and scenic objects creates the environment for a moving panorama of metamorphosis. The main idea uses the metaphors of the circle, earth, universe. The important part of the work was a storyboard. It helps to create and devise the development of the visual narrative. The process of transformation and the revelation of ideas happened on the background of the real stage elements and represented virtual space. Looking to the stage, spectators were supposed to experience the history (as past and present) and the memory which is presented to them. Represented space constitutes a kind of place. How to change environmental space without changing elements physically? How does global reflect the personal? And how, therefore, can the space be visually turned from public to private?

Theatre Company: Ensemble Productions
Director: A Slusarenk
Lighting Designer: Steve Nolan
Sound Designer: Sound by Design
Projection Consultant and video content realisation: Nina Dunn
Technical Director: Paul Godfrey
Set & Video Design: Anna Efremova
Photographer: N Dunn

INGRID HU   SET, COSTUME & LIGHTING DESIGNER

ON THE CUSP
Adi Lerer, 2009

Freedom Studio, Roundhouse, Camden, August 2009;
Venue 2, Rich Mix, London, August 2009, February 2010

On The Cusp was a solo performance conceived, written
and performed by Adi Lerer. The design started with a
scenographic idea; an object that could be manipulated
throughout the performance to respond to the narrative.
The design process and the performance evolved in
parallel, with the design playing an active role in shaping
the story, the character, and the physical performance. The
final design was an imaginative structure made of double-
layered fabric, crinoline and Spandex netting, suspended
on a pulley system, which suggested at different times
a basket of oranges, a boat, a dress, a shelter, as well as
more emotional and psychological aspects of the piece.
Creating full-size, working prototypes of set pieces – like
three-dimensional sketches – allowed play and further
refinement and offered fresh insights. The design process
became more transparent, and it encouraged collaboration
among the creative team.

Other creative collaborators: Gillian Foley and David Lockwood
Photographer: Tony Rizzo

DAWN ALLSOPP   SET & COSTUME DESIGNER

DEATH OF A SALESMAN
Arthur Miller, 1949

York Theatre Royal, November 2008

This classic story of the failure of the American dream
spans time frames and locations. All the elements needed
to set scenes were heaped together on two trucks; one
stage left and the other stage right. Things were seemingly
chaotically balanced as if at any given moment they might
come crashing down. These two trucks pivoted and could
swing up and down stage, thus bringing the relevant area
of the staging into focus. At other times the stage could be
open, revealing a huge billboard and its slogan: "It's lucky
when you live in America". Willy Loman could stand centre
stage and all the elements of his disintegrating life could
come to him. The image, from Act II, depicts the kitchen
and yard as everyone heads off for the ball game.

Theatre Company: York Theatre Royal
Director: Damian Cruden
Lighting Designer: Richard G Jones
Original music: Chris Madin
Photographer: Dawn Allsopp

'An echoing soundscape suggested the sinister world beyond, and bright white light flooding down into the rotunda told us that the roof was opening'

EMMA THOMPSON   SET & COSTUME DESIGNER

DAYS OF HOPE
Howard Goddall, 1991

Midlands Arts Centre, Birmingham, April 2007

In 2007 the Midlands Arts Centre shut its doors after 40 years for a much-needed refurbishment. This production was the last show put on there and, as the theatre was being gutted, both the lighting designer, Penny Gaize, and I used this to our advantage when considering the design. Never before had the theatre been used in the round, so we took seating from the auditorium and placed it at the back of the stage. We exposed the old proscenium arch that had been clad for years. The theatre was stripped out completely and we made features of objects that are usually hidden, such as backstage areas, flying wires, stacked chairs, even ladders and tins of paint. The story is about the end of a way of life for a family living in Spain during the Civil War, but It was also an exploration of the end of an era within a building, its staff and their memories.

Theatre Company: **MAC Productions**
Director/Choreographer: **Iqbal Khan**
Lighting Designer: **Penny Gaize**

ISABELLA BYWATER   SET & COSTUME DESIGNER

LA BOHÈME
Giacomo Puccini, 1896

Coliseum, London, February 2009

Updated to 1930s Paris, this romantic story of young love blighted by sudden tragedy unfolds on sets inspired by the iconic photographs of Cartier-Bresson and Brassaï. I studied at first hand the details of the streets and buildings of Paris; the cobbles, the staircases, skylights, door handles, window frames, and tried to make the atmosphere 'real and grubby and tired'.

Theatre Company: **English National Opera**
Director: **Jonathan Miller**
Photographer: **Christopher Simon Sykes**

JAMIE VARTAN   SET & COSTUME DESIGNER

LA TRAVIATA
Giuseppe Verdi, 1853

Malmö Opera, December 2008

The first instinct was to place Violetta's party around a swimming pool at night, providing a necessary danger and excitement. The decision to use projection was made later, as a response to that instinct. Violetta is dying of consumption; in a sense, drowning, her lungs slowly filling with water. The slow overture music was the opportunity to project, onto a gauze covering the stage, extreme slow motion footage of Violetta falling through the air in her party dress, breaking through the surface of the water and sinking slowly to the bottom of the pool. After sinking out of view, Violetta as a child appears on stage, observed by her adult self. The child Violetta then slowly descends and disappears through a circular opening in the floor, in a revolving motion, down a hidden spiral staircase. This dream-like moment is then interrupted by the crashing opening chords of the party rushing onto the stage, holding bubbling champagne flutes and singing Brindiamo!

Theatre Company: **Malmö Opera**
Director: **Thomas de Mallet Burgess**
Choreographer: **Maxine Braham**
Lighting Designer: **Sinead Mckenna**
Photographers: **Dennis Trulsson and Malin Arnesson**

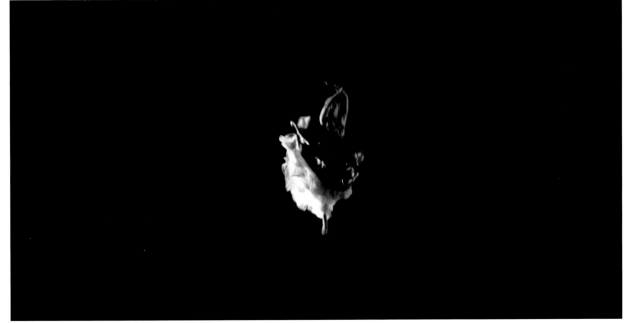

MIKE BRITTON   SET & COSTUME DESIGNER

THE LADY AND THE SEA
Henrik Ibsen, 1888

Birmingham Repertory Theatre, March 2008

The Lady and the Sea centres around the character of Ellida, a lighthouse keeper's daughter who previously lived all her live by the sea, but is now married to Doctor Wangle and lives inland with him and his two daughters. She is haunted by the memory of a stranger, a sailor who she once promised herself to, and is torn between him and the reality of life with her husband. I used the full scope of Birmingham Rep's stage and created a large, black, reflective room. It is a haunted space, a place that Ellida needs rescuing from, where she feels trapped and suffocated; a space that deprives her of light and the sea. When we first see Ellida she is in a white dress, echoing the white flowers struggling to exist in this dark, oily abyss. The veranda of the Wangle house is portrayed as an open limed wood box floating over the flowers, which drifts as if lost at sea, up and down stage. It is not until the end of the play, when the stranger comes to claim her, that she is able to make the free choice to stay with her husband, and the back of the black room she has been encased in breaks open, letting the light and the sound of the sea pour back into her world.

Theatre Company: Birmingham Repertory Theatre Company
Director: **Lucy Bailey**
Lighting Designer: **Oliver Fenwick**
Sound Designer: **Dan Hoole**
Other creative collaborator: **Luke Stoneham**
Photographer: **Manuel Harlan**

CATHERINE MORGAN   SET & COSTUME DESIGNER

MACBETH
William Shakespeare, 1606

Broadway Theatre Studio, Catford, 2010

Keen to accentuate the militaristic nature of Macbeth, the director, Alice Lacey, and I wanted to create a sense of immediate threat permeating the whole landscape. Researching the Spanish Civil War, with its disorganised fighting in the hills and inter-family conflict on the streets, made us very aware of the visceral nature of civil strife and the oppressive ambition of ruling elites. These have their parallels in Jacobean England and 11th-century Scotland. I created a set that played with the idea of encampment. A camp is a temporary space in a state of flux and, in a play of rapid scene changes, the set could be swiftly transformed from military to rebel to dispossessed boys' camp. Benches, a trestle table and ammo crates were set out in different configurations to prompt the audience's imagination and to suggest thematic ideas. Towers of army duckboards might make the audience consider aspiration and fragility, 'vaulting ambition' and imminent destruction, while the slats, through which different shadows could be cast, might suggest porous barriers, eavesdropping, Macbeth's spy in every castle. The aim was to reveal more about the play through the addition of interpretive location choices, created by humble objects which the audience imaginatively transforms.

Theatre Company: Broadway Theatre
Director: **Alice Lacey**
Lighting Designer: **Cath O'Sullivan**
Sound Designer: **Adam Harper**
Choreographer: **Jules Vandoorne**
Photographer: **Adam Levy**

JUDITH CROFT   SET & COSTUME DESIGNER

WAITING FOR GODOT
Samuel Beckett, 1948

Library Theatre, Manchester, February 2008

This design for *Waiting for Godot* provides a pared-down, minimalist setting, influenced by works by Klee and Ernst, and images of post-war landscapes. It is a theatrical set, non-naturalistic, where in the intimacy of the Library Theatre details such as tyre tracks in the texture of the floor can be noticed. In the same way that the set hints at previous habitation, I wanted the costumes to suggest the previous lives of the characters. So, within the parameters of a tramp's costume, I have chosen garments and accessories which carry their own messages, such as Vladimir's silk hanky, Estragon's 50s car coat and Lucky's battered steward's tailcoat. Pozzo's dominant mustard coat and checked suit contrast strongly with the otherwise muted tones of greys, blues and browns used for the other clothes, and his is the only costume which has not been broken down and dusted with the ashy quality of the set.

Theatre Company: Library Theatre Company
Director: Chris Honer
Lighting Designer: Nick Richings
Sound Designer: Paul Gregory
Other creative collaborator: Renny Krupinski

CONOR MURPHY   SET & COSTUME DESIGNER

THE MAGIC FLUTE
Wolfgang Amadeus Mozart, 1791

LG Arts Centre, Seoul, South Korea, March 2009

The idea of a transformative journey is central to the design for *The Magic Flute*. There is a real sense of moving from darkness and chaos, at the beginning of the piece, towards some kind of enlightenment as we move through it. There are moments of playfulness, overtly theatrical performance, seriousness and naivety in the piece, all of which I have tried to capture in some way in the design. We have used a stripped-back aesthetic to allow the opera to unfold clearly, but within that we have used strong colour, simple shapes, childlike drawings and projected animations to enhance the more illusionary aspects of the opera. My main interest in designing for the stage is that, through the spatial geometry of the design, we can influence the emotional journey. I am fascinated by the spatial relationships between the performers, and in the early stages of the design I try to imagine how the key relationships will appear on stage and to allow the design to develop from there.

Theatre Company: Korean National Opera
Director: Mike Ashman
Lighting Designer: Paul Keogan
Photographer: Namgoong Sun

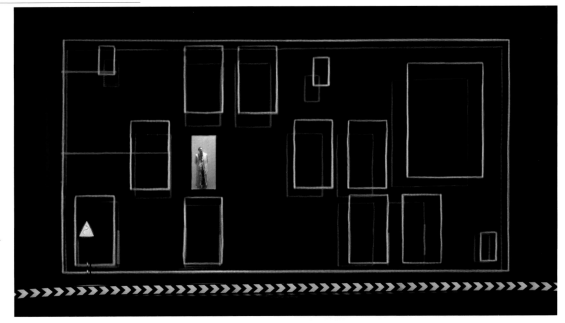

3 Boys_v3   Queen_v3   Papageno_v3

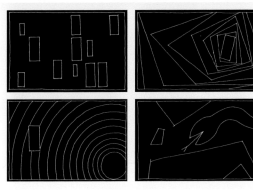

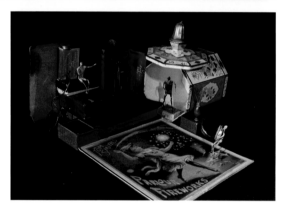

PAUL BARRETT   SET DESIGNER

CAT AND MOUSE
Julia Smith, 2009

B2 Studio, Belgrade Theatre, Coventry, January 2009

Cat and Mouse tells the story of a young boy, Chaim, and his survival of the Warsaw ghetto and Auschwitz. As he withdraws into the security of a fantasy mouse world, parallels are drawn between the Nazis' Final Solution and the population of mice under threat from a feral cat invasion. It was clear from early discussions with the writer and director Julia Smith that the design needed to work on a variety of symbolic levels. We were keen to explore an outsize collection of objects that would engage the young performers, totally transform the theatre space and could be adapted quickly to support the momentum and the various locations within the narrative. The Bakelite radio, for example, was used for the mouse orchestra, the gas chamber and the presence of the feral cat. I always begin my designs by developing a series of Found Object Sketches. Often these are abstracted shapes, forms and textures that jump-start the design process, as I find it disheartening staring at a blank piece of paper. For this production I was able to sketch with objects, many from the period, that became key to the final stage design.

Theatre Company: Imagineer Productions
Director: Julia Smith
Costume Designer: Anna Lewis
Lighting Designer: Wayne Dowdeswell
Sound Designer: Ilona Sekacz
Photographer: Martin Hewitt

CHRIS DE WILDE   SET & COSTUME DESIGNER

CANDIDE
Leonard Bernstein, 1956

Värmlandsoperan, Karlstad, Sweden, March 2008

Setting the story in 1956 (the date of the original stage production) gave us access to a diverse vocabulary of 20th-century images and styles, illuminating Candide's picaresque adventures around the world and allowing us to switch in a moment from the comic to the touching, from the bizarre to the profound. Candide escapes with his companions to Cadiz and a boat to the new world. A literal interpretation of their flight on horseback, combined with the strong thread of surrealism to be found in Spanish art, suggested this response to a thrilling moment in the score. A pink formica disc set against a plain blue background creates a basic space which acquired the geographical setting and mood of each stage of the journey with the addition of simple scenic elements. Arriving in Venice, Candide and Martin discover Paquette among the dockside whores.

Theatre Company: Värmlandsoperan
Director: Vernon Mound
Choreographer: Anthoula Papadakis
Lighting Designer: Frederik Magnusson
Sound Designer: Gary Dixon

HAZEL BLUE   SET & COSTUME DESIGNER

CLUTTER KEEPS COMPANY
Davey Anderson, 2010

Tramway 4, Glasgow; touring Scotland, Italy, Bulgaria,
February 2010

The design for this production developed out of having the
privilege of being able to be involved in the development
of the writing. It meant that I could formulate ideas based
on the observation of workshops and discussions which
contributed to the final text. I researched the concept
of clutter/chaos/organisation – the cathartic experience
that 'de-cluttering' our lives can be. The play works with
this theme on both a visual and psychological level, and
the design reflects the juxtaposition of order and chaos.
It is a small set, designed primarily for touring. It required
many different scene changes, ranging from domestic
interiors to a night-time fairground. These were facilitated
by the actors, who expertly rearranged the five nesting
tables which, accompanied by clever lighting, transformed
the set. Movement was choreographed throughout, and
contributed to the fluid manipulation of set pieces. Birds
of Paradise is committed to ensuring that all productions
are fully accessible. We wanted to make the production as
visually exciting as possible for hearing-impaired audience,
and I made around 60 charcoal drawings which combined
with and related to the text. This ran throughout the piece
as a back projection, revealing the text through imagery.

Theatre Company: Birds of Paradise Theatre Company
Director: Morven Gregor
Choreographer: Lindsay John
Lighting Designer: Paul Sorley
Sound Designer: Davey Anderson
Photographer: Eamonn McGoldrick

RICH EVANS   SET & COSTUME DESIGNER

THE SEAGULL
Anton Chekhov, 1895
New translation by Stewart Paterson, 2009

Main Stage, York Theatre Royal, April 2010

Working with this new translation, the director and I
played with the façade of society being mirrored by that
of a play, allowing the audience to see the workings of the
production. Through the design I worked to evoke a feeling
of vastness, isolation and personal tension. I increased
the stage area with a series of large, stepped platforms
that broke the line of the proscenium and linked the stage
and the stalls. This area aided the feeling of vast open
land in Acts I and II, before becoming a barrier between
audience and performance as the characters become
more isolated in the closing acts. In Act IV all masking was
removed to open up the full expanse of the stage, showing
behind the scenes of both the production and the world
the characters inhabit. The dramatic transformation of the
elegantly regimental trellis and frame in the first three acts
to the disintegrated state of Act IV reflected the ruined
lives of the characters and aimed to create the impression
of an oppressive, isolated and unhappy existence.

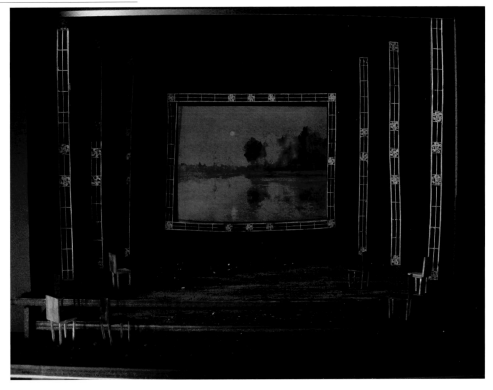

Theatre Company: York Theatre Royal and Royal Scottish Academy of
Music & Drama
Directors: Hugh Hodgart and John Kazek
Lighting Designer: Kai Fischer
Sound Designer: David Simpson
Other creative collaborator: Damien Cruden
Photographer: Kai Fischer

ELANOR HIGGINS   LIGHTING DESIGNER

SWEENEY TODD
Stephen Sondheim, 1979

Weston Studio, Wales Millennium Centre, Cardiff, July 2009

In our conceptual conversations we discussed the horrors of the show, and its many locations. One of the themes discussed was of the characters as rats in the sewer. This formed the backbone of both design and lighting design. Max's set design was an open, raised stage with trapdoors, one being a chute down from Todd's barber chair. In the upstage right corner was a silhouette of St Paul's Cathedral with a small cyclorama behind. With the space being so open, my lighting design played a crucial role in transforming the space into its many different locations, from the pie shop and Sweeney's barber shop, to the judge's house, to Bedlam, the docks and market squares of London. Through selective lighting and choice of colour, I was able to communicate a sense of time through backlighting the cyclorama, from sunrise through to sunset, and also to use it to heighten the drama of the moment, building the tension along with the music and performances. I see lighting design as a visual language and in this image the lighting design is specifically used to reveal the horrific consequences of Beadle Bamford's acceptance of a free shave.

Theatre Company: Welsh National Youth Opera, Welsh National Opera MAX
Director/Choreographer: Peter Harris
Set & Costume Designer: Max Jones
Movement Director: Ayse Tashkiran
Musical Director: Fergus Shiel
WNO Max Producer: Paula Scott
Photographer: Kirsten McTernan

DODY NASH & SIMON BENNISON
SET, COSTUME & LIGHTING DESIGNERS

SWANHUNTER
Jonathan Dove (composer) and Alasdair Middleton (librettist), 2009

Howard Assembly Room, Leeds, and tour, November 2009

DN: For this shamanic epic from Finland, our focus was to create a concise palette of discreet elements for Clare Whistler to choreograph, to support the flow and clarity of her narrative. These elements were to carry the same physical weight as the bodies on stage, so all could be moved around to represent locations, journeys or more abstract concepts.
SB: We experimented in the model with shades of blue to convey the icy setting and find an environment of pervasive colour as used in artworks made from fluorescent light.
DN: It was about achieving the potency and 'strangeness of context' of sculpture in a gallery space. Rather than pieces of a set, I aimed to give the objects the attributes of sculptures. This was in keeping with the experimental programming style of the Opera North projects team. I wanted to bring a sense of installation into the performance. It was also a development of my non-theatre projects, like the Listening Shell.
SB: I then applied the idea of an installation to a touring design, making a minimal set of carefully placed instruments that would light well, complementing the sculptural qualities. Mobile fluorescent tubes handled by the singers further expressed this idea.

Theatre Company: Opera North
Director: Clare Whistler
Lighting Designer: Simon Bennison
Photographers: Simon Bennison and Dody Nash (model)

OLIVIA GASTON   CHOREOGRAPHER & SET DESIGNER

A CHORUS OF DISAPPROVAL
Alan Ayckbourn, 1984

Altrincham Garrick Playhouse, February 2009

The director and I agreed that the set would be composite, to serve a number of scenes, so we concentrated on two multifunctional doors. Scenes included a rehearsal room, an opera stage of *The Beggar's Opera* (a play within a play), two different living rooms, a pub, a garden, a restaurant and a street. I did not include a kitchen and dressing room area on view because I felt that this was understood. To create surprise, the street scene could be seen as the gauze was opened at the rear. For part of my research I watched the film, which gave me some inspiration for the use of colour and furnishings. I also choreographed the dancing, which meant taking into consideration designing a set with adequate dancing space.

Theatre Company: **Altrincham Garrick Playhouse**
Director: **Nick Johnson**
Costume Designer: **Garrick Wardrobe**
Lighting Designer: **Fred Isaac-Dixon**
Sound Designer: **Chris Mills**
Photographer: **Martin Oldfield**

ADRIAN LINFORD   SET & COSTUME DESIGNER

ORFEO ED EURYDICE
Christoph Willibald Gluck, 1762

Ordway Centre, Minnesota, September 2010

Our thoughts on *Orfeo ed Eurydice* began almost five years ago, when we didn't have a theatre space confirmed. The process has always been exciting in that we have revisited the themes of the piece over the time period. The wall was the first image that came to mind: not only did it create barriers and separate the stage space, but the act of it moving, splitting, twisting and turning made a good physical narrative to Orpheus' mental state. Through time and development the surrounding stage elements took on the form of an old theatre, using front-of-house as the known living world and the backstage as the unknown world of death. Ideas developed and the Act II backstage space became the Elysian Fields, where the newly dead are lowered to their new resting place. The music in this act made us question why Eurydice would ever want to return, which then had us look again at how we design and stage the final ballet. The wall has always

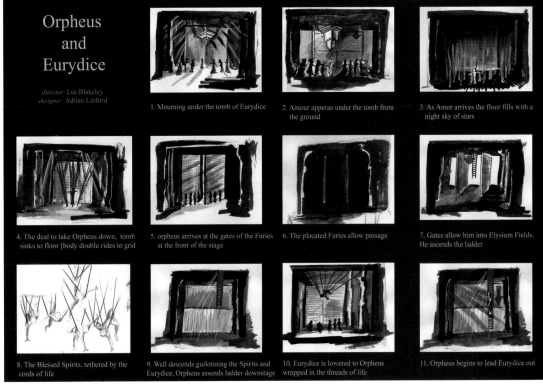

Orpheus and Eurydice

director: Lee Blakeley
designer: Adrian Linford

1. Mourning under the tomb of Eurydice
2. Amour apperas under the tomb from the ground
3. As Amor arrives the floor fills with a night sky of stars
4. The deal to take Orpheus down, tomb sinks to floor [body double rides to grid
5. orpheus arrives at the gates of the Furies at the front of the stage
6. The placated Furies allow passage
7. Gates allow him into Elysium Fields. He ascends the ladder
8. The Blessed Spirits, tethered by the cords of life
9. Wall descends guilotining the Spirits and Eurydice, Orpheus assends ladder downstage
10. Eurydice is lowered to Orpheus wrapped in the threads of life
11. Orpheus begins to lead Eurydice out

been the design driving force though the production; it has undergone many changes and developments as we have revisited the music and text, finding different ways to tackle the show's needs and themes.

Theatre Company: **Minnesota Opera**
Director: **Lee Blakeley**
Lighting Designer: **Jenny Cane**
Other creative collaborator: **Adrian Linford**

FRANCIS O'CONNOR   SET & COSTUME DESIGNER

PINOCCHIO
Jonathon Dove, 2007

Leeds Grand Theatre, 2007

In *Pinocchio* there were many spaces to realise: forest workshops, puppet shows and the inside of a whale! The story is told thick and fast, and I wanted a space that allowed the action to unfold. I came up with a box of tricks using old fashioned theatre technology, pulleys, cloths and flying… the kind of things I played with in my cardboard box theatres as a child. My son Finton was six at the time. I asked him to design the front cloth. I wanted to see the show through the eyes of a child.

Theatre Company: Opera North
Director: Martin Duncan
Choreographer: Nick Winston
Lighting Designer: Davy Cunningham
Photography: Robert Workman

XRISTINA PENNA   SET & COSTUME DESIGNER

HOLES – A SITE-SPECIFIC PERFORMANCE
Gabriella Svenningsen, 2005

Round Chapel, Hackney, May 2007

The text, *Holes*, set the structure for a metaphorical journey within the self, from Home to Forest, Limbo, Inferno, Purgatory and back. The writer, the director and the scenographer developed a collaborative way of working that was later enriched by the input of 20 artists from various disciplines. The choice of venue, the Round Chapel, provided several spaces, levels and perspectives, and therefore facilitated scenographically the visual narrative of the journey. The transition from Home to Forest signified the physical deconstruction of the characters' reality and their entrance into the unknown lands of the self. This was interpreted by a built set of two rooms in the main chapel hall. These two rooms were built at an early stage in rehearsals, allowing the performers and the scenographer to familiarise themselves with them and develop them further. The watcher was free to walk around the rooms and observe the characters in the comfort of their own space. Seven performers wearing animal masks entered the space, pulling down the set, transforming the domestic environment into chaos. The audience was then invited to follow these animal creatures into new levels and secret rooms throughout the venue, where other stages of the journey were revealed.

Theatre Company: Poemstomyotherself
Director: Anastasia Anapolytanou
Choreographer: Caroline Thompson
Lighting Designers: Sien Chi Theng with Yi Chen
Sound Designers: William Huckerby and Nik Paravatos
Photography: Anastasia Anapolytanou, Xristina Penna, Poemstomyotherself

CELIA PERKINS   COSTUME DESIGNER

THE SOLOS PROJECT
Susie Crow, 2008

Burton Taylor Studio, Oxford Playhouse, January 2008

The concept driving the Solos Project was to bring together six artists working in the field of dance to present and develop new solo work reflecting their individual dance traditions, ideas, experience and skills. My challenge was to unite six very diverse performers through design, while maintaining the individual narrative of each choreographer and their piece. Collaborating with the artists through the design process I employed colour, texture and form with each costume, taking the spectator on a visually designed journey from piece to piece, while enabling the revelations of each unique performance and the transformation of the space, challenging the audience's idea of what dance is. "Oh, note, watch. Find in dance what it is to be me" (*Dancer*, Shane McCauley). On a personal level this project was a delight to me as I love to design around movement and the body; to use form, colour and texture to reveal a character, their mood, thoughts and story.

Theatre Company: Ballet in Small Spaces
Director/Choreographer: Elly Crowther, Jane Connelly, Joelle Pappas, Adrienne Hart, Ana Barbour, Susie Crow with Lisia Moala
Choreographer: Susie Crow
Lighting Designer: Scott Stewart
Sound Designer: Scott Stewart
Costumes: Becca Ogden

POST WORKS   SET DESIGNERS

EPISODES OF FLIGHT
A collaboration between choreographer Rosemary Butcher, art and design collective Post Works and composer Cathy Lane, 2008

Riverside Studios, London, and Muffathalle, Munich, November 2009

Episodes of Flight was a multi-disciplinary collaboration, commissioned as part of the Dance Umbrella Festival 2008. The concept of the choreography centred on an interaction with a remembered past, specific to the urban environment of New York where Rosemary Butcher studied in the late 60s and early 70s. In the choreography, a rigorous physical journey is marked by a single figure measuring out a pathway within a confined space. The installation consisted of two projection screens that framed the movement of the dancer around the rectangular performance space. Projected onto the screens, a series of fictional gridded landscapes and movement notations provided echoes and fragments of narrative strands within the choreography. The two-dimensional movement notations developed from watching Elena Giannotti's choreographed movements and translated the physical space transcribed by the movement of the dancer into drawing. Celebrating the processes of translation and transformation, the work expands on the inherent slippages that occur as we move from one language, physical state, space or discipline to another.

Theatre Company: Rosemary Butcher Dance Company and Post Works
Director/Choreographer: Rosemary Butcher
Lighting Designer: Charles Balfour
Sound Designer: Cathy Lane
Dancer: Elena Giannotti
Photographer: Tim Brotherton

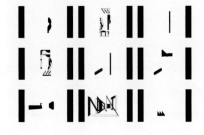

REBECCA PRIDE   SET & COSTUME DESIGNER

THE THREEPENNY OPERA
Bertolt Brecht, 1928

The Studio, Bournemouth, April 2007

The core idea behind this production was to reposition Brecht's masterpiece from the late 19th century and the coronation of Edward VII to the imaginary coronation of Edward VIII. Christopher Littlewood's idea was to place Mosley's Blackshirts as a political backdrop to the performance. This said, Tiger Brown became a leading Blackshirt in the manner on Mosley and Mac the Knife, and his gang became stereotypical 1930s gangsters. The 1930s setting reinforced the power of Kurt Weill's musical score and its reliance on the jazz idiom. Creatively, my greatest influence was the *Glitter and Doom* exhibition at The Metropolitan Museum of Art in New York, which I had seen in the autumn of 2006. This exhibition showcased the work of the German Expressionist painters, including Otto Dix, an artist who became a major influence on my design. His example inspired me to recreate the often vibrant and jarring colour schemes favoured by the German Expressionists. The space was a simple black box, and the costumes were all made by the students at The Arts University College.

Theatre Company: **AUCB Acting Company**
Director: **Christopher Littlewood**
Lighting Designer: **Peter Clifton**
Sound Designer: **John Camble**
Photographer: **Andrew Cope**

SIMON CORDER   SET & LIGHTING DESIGNER

KAFKA AMERICA
Jochen Ulrich and Kurt Schwertsik, 2009

Großes Haus, Landestheater Linz, Austria, October 2009

This was a new full-length dance piece, inspired by Franz Kafka's unfinished first novel, *Amerika* (1913–27). It is placed in an impression of early 20th-century America, a place Kafka had not visited. The process starts with a conversation of ideas with the author/choreographer, reading the book and watching relevant movies: *Metropolis* (Fritz Lang, 1927), *The Trial* (Orson Welles, 1962), and *Europa* (Lars von Trier, 1991). Image research follows, ruminations on a bicycle, and a few photographs of my own. This was my first scenographic venture with Jochen, with whom I had previously made lighting designs, and I was keen to draw on my experience with Lea Anderson and The Cholmondeleys & The Feather-stonehaughs. This involves creating a physical environment which challenges the dancers and moulds the choreo-graphy, not simply a decorative vessel for whatever the choreographer comes up with in a bare studio. I arrived at the idea of a steel-frame tower, with a boardwalk ramp, sitting on a disk of grass. These materials – riveted steel painted with red oxide and a bleached wooden boardwalk, placed on grass to represent the virgin land – evoke, somewhat formally, and somewhat abstractly, the early 20th-century European impression of the New World.

Theatre Company: **Landestheater Linz and Bruckner Orchestra**
Choreographer: **Jochen Ulrich**
Costume Designer: **Bjanka Ursulov**

PETER MUMFORD   SET DESIGNER

E=mc²
Matthew Hindson, 2009

Birmingham Hippodrome, September 2009

When David Bintley first approached me to design
this piece, his notion was to ask for a design that was
defined predominantly by light. As someone who trained
originally as a stage designer but has probably become
better known for my lighting work, this was terrific: a real
opportunity to create a space that was a canvas for light.
Matthew Hindson's score is a truly exciting and inspiring
piece of music divided into four parts: Energy, Mass,
Manhatten Project, Speed of Light. I created four versions
of a space that revealed and used light in different ways,
both painterly and using the physical power of intense
light, particularly in the final section. In order to do this
I designed a number of physical ways to let light into
the space. As a designer who continues to design sets
but works predominantly with light, my design work
has, over the years, evolved towards a position where
I'm specifically interested in a very direct and deliberate
relationship between the space and the way it receives,
reflects and is defined by light, and if I'm asked to design
a project, I'm looking to create a space that is a considered
a canvas for light and performance.

Theatre Company: Birmingham Royal Ballet
Director/Choreographer: David Bintley
Set Designer: Peter Mumford
Costume Designer: Kate Ford
Lighting Designer: Peter Mumford

PATRICK CONNELLAN   SET & COSTUME DESIGNER

COPENHAGEN
Michael Frayn, 1998

New Vic Theatre, Newcastle-under-Lyme, May 2010

The essence of this set design was used in repertoire between *Copenhagen* and *Alphabetical Order*, also by Michael Frayn. Therefore, I explored the common themes of the plays; order and chaos, the mass production of information and transformation. The overall geometry of the design, sitting within the 'perfect' in-the-round space, assumes the structure of the atom with the centre being the nucleus and the intellectual response of the audience racing around as electrons. The halo of paper suspended above represents a whirlwind of information and understanding, as well as alluding to the mushroom cloud of a nuclear explosion. The floor and carefully placed furniture, charred documents and historical artifacts is the scene of a crime; burnt and violently damaged, leaving historical relics as pieces of evidence. Each relic is tagged and apparently archived, as though it may have some significance in the investigation and understanding the audience carries out. In recent times I have become more interested in how the real and authentic object, thoughtfully placed in the appropriate context, may reveal more than the self-consciously designed artificial object. The resonance and power of the authentic may be a more useful and meaningful visual metaphor. It is this that I have explored in my design for *Copenhagen*.

Theatre Company: **New Vic Theatre, Newcastle-under-Lyme**
Director: **James Dacre**
Lighting Designer: **Daniella Beattie**
Sound Designer: **James Earls-Davis**
Photographer: **Andrew Billington**

MAX JONES   SET & COSTUME DESIGNER

MEASURE FOR MEASURE
William Shakespeare, 1603–4

Clwyd Theatr Cymru, Mold, Flintshire, May 2008

When designing for a production, my starting points are both text and space. It's very important for me to complement and satisfy them equally. *Measure for Measure* is a production with multiple interior and exterior locations. It was clear that we would require a composite environment, one that would not technically hinder the pace and intensity of the piece, yet was still bold enough to evoke, for instance, the grandeur of the Duke's palace versus the grotesque underbelly of a turn-of-the-century Vienna. "Some rise by sin, and some by virtue fall." My response was both to exploit and to adapt the virtues inherent to the studio. Reconfiguring the seating into a deep thrust formation with one strong central entrance through the auditorium put the intense action in the laps of our audience. In the upstage area a huge dam-like wall was built. It spanned both the full width of the studio and sunk to the depths of the theatre's pit below. This was detailed using period architectural features, whilst also integrating elements from the contemporary constructed studio walls and, although bold in scale, the audience could have walked in assuming that it was an existing feature of the theatre; a subtle and foreboding manipulation of both audience and the space.

Theatre Company: **Clwyd Theatr Cymru**
Director: **Phillip Breen**
Lighting Designer: **Tina MacHugh**
Photographers: **Max Jones (model), Catherine Ashmore (mistress)**

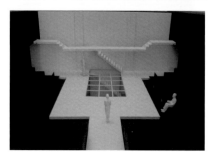

RAJHA SHAKIRY   SET DESIGNER

FEEBLE MINDS
Devised by inc. Theatre Ensemble and HotPots, 2009

Albany, London, July 2009

Spare Tyre make theatre that enables voiceless
individuals and communities to tell their stories and to
challenge social prejudices. This piece was devised by
the company's two ensemble groups, and is loosely
based on Shakespeare's *Timon of Athens*. Following
several discussions with the director, Arti Prashar, the
design inspiration was based on the themes of greed,
the definition of currency, insanity, neurology, order, the
four elements, nature and the gods. The architecture
of the venue strongly influenced the design shape and
transformation of the space. We created a corridor of
opaque screens, shadows and sounds to disorientate
the audience as they entered. In placing a large convex
screen, I also wanted to redefine and work against the
familiar playing area. The multi-sensory effects and
materials used enabled the performers and audiences
to be transported to an unfamiliar and unsettling world,
a world where the bouffon characters come out of the
shadows to play for their audience.

Theatre Company: Spare Tyre
Directors: Arti Prashar and Isaac Ngugi
Costume Designer: Lieutske Visser
Lighting Designer: Philip Gladwell
Sound Designer: Tayo Akinbode
Multi-media Artist: Matt Spencer
Photographer: Patrick Baldwin

NICKY SHAW   SET & COSTUME DESIGNER

ALCINA
George Friderick Handel, 1735

Irish tour of eight venues, commencing at
Soltice Arts Centre, Navan, October 2009

Alcina is an enchantress, and the opera is set on her
magical island where her many ex-lovers are rumoured
to live, transformed by her into wild beasts. We decided
to set the opera in the 1890s, as this period allows for a
formality of ritual behaviour: there is still a clear definition
between male and female dress (useful because the
heroine, Bradamante, turns up in disguise as her brother,
to rescue her betrothed Ruggiero from the power of
Alcina's magic) and, finally, to contrast smart formal dress
with nature. I designed a 'magic box' that opened into
different configurations. The design on the inside and
outside walls was of repeating trees, which were used
both as a literal image for exterior scenes on the island
in the forest and also served as a painted *trompe l'oeil*
interior room in Alcina's palace. During the last scenes,
when Alcina's magic has finally been broken, the forest set
closes around her, locking her up inside the now black box
– the trees are gone, all enchantments are broken.

Theatre Company: Opera Theatre Company
Director: Annilese Miskimmon
Lighting Designer: Tina MacHugh
Conductor: Christian Curnyn

RUARI MURCHISON   SET & COSTUME DESIGNER

MACBETH
William Shakespeare, 1603–7

Quarry Theatre, West Yorkshire Playhouse, March 2007

A war is being fought when *Macbeth* opens. Fear, superstition, religion, blood and nature force their way into the human world, evoked in a design that used natural materials manipulated by mankind. A steel wall – out of which a section has fallen onto a clotted blood floor – formed the acting area, which was enclosed by a curved rock wall. This wall could rise and fall, showing thin strips of landscape lit by intense colour. In this way we represented Burnham Wood. Nature: acidic green; war: more blood red; fear: grey. In a final comment on the state of the nation at the end of the piece, the wall closed emphatically; although Macbeth is conquered, the world carries on in the same way, as before, in turmoil somewhere!

Theatre Company: West Yorkshire Playhouse
Director: Ian Brown
Lighting Designer: Guy Hore
Sound Designer: Mic Poole
Fight Director: Kate Waters
Photographer: Keith Patterson

IONA McLEISH   SET & COSTUME DESIGNER

HELDENPLATZ
Thomas Bernhard, with English translation by Andrea Tierney and Meredith Oakes, 1988

Studio One, Arcola Theatre, London, February 2010

For over a decade I have worked with directors Annie Castledine and Annabel Arden, investigating the visual possibilities of language and meaning, reality and illusion, and the exploration of the movement of character(s) in space. *Heldenplatz* insists that space is left for the absent characters and the echoes from the past. It demands emptiness, yet requires the imprint of fleeting glimpses, shifting shadows, ghosts from the past and the significance of objects alongside those living. For me, work on this production started 18 months before the opening. I attended read-throughs of the new translation in Meredith's kitchen. I considered the spatial opportunities of the venue. I worked with the Arcola's three supporting pillars, cladding them with mirror, allowing them to underscore the traces of the absent characters. In the late summer of 2009 I met up with Annie with a rough model. The traverse arrangement was right for this piece, not only allowing the audience to consider each other and the role of the silent witness in history, but also empowering full movement within the space. Everything in the space was a distillation, essential for the telling of this story, and all characters inhabited the created world, observing the action as eyewitnesses and our consciousness.

Theatre Company: Arcola Theatre Production Company
Directors: Annie Castledine and Annabel Arden
Lighting Designer: Ben Payne
Sound Designer: Andrew Pontzen
Photographer: Robert Workman

GWYN EIDDIOR PARRY   SET & COSTUME DESIGNER

BOBI A SAMI... A DYNION ERAILL
(BOBI AND SAMI... AND OTHER MEN)
William Samuel Jones and Samuel Beckett, 1988

Studio tour in Wales, February 2009

The main challenge was to accommodate three separate pieces of theatre within one space, each piece separately punctuated, but also flowing smoothly from one to the other to create a cohesive night of theatre. As the production was touring and performed in traverse, the whole theatre space needed to be designed from scratch: onstage, backstage and the auditorium. My reaction was first to find the similarities and common ground of all three plays to create the shell of the set. This led me to design a series of simple concrete walls that would accommodate all technical needs and suggest the ambiguous, uncomfortable environment in which all the characters were trapped. It also served as a blank canvas on which we could introduce the other set elements to transform the space as and when requested. As Beckett directs in Act Without Words I, a tree, a carafe of water, three boxes, a length of rope and a pair of scissors were flown in sequence to create a puzzle in which the man unsuccessfully attempts to find shade and quench his thirst. In Act Without Words II, a big red goad rolls onstage to prod and wake the two men from their sacks. To create the inside and outside of the enclosed yard in which Bobi and Sami live and later escape from, I simply revealed a sliding gate at one end and a revolving door at the other which they go through and come back into between scenes. All three pieces leave plenty of food for thought for the audience. They are anything but black and white, therefore I didn't want to set any preconceptions about the characters or their habitat. The set and costumes needed to be flexible and broadly open for interpretation.

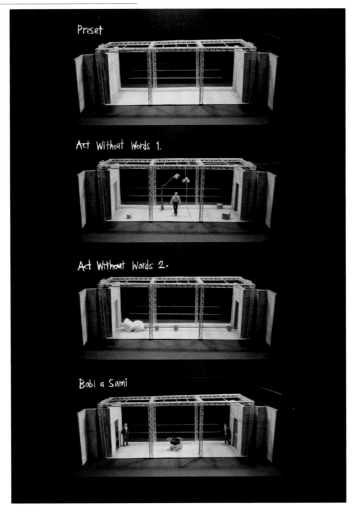

Theatre Company: Theatr Genedlaethol Cymru
(Welsh Language National Theatre)
Directors: Cefin Roberts and Judith Roberts
Lighting Designer: Nick Mumford
Sound Designer: Osian Gwynedd
Photographers: Gwyn Eiddior Parry and Warren Orchard

STUART TARGETT   SET & COSTUME DESIGNER

L'ELISIR D'AMORE
Gaetano Donizetti, 1832

Piazza del Popolo, Anghiari, Tuscany, Italy, July 2008

The whole show was about transformation and revelation. Stuart, the director, initially asked me to come up with a design that transformed the piazza in Anghiari, a walled town in Tuscany, but with sympathy to the location and using the orchestral stage/platform that was already there. Both the fairy-tale quality of the opera and the shape of the platform inspired me to create a picture book with fly-away pages, including a portrait of Anghiari itself, across the buildings of the square that incorporated windows from which action could be played. The book initially lies open and flat and then, during the overture, pop-ups rose from the stage surface to transform it into a workable set for the opera. Characters from out of town came from other books to transform the storyline, and I used defined colour schemes to highlight this. Dulcamara's carriage was the ultimate example of transformation in the show. I transformed the town's historic dustcart into a covered wagon which itself, with the help of several mousetraps, transformed into a travelling medicine show with a vibrant display of bottles. These had themselves been transformed from pound-shop vases by the commissioning of Chianti-style baskets from local craftsmen.

Theatre Company: British Youth Opera
Director: Stuart Barker
Lighting Designer: G P Service, Arezzo
Sound Designer: G P Service, Arezzo
Other creative collaborator: Simon Over

MARK HOWLAND   LIGHTING DESIGNER

PAINS OF YOUTH
Ferdinand Brückner, 1926

B2 Studio, Belgrade Theatre, Coventry, September 2007

The visual concept began with our decision to transform the then-new studio space at Coventry's Belgrade Theatre into a modern environment that would best allow the elements of danger and self destruction that run through the play to be expressed. The lighting developed to match the elements within the set. The room, perched on top of the hydraulic lifts, was illuminated entirely by domestic fittings within. The surrounding space was transformed from intimate and sensual to stark and foreboding, using a range of light sources. Fluorescent, sodium, HMI and tungsten sources were all used individually to heighten the atmosphere within each scene. One of the most effective elements of the whole lighting design was the shadow cast onto the back wall of the theatre by the two sodium floods, as shown in this image. As the floods warmed up and increased in level over the start of the scene the image of a quintessentially caricatured house was revealed on the back wall, complete with chimney and windows. This provided a very effective backdrop to scenes where the young students argue about not wanting to enter into the boredom of domesticated adult life.

Theatre Company: Belgrade Theatre
Director: Gadi Roll
Set Designer: Roni Toren
Costume Designer: Monika Nisbet
Photographer: Roni Toren

ANNA BLISS SCULLY   SET & COSTUME DESIGNER

THE EXQUISITE CORPSE
Branwen Davies, Angharad Devonald, Tracy Harris, Kit Lambert and Othniel Smith, 2009

Weston Studio, Wales Millennium Centre, Cardiff, and Southwark Playhouse, London, July 2008

Consisting of 16 scenes, *The Exquisite Corpse* was a 4D version of the eponymous surrealist parlour game. The scenes contained no common characters or plot, only recurring imagery and themes. Every scene was numbered, and the audience sequenced the play before each performance by re-ordering a row of randomly numbered objects in the theatre foyer. The cast were never shown this order. After a fixed opening sequence, the first of the evening's scene numbers was projected behind them. They set up the scene, performed it and, when complete, looked behind them, where the next number in the sequence appeared. With short scenes, a need for dynamic, choreographed scene changes and shifts in pace and tone, we developed a designed framework: five actors sat on stools around the stage, each with a coatstand decked in highly-specific costumes and props; on the floor, coloured tape marked out the positions of furniture, with hard lighting locking down each area; on the cyclorama, projected images set the tone of each scene. In performance it had the rigour of a sport: between each scene a poised potential, then the flash of a number and an underscored transformation into a newly-shaped space, new characters, and a new story.

Theatre Company: True/Fiction Theatre
Director: Matt Peover
Lighting Designer: Nicki Brown
Sound Designer: Blair Mowat
Creative Associate: Matthew Bulgo
Photographer: Kirsten McTernan

JANET BIRD   SET & COSTUME DESIGNER

ENJOY
Alan Bennett, 1980

National tour, 2008

"Dear lady. Put one or two things together, but only the barest essentials. Packing is unnecessary as these trained staff will shortly transfer your home and its contents to its new setting". Connie and Wilf live in one of the last back-to-backs in Leeds. Their house is shortly to be demolished, but before this is to happen the council try to identify the source of their community contentment by way of a survey conducted by silent observers. The process of this close scrutiny opens many old (and new) wounds. Eventually it is decided that instead the house is to be transferred to a living museum on the outskirts. The stage direction simply says: 'at this point Gregory, Adrian, Rowland and Charles begin to dismantle the house'. We made a decision to expose the theatricality of the process. The family's whole world is being taken apart, not just their house. So for us, seeing the structure of the set as their lives are taken apart is about revelation and exposure. Families spend their time not saying what they mean, for all sorts of reasons: honesty is a refreshing and dangerous thing. The set is honest about what it is happening in that transformation. The illusion is being stripped away, we're being taken behind the mirrors.

Theatre Company: Bath Royal Theatre
Director: Christopher Luscombe
Choreographer: Jenny Arnold
Lighting Designer: Paul Pyant
Sound Designer: Jason Barnes
Photographer: Manuel Harlan

ZOE SQUIRE   SET & COSTUME DESIGNER

ERNEST AND THE PALE MOON
Oliver Lansley, 2010

UK tour, March 2010

I worked closely with director Emma Earle to create an inventive design with various narrative twists and turns through physical storytelling and creative use of set and props. The terrifying tale of *Ernest and the Pale Moon* transforms the stage into a series of visual events and motifs to tell the journey of a man who spends his days watching the beautiful young woman who lives in the apartment block opposite. Upon seeing her with another man he is thrown into a jealous rage and driven to murder. All is not what it may at first seem, for it is not only the space that has appeared to transform. The audience watch as Ernest's guilt sends him on a spiralling descent into madness.

Theatre Company: Pins & Needles Productions and Les Enfants Terribles
Director: Emma Earle
Lighting Designer: Paul Green
Sound Designer: Thomas Gisby
Photographers: Charlie Mudie and Jude Palmer

MARTIN JOHNS   SET & COSTUME DESIGNER

A MIDSUMMER NIGHT'S DREAM
William Shakespeare, 1595–6

Main House, Theatre by the Lake, Keswick, July 2009

The early court scenes were played in Jacobean costume against a vast gauze wallhanging of a hunting scene: a formal, male-dominated world. The transformation from court to wood was effected by first bleeding-through, then flying out the gauze, revealing a huge, blasted tree-stump with fallen boughs: an image of the chaos caused by Oberon and Titania's quarrel. The tree was set against a tilted circular canopy of branches and a large full moon; it was also on a revolve and seen from different perspectives as the revolve turned, to create different locations within the wood. The elements of the wood were painted in silvers, whites and greys, responding to lighting to create the changing moods of the wood from naturalistic to magical, to hostile. Thematic sound collages were also used in the fairy scenes, in contrast to the period music of Dowland in the court. With most actors doubling or trebling roles, a strong contrast was vital between the elaborate Jacobean court costumes, the servants' livery of the mechanicals, and the fairy world: ragged cloaks and half-masked heads inspired by forest vegetation – chestnut, fungus, seedheads. Finally, the blasted tree stump joined with the branched canopy to create an image of regeneration, order restored to the wood.

Theatre Company: Theatre by the Lake
Director: Ian Forrest
Choreographer: Lorelei Lynn
Lighting Designer: Nick Beadle
Sound Designer: James Earls Davis
Fight Director: Kate Waters
Photographer: Keith Pattison

BECKY MINTO   SET & COSTUME DESIGNER

WHITE TEA
David Leddy, 2009

Assembly Rooms, Edinburgh, August 2009

The piece deftly used the role of tea in British and Japanese life as a way to explore colliding cultures and clashing personalities. Our performance space was a 4.2 × 4.8 m office within the Assembly Rooms, complete with connecting doors to internal corridors, a large bay window overlooking George Street (where the deputy stage manager was concealed), carpet tiles, plastic coving and a suspended ceiling. Inside this sterile room we created an installation inspired by Japanese tea houses. A metal frame was designed to fit inside the room, onto which the set and LED-panelled ceiling were clad. A cocoon of paper prayer flags and origami birds layered the walls. The audience, dressed in white paper kimonos, sat on black lacquer benches around the walls, with tatami matting under their feet. Traditional floor lanterns concealed the speakers, lighting and projectors, from which lush images of Japan and cutting-edge LED and laser-projected messages were thrown onto the walls, ceiling and performers around them. In the corners of the room on delicate stones, teacups sat waiting to be served. The audience were so close that attention to detail was vital and, though the space was so tiny, every inch was used creatively.

Theatre Company: Fire Exit Ltd
Director: David Leddy
Lighting Designer: Nich Smith
Sound Designer: Graham Sutherland
Video & Projection: Tim Reid
Assistant Director: Stef Smith
Photographers: Tim Morozzo (production shots), David Leddy (pre-production shot)

RYSZARD ANDRZEJEWSKI   COSTUME DESIGNER

THE SOFA
Elizabeth Maconchy, 1957

Lilian Baylis Theatre, Sadler's Wells, London, November 2007

With the premise of an East End, Hoxton, house party, this is the story of 'a dissolute young man (Prince Dominic) who is punished by his grandmother for his fast living and predatory womanising by being turned into a sofa'. The magical transformation from man to inanimate object is the result of the influence of his grandmother, 'the Witch', a Zandra Rhodes figure who has tailored a 'sofa suit' for her grandson to initiate his transformation into the sofa itself. He is then released from his grandmother's spell and transformed back into a man as his girlfriend is seduced upon the sofa by another man.

Theatre Company: **Independent Opera**
Director: **Alessandro Talevi**
Set Designer: **Madeline Boyd**
Choreographer: **Hanna Gilgren**
Lighting Designer: **Matthew Haskins**
Other creative collaborator: **Dominic Wheeler**
Photographers: **Belinda Lawley and Robbie Jack**

SUE CONDIE   SET & COSTUME DESIGNER

A MIDSUMMER NIGHT'S DREAM
William Shakespeare, 1594–6

The Round, Stephen Joseph Theatre, Scarborough, June 2010

Set loosely around 1910–20s against a background of tango, we chose the simplicity of a circle echoing the phases of the moon for our more formal setting of Theseus's country estate. As the play progresses we see this shape shattering to become a forest with no actual trees but an abstract place of different shapes and reflective surfaces providing a ramp and playful levels. Here we see Puck, our master of ceremonies, controlling the action as the set is pieced back together by the fairies. The lovers are choreographed in a dream-like state to find themselves awaking from their sleep, shifting the narrative back to the estate where *Pyramus and Thisbe* is played. My recent work reflects my passion for textiles. I often draw inspiration from decorative patterns and enjoy discovering ways of altering them to create a particular atmosphere on stage. In *A Midsummer Night's Dream*, for example, we looked at Art Deco patterns and echoed the repetitive shapes and forms in the painted floor to create a forest feel, and also for the choice of fabrics for costumes and soft furnishings. Designing for the round allows us the opportunity to relish details, as the audience is close enough to appreciate the textures and even the buttons we select. I love the variety of fabrics nowadays, and enjoy the challenge of choosing sometimes surprising contemporary cloth to recreate period frocks on a tight budget!

Theatre Company: **Stephen Joseph Theatre**
Director: **Chris Monks**
Choreographer: **Beverley Edmunds**
Lighting Designer: **Jason Taylor**
Sound Designer: **Paul Stear**
Video Design: **Paul Stear**

JANET VAUGHAN   SET & COSTUME DESIGNER

FOREVER IN YOUR DEBT
Nick Walker, 2010

Touring, February 2010

The design developed alongside the script, each slightly influencing the other, with my feeling that there was a need for some sort of physical transformation in the design, leading to the writing of the building demolition denouement. It was the first time these two theatre companies had collaborated, bringing together two quite different processes for making work, with Foursight's emphasis being on devising around the scripted material throughout the rehearsal process. I've done a lot of design for devised work and so am used to building possibilities into a set – usually in the form of cupboards or hatches out of which to produce props unthought of at the point of design, or putting everything on wheels so that the elements of the set can be moved about if it becomes necessary once the show begins to unfold. In this case, once I had the visual start and end points I designed the set to break up into several moveable units and left it up to the acting company to devise the exact sequence of the transformation from rooftop to rubble – via slide, boat, cowboy steer, row of terraced houses and maternity ward.

Theatre Company: Talking Birds Theatre Company and Foursight Theatre Company
Director: Sarah Thom
Co-director: Kate Hales
Lighting Designer: Arnim Friess
Sound Designer: Derek Nisbet

NAOMI WILKINSON   SET & COSTUME DESIGNER

LA DISPUTE
Pierre de Marivaux, adapted by Neil Bartlett

Peacock Stage, Abbey Theatre, Dublin, January 2009

Marivaux's play is set at the point when four adolescents kept in confinement from each other since birth are allowed to meet each other for the first time (and fall in love), an experiment perpetrated for the idle amusement of an aristocrat who wishes to determine whether women are inherently more fickle in love than men. By creating a series of sliding trap doors suggesting hidden enclosures, like those used for animals in a zoo, circus or laboratory, I wanted the set to display similarly clinical and brutal characteristics as those behind the experiment on these hapless children. The printed forest around the walls acted as a cipher for the deception wrought on the children, who never saw the real thing and so would know no better, while the giant rabbit sits menacingly reminding us further of these children's cheated childhood.

Director: Wayne Jordan
Lighting Designer: Sinead Wallace

IAN WESTBROOK   SET & COSTUME DESIGNER

ALL THE FUN OF THE FAIR
Jon Conway and David Essex, 2008

Garrick Theatre, London, September 2008
Churchill Theatre, Bromley, April 2010

The design emerged from a request by producer Jon
Conway: "Ian, if this show has any hope of coming in
on budget, we need to unload, fit up and light in eight
hours, to open that night touring all major UK theatres".
With this in mind I chose a set with adaptable portals that
represented structures of an old wooden roller coaster.
Using three colours – red, yellow and blue lights used in
the real fairgrounds – to edge these portals and stage
rostra, along with side-moving fairground stalls and flown
illuminated sign boards, the set was born. To fit three
life-size dodgem cars, a large sweet cart and five flying
galloper horses, along with railway station platform,
flying motor bike and rider moving over the audience,
was a challenge, but also fun. The Wall of Death features
heavily in the story; we could not tour a real Wall of Death,
but simulated this by sound effects and clever lighting.
Act I starts with a drab and scruffy funfair in need of
refurbishment: this reflects the underlying tensions and
tragic lives of the characters. Throughout the show a
transformation occurs, not only in the characters but the
sets. Act II opens with an upbeat musical number and the
fairground being redecorated, reflecting the developing
optimism; but also with an underlying sub-plot of disaster
and the death of the most loveable of the characters.

Management: Alan Darlow Productions, Jon Conway and
Lee Dean Productions
Director: David Gilmore
Choreographer: Sophie Lawrence
Lighting Designer: Ben Cracknell
Sound Designer: Sebastien Frost and Steve Jones
Other creative collaborator: Pete Kramer and The Twins

MALCOLM RIPPETH   LIGHTING DESIGNER

BRIEF ENCOUNTER
Noël Coward, 1945, adapted for the stage by
Emma Rice, 2007

Cineworld Cinema, Haymarket, London, then UK and US tours,
February 2008

In February 2008 we took over an art deco West End
cinema and transformed it into a theatre for this production,
which used a combination of Coward's original stage play,
Still Life (1936), and the screenplay of *Brief Encounter*,
switching seamlessly between theatre and film. I was
interested in how filmically our stage could be lit, with
an ever-present ensemble in widescreen, but also in
contrasting the scale of the projected image with intimate
human environments. I used facial-sized specials and wide
crosslight to pull people out of the backgrounds and put
our various lovers into close up, and played throughout
with colour temperature – ranging from firelight through
sepia to daylight and the cold light of the largely
monochrome projections. Here we see Alec and Laura,
finally alone in a boathouse, lit by the glow of a stove.
A moment later their reverie is broken: a piercing train
whistle and a snap shift from firelight to cold white takes
them from intimacy to exposure, from private to public,
and, significantly, from colour to black and white.

Theatre Company: Kneehigh Theatre, originally produced by David Pugh,
Dafydd Rogers and Cineworld
Director: Emma Rice
Set & Costume Designer: Neil Murray
Sound Designer: Simon Baker
Video & Projection Design: Jon Driscoll and Gemma Carrington
Photographer: Steve Tanner

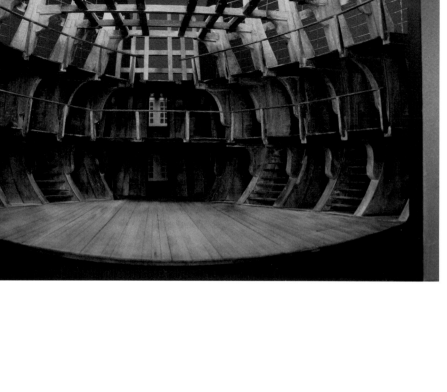

CHRISTOPHER ORAM   SET & COSTUME DESIGNER

BILLY BUDD
Benjamin Britten, 1951

Glyndebourne, May 2010

The thing that first struck me when I came to Glynde-bourne was the relationship of the auditorium and the stage, and that its materials, finishes and forms are very evocative of nautical architecture. With this in mind, I then wanted to create a sense of claustrophobia and of being trapped onboard a Napoleonic man o'war, taking reference for its structure from that of a ship stripped of its cladding, and the ribcage of a whale. We consequently created a structure with decks and galleries following the lines of the auditorium, bringing the audience into the belly of ship and the action onboard. Creating this abstracted, yet realistic, setting allowed the company to work the ship in a naturalistic way, helping tell the story of the relationships and hierarchy onboard an 18th-century warship.

Director: Michael Grandage
Lighting Designer: Paule Constable
Movement Director: Tom Roden
Conductor: Mark Elder
Associate Designers: Andrew Edwards and Richard Kent
Assistant Designers: Ben Davies and Chiara Stephenson

PIP NASH   SET & COSTUME DESIGNER

URBAN DREAMS
2008

Open-air touring in south east London, 2008

Urban Dreams was an inter-generational community performance created for open air spaces in south east London, on the banks of the Thames and in parks from Tower Bridge to Greenwich via Deptford. It explored collective ideas of dreams: daydreams, night dreams and fears, and the five stages of sleep. The cast, which included 56 performers between the ages of seven and 70, presented the piece through movement, text, live music, puppetry, mask and projection. *Urban Dreams* was created through imaging, music and poetry workshops, led by a creative team of professional theatre practitioners. The aim was to explore the ideas through a range of media, so that the piece was driven by a variety of performative forms, not only text. The material was gathered initially through workshops with both the London Bubble and Face Front participatory youth, adult and elders' drama groups. Drawing the collected ideas together, the creative team formed a narrative and scenographic framework through discussions, drawings and exercises. This was then taken into the production and rehearsal process with the performers, and finally presented outside at night against the background lights of the Thames and city skyline.

Theatre Company: London Bubble Theatre Company
Director: Jonathan Petherbridge
Choreographer: Linda Dobell
Lighting Designer: Nao Nagai
Musical Director & Composer: Martina Schwartz
Text: Jennifer Farmer
Puppeteer: Aya Nakamura
Performer: Eric MacLennan
Photographer: Steve Hickey

JULIET SHILLINGFORD   SET & COSTUME DESIGNER

THE LONG ROAD
Shelagh Stephenson, 2010

Curve, Leicester, March 2010

The Long Road explores the way in which a family deals with the random killing of their teenage son. The language is very poetic, and I was struck by the way the mother describes the objects that are left behind when her son died – the used cup, the pillow, the clothes that still contain his smell. The belongings that make up a person take on more significance when he or she dies. I am interested in how, as designers, we make choices about the meaning of objects – props, set dressing, furniture or clothes – in order to reveal a narrative. A simple wire grid was hung with Danny's possessions. Careful choices were made about the type of objects and their original colour; then everything was sprayed with a dusting of grey as if covered in ash and echoing the fog that has descended over the lives of the family. This was then used as the screen for the projected film of the boy's face, which faded in and out during the course of the play as if he were witnessing the anguish of the family he left behind.

Management: Leicester Theatre Trust
Director: Adel Al-Salloum
Lighting Designer: Arnim Friess
Sound Designer: Jack C Arnold
Photographer: Johan Persson

DICK BIRD   SET & COSTUME DESIGNER

SNEGUROCHKA
Nicolai Rimsky Korsakov, 1881

Wexford Opera House, October 2008

Snegurochka, the Snow Maiden, is based on an old Russian folk tale, and tells of a land where the sun has refused to appear for 13 years, out of fury at an illicit union between Winter and Spring that has produced a beautiful but aberrant child. We chose to tell the story in contemporary landscapes and communities that have been transformed by environmental catastrophe; the rusting, abandoned fairground at Chernobyl, and the dried up Aral Sea – a desert littered with ships, where fishing villages now stand 200 kilometres from the water. Each setting tends to plant an enigma, the answer to which is revealed by the setting of the following scene. We begin with a forest of oil pipes growing out of the snow. In the far distance is a circle of lights. In the next scene we find ourselves between the giant legs of a ferris wheel, where Snegurochka's adoptive parents have made their home in one of the detached gondolas. Tsar Berendey holds court from his bath in a decrepit cabin at an alarming angle. In the next scene he descends from the side of his ship, which we see leaning, stranded on the frozen ocean floor.

Theatre Company: Wexford Festival Opera
Director: John Fulljames
Lighting Designer: Paul Keogan
Photographer: Patrick Redmond

KIMIE NAKANO   COSTUME DESIGNER

MURAL STUDIES
Jamie Hamilton, 2010

Rich Mix, London, and world tour, May 2010

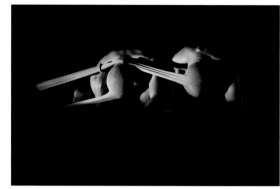

The empty space becomes a canvas on which movement is spilt, flung, dripped and scraped by five mural-painting coloured costumed dancers. The dancer stands at the core. The opening scene is inspired by strange surrealistic Dali characters.

Theatre Company: Van Huynh Company
Choreographer: Dam Van Huynh
Lighting Designer: Antony Hateley
Composer: Jamie Hamilton
Photographer: Agnieszka Janiszewska

SOUTRA GILMOUR   SET & COSTUME DESIGNER

THE TRAGEDY OF THOMAS HOBBES
Adriano Shaplin, 2008

Wilton's Music Hall, London, November 2008

This ambitious play for the RSC is set in 1650s London, when the closing of the theatres led to the rise of experimental science and public demonstrations as the new performance, and The Royal Society was born. It presented an amazing opportunity to work in the once-lost Wilton's music hall, with its famous 'barley sugar' cast iron pillars and its faded plasterwork. A wooden scaffold was built in the void of the proscenium opening, allowing access to all areas, down into the understage, across the second floor galleries and up into the dome of the ceiling. Have we walked into a closed and barred theatre space? Is Wilton's undergoing a facelift for reopening? Is it the gallows, the framework for a scientific machine, or the burning timbers of the fire of London? In the triple-height room the audience was taken on a journey through London's basements, streets and attics, its coffee houses, palaces and the private studies of its most famous and infamous scientists; up to the heavens of Boyle's prayers and down to the underworld of Hooke's gruesome anatomical antics with dogs, via Newton's flighty notions of gravity. By transforming Wilton's shallow stage and flat auditorium, I hope its volume, circulation, height and, indeed, history were revealed.

Theatre Company: Royal Shakespeare Company
Director: Elizabeth Freestone
Lighting Designer: Johanna Town
Sound Designer: Adrienne Quartly
Photographer: Hugo Glendinning

FRANCISCO RODRIGUEZ-WEIL   SET & COSTUME DESIGNER

KATYA KABANOVA
Leoš Janáček, 1921

Royal Northern College of Music, Manchester, March 2008

We wanted the set to reflect the sense of oppression that pervades the opera. The storm taking place in the third act was used as a metaphor for Katya's inner turmoil (the book is based on a play called *The Storm*). The main action took place in what became the eye of the storm, a revolve on a rake that was engulfed by portals representing a brewing tempest. Katya's actions were confined to this area, as if showing her limited freedom. The back of the revolve went up to reveal the ruins, and the floor split to disclose a river underneath. A lonely tree changes as the acts progress, reflecting Katya's inner turmoil. During the storm scene in the third act, lightning strikes the tree: it breaks in full view of the audience as the revolve turns. It is also in this scene that we first see Katya break down.

Theatre Company: Royal Northern College of Music
Director: Stefan Janski
Lighting Designer: Phillip Edwards

KATHRINE SANDYS   SCENOGRAPHER

HUSH HOUSE
Kathrine Sandys, 2010

Bentwaters Parks, Suffolk, March 2010

Hush House is an installation that uses natural light and infrasound to create 'presence' in the de-commissioned Cold War test hangar. The third in a series of pieces exploring empty Cold War sites, *Hush House* positions the space, location and journey to the space, as the focus of the work. The spectator becomes participant through their exploration of the site, ordinarily only experienced in fictional representation. Using apparently invisible scenographic devices – carefully contrived journey, controlled light and sound that appears to creep from the building – the space and site adopts a sense of its previous activity. I am interested in how a journey through the landscape of late 20th-century military spaces is relatively unexplored and therefore holds an air of mystery that encourages an imagined narrative about the site. The myths of the Cold War have a resonance when encountering architecture of unknown purpose. Infrasound (sub-audible sound) is never experienced as a tangible sound object in itself. By reducing sound and to its experiential waves of sensation, this scenographic device transforms a derelict space into a sensory environment.

Theatre Company: Aldeburgh Music/Faster Than Sound
Sound Designer: Kathrine Sandys
Photographer: Simon Sandys

Biographies

PAGE NUMBERS FOR THE DESIGNER'S SUBMISSION FOLLOW EACH NAME.

DAWN ALLSOPP   103

Dawn trained at The Bristol Old Vic Theatre School, having originally completed a degree in Fashion and Textile Design.

She was resident designer at Swan Theatre in Worcester from 1994 to 2000 before going freelance.

Over the past ten years she has worked for a variety of directors and venues and has also become involved with the Birmingham-based theatre-in-education company Language Alive, designing sets and costumes which then tour into schools.

Recent theatre credits include; *The Importance of Being Earnest* (New Wolsey, Ipswich); *The Grapes of Wrath* (Colchester Mercury Theatre); *Town* (Theatre Royal, Northampton); *The Hired Man* and *Oliver Twist* (Octagon, Bolton); *The Dumb Waiter* and *A Kind of Alaska* (Derby Live); *Beautiful House* (Library Theatre, Manchester); *Fireflies* (The Lowry, Salford); *Blithe Spirit* (Nottingham Playhouse); *Death of a Salesman* and *The Homecoming* (York Theatre Royal); *A Chorus of Disapproval* (New Wolsey, Ipswich/Colchester Mercury); *Quartet* (Oldham Coliseum); *Accidental Death of an Anarchist* (Northern Broadsides).

BECS ANDREWS   63

Becs designs mainly for opera, dance and site-specific projects. She also works in a wide range of educational contexts. She is interested in designing sets, costumes and video-projection concepts that are fully responsive to the performer's movement in space.

Operas she has designed include *On the Rim of the World* and *La Serva Padrona* for Royal Opera House, *Eugene Onegin* for Scottish Opera and Royal Scottish Academy of Music and Drama; *Albert Herring* for British Youth Orchestra; and *Fiesque* for University College Oxford.

Dance work includes *The Art of Not Looking Back* and *Untitled* for Hofesh Shechter Company; *Session* (Introdans) and *Momo* (Stadttheater Bern) with Didy Veldman; and *Itinerarium, Set and Reset, Clepsydra* and *Lounge* at The Place.

Site-specific work includes *The Hotel* (Fringe First at Edinburgh Festival); *The Quiet Little Englishman* (Liverpool Capital of Culture); *Twos* (The Crypt Gallery, St Pancras Church); and *Aperture*, which Becs directed in Battersea Arts Centre's gallery.

Becs has also designed plays in many theatres around the country and worked in India, Lebanon, Belgium, Netherlands, Switzerland and Ireland.

She was overall winner of the Linbury Prize in 2003, trained as a fine art film maker at Oxford University (Ruskin School of Fine Art) and studied theatre design at Wimbledon School of Art.
www.becsandrews.com

RYSZARD ANDRZEJEWSKI   125

Ryszard trained at Central Saint Martins College of Art and Design, graduating in 2001 with BA(Hons) in Theatre Design for Performance. He has assisted theatre and opera designers as a researcher, model-maker and draughtsman.

Set and costume design for theatre: *Ubu Roi, Baby with the Bathwater, Auction of Promises, The Promise.* For Stonecrabs Theatre Company Ryszard has designed *Josephine the Singer, Waltz #6, Charity Wars* and *All Nudity Shall Be Punished.*

Design for opera, music and dance: *Russalka*, Rococo-à-Gogo for The Irrepressibles arts band; costume designs for *The Legend of Beowulf*, Independent Opera's double bill *The Sofa* and *The Departure* at the Lilian Baylis Theatre, Sadlers Wells; *Ballet Black* at the Linbury Studio, Royal Opera House; and University College Opera's production of *Genoveva.*

Examples of Ryszard's work can be viewed online at www.skirich.co.uk

LIZ ASCROFT   27

Liz trained at Wimbledon School of Art. She has been awarded the Arts Council Trainee Design Bursary, the UNESCO award for Promotion of the Visual Arts (Prague Quadrennial), and Theatrical Management Association Best Designer.

Credits include *Lucia di Lammermoor* (Houston Grand Opera, Texas, and Scottish Opera), *Alice's Adventures in Wonderland, A Midsummer Night's Dream, Death and the Maiden, Robin Hood* (Dukes Playhouse, Lancaster), *Blithe Spirit, Three Sisters, Children's Hour, Mary Barton, Hedda Gabler, As You Like It, Fast Food, So Special, The Seagull, The Rise and Fall of Little Voice,* and *On the Shore of the Wide World,* which transferred to Cottesloe Theatre (Royal Exchange Theatre, Manchester), *Katherine Howard* (Chichester Festival Theatre), *Vincent River, Apocalyptica, Give Me Your Answer Do, Yellowman, Anna in the Tropics, Losing Louis* and *The Rubenstein Kiss* (Hampstead Theatre), *Peggy For You* (Comedy Theatre, London, and tour), *Two Gentlemen of Verona* (Royal Shakespeare Company Swan Theatre and national tour), *Honour* (Wyndham's Theatre, London).

For Gate Theatre, Dublin: *All My Sons, Uncle Vanya, Dublin Carol, See You Next Tuesday* (The Duke of York's, London), *Afterplay/The Bear* (Spoleto Festival, South Carolina and Gielgud Theatre, London), *Faith Healer, Yalta Game* and *Afterplay* (Sydney Festival), Harold Pinter's *One for the Road* (St Martin's Theatre, London), and *A Kind of Alaska* (Lincoln Centre, New York) for the Pinter Festival.

ELROY ASHMORE   87

After studying design on the Motley Theatre Design Course, Elroy assisted various designers at the National Theatre, the English National Opera, the Young Vic and the Thorndike Theatre in Leatherhead. He went on to become Head of Design for the Haymarket Theatre, Basingstoke, the Pitlochery Festival Theatre and the Belgrade Theatre, Coventry.

Elroy now works as a freelance designer. He has designed drama productions throughout the UK as well as in Germany, Austria, America and Malta. Elroy regularly designs pantomimes in Ireland.

Apart from drama Elroy is most at home designing for theatre with music. He has designed musicals, ballets for companies in New Zealand, America, Japan, and South Africa as well as operas for many UK companies and in Iceland.

Musicals include *Aspects of Love, The Boyfriend, Cabaret, Godspell, Gypsy, Les Miserables, Little Shop of Horrors, Little Tramp, Rockin' Mikado, Pump Boys and Dinettes, Rocks Progress, Sticky Fingers, They're Playing Our Song* and *Wallop Mrs Cox.*

Ballets include *Little Red Riding Hood, Melodrame, Namouna* and *The Natives of Dreamland.*

Operas include *Così Fan Tutti, The Barber of Seville, La Bohème, Carmen, La Cenerentola, Eugene Onegin, The Elixir of Love, Don Giovanni, Die Fledermaus, Fra Diavolo, Un Giorno Di Regno, Lucia di Lammermoor, Il Mondo Della Luna, Pagliacci, Rigoletto, Rusalka, Stiffelio* and *La Traviata.*

SARAH BACON   60

Sarah studied architecture at University College Dublin, and 3D design at Brighton University. She trained in theatre design at Motley. In 2009 she was a Linbury Prize finalist, and Jerwood Young Design.

She has designed for theatre, opera, dance and film. Recent designs for opera include new opera *The Raven, Les Enfants Terribles, The Rape of Lucretia* (Grimeborn, 2010); *La Clemenza di Tito,* and *Susannah* (Hampstead Garden Opera), *Suor Angelica, La Voix Humaine, Il Signor Bruschino, Rita, The Old Maid and the Thief, La Tragedie de Carmen* (Wexford Festival Opera); *La Tragedie de Carmen* (English Touring Opera); and *Xerxes* (Opera Theatre Company).

Theatre designs include *Medea/Medea* (dir. Dylan Tighe, Gate/Headlong), costume designs for *Hamlet: Rehearsing the Dane* (Pan Pan Theatre Company, Dublin Theatre Festival), *Still the Blackbird Sings* (dir. Caitriona McLaughlin, Derry Playhouse); and *Starvin'* for dance company Fitzgerald & Stapleton. Film credits include production design on feature films *Coney Island Baby* (2002, dir. Amy Hobby), *King of Nothing* (2006, dir. Damian Chiapas), and short films *To the Marriage of True Minds,* and *The Sparrow* (2009, 2010, dir. Andrew Steggall).

MARK BAILEY   67

Mark Bailey has designed over 150 productions of theatre, opera and ballet in Britain, Europe and North America. He has worked for the National Theatre, English National Ballet, Opera North and the Gate Theatre Dublin including Clwyd Theatr Cymru where he is an Associate Artist.

His many West End credits include: *The Importance of Being Earnest* (also Toronto), *The Winslow Boy, Present Laughter, Iolanthe, The Gondoliers, Rat Pack Confidential, Which Witch* (costumes), *Mack and Mabel, Legal Fictions* and *Rent.*

Opera and dance includes *Ariadne auf Naxos* for Maggio Musicale Florence and Opera de Lausanne; *Carmen* for Royal Opera House Linbury Studio; *The Rise and Fall of the City of Mahagonny* (sets) for Los Angeles Opera; *Madama Butterfly* (Nevill Holt and Grange Park Opera); *Melody on the Move* and *The Snow Queen* (English National Ballet); *The Sleeping Beauty* (Hong Kong Ballet); and *Varii Capricci* for Sir Peter Wright's 80th birthday celebrations.

Other designs include *The Threepenny Opera* (National Theatre), *The Pretenders* (National Theatre of Norway), *Hamlet* and *Macbeth* (Chicago Shakespeare Theatre), Robert Lepage's *Polygraph* (Nottingham Playhouse) and national tours of *Look Back in Anger, A Chorus of Disapproval, Hadrian VII, Peace in Our Time, Entertaining Mr Sloane, A Judgement in Stone, To Kill a Mocking Bird* and *The Rivals.*

Mark designed *Broken Lives* for the BBC.

MARTYN BAINBRIDGE   76

Martyn Bainbridge is an Associate Designer of Clwyd Theatr Cymru.

Martyn's productions for Terry Hands at Clwyd Theatr Cymru are *Arcadia; The Crucible; Under Milk Wood; Night Must Fall; The Norman Conquests: Table Manners, Living Together* and *Round and Round the Garden; Memory;* and *Arden of Faversham.* Other productions for Clwyd Theatr Cymru include *Gaslight, A Christmas Carol, An Inspector Calls, The Birthday Party, A Toy Epic, Cariad, The Drawer Boy, Memory* (New York and London) and *Festen.*

Among his other theatre designs are *A Midsummer Night's Dream* (open air production for Singapore Repertory Theatre), *Brief Encounter* (The Lyric Theatre, Shaftesbury Avenue) and a series of productions for Theatre Royal Plymouth, namely *A Little Night Music, The Birthday Party, Kes, Absurd Person Singular, My Cousin Rachel, Charley's Aunt, Master Forger, I Have Been Here Before, Pump Boys and Dinettes* and *The Shadow of a Gunman.* He designed *Deathtrap* and *Intimate Exchanges* for the Northcott Theatre, *The Soldier's Tale* for the Oxford Playhouse, *On the Razzle* for the Leeds Playhouse and *Measure for Measure* for the Oslo Nye Teatre.

Opera designs include, most recently, *Don Giovanni* (Royal Scottish Academy), *Ariadne auf Naxos* (Garsington Opera), *The Magic Flute* (Kent Opera), *The Trial* (Bloomsbury Theatre), *Madama Butterfly* (Phoenix Opera) *Norma, La Traviata* (Northern Ireland Opera), *Le Nozze di Figaro* (Guildhall), *La Rondine* (Royal Academy of Music).

Martyn Bainbridge's ballet designs include *Daphnis and Chloë* (Royal Ballet at Covent Garden).

He has also designed exhibitions, among them *The Astronomers* (London Planetarium), *Lawrence of Arabia* (National Portrait Gallery), *Daendels* (Rijksmuseum, Amsterdam), *Armada 1588–1988* and *Peter the Great* (National Maritime Museum, Greenwich), *Madame Tussaud Scenerama* (Amsterdam), *EMI Centenary Exhibition* (Canary Wharf) and *The Chamber of Horrors* (Madame Tussaud's London).

KEITH BAKER 74

Keith read drama at Royal Holloway and theatre design at Nottingham Trent University before beginning his career at The Swan Theatre in Worcester and then becoming resident designer at The Oldham Coliseum. His work has toured both nationally and internationally, and as well as theatre in all forms includes short films, music videos, rural touring and theatre for young people.

Favourite designs include: *River's Up*, *To Be a Farmer's Boy*, *Who's Afraid of Virginia Woolf?*, *Macbeth*, *Night Must Fall* and *Educating Rita* (Swan Theatre, Worcester), *The Houses In Between*, *One for the Road*, *Abigail's Party* and *The Mysterious Mr Love* (Oldham Coliseum), *Entertaining Mr Sloane*, *Educating Rita* and *The Rise and Fall of Little Voice* (Courtyard Theatre, Hereford), *Fantastic Mr Fox* (Belgrade, Coventry), *September in the Rain*, *Intimate Exchanges* and *Hansel and Gretel* (Theatre Royal, Bury St Edmunds and tour), *Under Milk Wood* and *The Falling Sky* (Old Town Theatre Company), *Postcards From Maupassant* (Old Red Lion), *Two Sisters* (Buxton Festival and 24:7), *Bentwater Roads* (Eastern Angles), *James and the Giant Peach*, *The BFG*, *Sweetpeter*, *Kadouma's Island*, *Little Angels*, *The Silver Sword* (Polka Theatre), *Secrets* (Polka/Watershed Tour), *Into the Woods* (Royal Academy of Dramatic Art), *The Bald Prima Donna*, *The Orchestra*, and *The Fix* (Mountview).

SIMON BANHAM 22

A freelance designer for 25 years and senior lecturer in scenography and theatre design at Aberystwyth University, Wales, UK. He is a founder member of Quarantine Theatre research and creation (www.qtine.com) and is responsible for the scenography on all their productions. In 2005 Quarantine were awarded the Art 05 prize for outstanding achievements in the arts.

His work was part of the Gold Medal-winning British entry to the 1995 Prague Quadrennial.

Two of his designs, *Ion* (Opera National du Rhin) and *Rantsoen* (Quarantine and Victoria Theatre Company) were chosen for presentation at the inaugural World Stage Design 2005 exhibition. For WSD 2009 he was invited to exhibit *For You* (Music Theatre Wales), *Grace* (Quarantine) and *Rebekka* (Norwegian National Opera).

DONATELLA BARBIERI 29

Donatella Barbieri is a scenographer, a researcher and an academic. In her current role as London College of Fashion Senior Research Fellow in Design for Performance at the Victoria and Albert Museum she is making a film, working on publications that analyse scenographic practice, in particular costume, and creating costume-based, site-responsive performance. As an academic she has created and run courses at London College of Fashion and at Rose Bruford College, most recently the MA in Costume Design for Performance, where she has been able to experiment in methodologies for the creation of performance around the body, movement and dress. She has also designed for theatre and opera nationally and internationally since graduating from Central Saint Martins.

PAUL BARRETT 110

Paul Barrett has a BA in Theatre Design and an MA in Scenography from Birmingham Institute of Art and Design. He was awarded a design bursary in 2000 at the Royal Exchange Theatre in Manchester where his design experience included *As You Like It*, *The English American* and *Bring Me Sunshine*.

His freelance credits as a theatre designer include, *Pigtales*, *The Wild Party* and *Go and Play Up Your Own End*, along with designs for the outdoor touring theatre company Heartbreak Productions, where credits include *A Midsummer Night's Dream*, *Macbeth*, *Hamlet*, *Much Ado About Nothing* and *Romeo and Juliet*.

Most recently he has designed set and props for Imagineers' production of *Cat and Mouse* at the Coventry Belgrade, as part of the National Holocaust Memorial Day.

He is the course director of the BA(Hons) Theatre, Performance and Event Design course at Birmingham City University and company director of Heavyfoot Ltd.

SIGNE BECKMANN 25

Signe was born in Copenhagen, Denmark, and trained at the Danish Design School and at the Motley Theatre Design Course. She has designed plays, operas, circus and dance throughout the UK, Denmark, Portugal and Japan.

Design for opera includes: *La Serva Padrona* (Sá de Miranda, Portugal), *Eugene Onegin* (Iford Arts), *Giasone* (Early Opera Company, Iford) and *Albert Herring* (Royal Scottish Academy of Music and Drama),

Design for theatre includes: *Dr Faustus* (Watford Palace Theatre), *House of Bernarda Alba*, *Dealer's Choice* (Embassy Theatre), *Ghosts* (Young Vic), *About Tommy* (Southwark Playhouse), *Dancing at Lughnasa* (Aubade Hall, Japan), *King Ubu* (Corona La Balance, Denmark), *Blackbird, Sexual Perversity In Chicago* (Norwich Playhouse), *Scenes From an Execution* (Hackney Empire), *Pedro and the Captain* (Arcola), *Love In Idleness* (Bristol Old Vic), *Breaking News* (Theatre 503) and *Good* (Sound Theatre).

Design for circus includes: *A Night For One* (touring Europe), *Quiproquo* (Lille Carl, Copenhagen).

Design for dance includes: *Meridian*, *Phantasy* (Ballet Rambert and Rambert Dance Company, Queen Elisabeth Hall).

Other: Stylist on *A Portrait of London* (Trafalgar Square) and *Kate Moss Liberation* (Liberation Magazine), both directed by Mike Figgis.

She was nominated for the Linbury Prize 2005 and has exhibited in Seoul, Korea.   www.signebeckmann.com

SIMON BENNISON 112

Simon trained in lighting design under Neil Fraser (Royal Academy of Dramatic Art), and then with Jennifer Tipton and Bill Warfel (Yale School of Drama). He also studied architecture (University of North London). He has designed principally for dance and drama, creating a series of 14 works with choreographer Cathy Marston (both *The Tempest* and *Asyla* were filmed for the BBC), and plays with directors Sean Holmes, Dominic Dromgoole, Simon Usher and Mike Bradwell. Works of note are *Howie the Rookie* (Bush Theatre); *The Price* (Tricycle and West End); *Scenes From an Execution* (Dundee Repertory Theatre, nominated for a Scottish Theatre Critics' Lighting Design Award); and *Black Milk* (Royal Court). He has lit many original works for the Royal Ballet, and pieces for the English National Ballet and Bern Ballet. Work for opera includes *Carmen* (English Touring Opera); *Rita* and *The Bear* (Royal Opera); and *Swanhunter* (Opera North). He is also lighting manager for the Royal Opera House Covent Garden, working with visiting designers on new works, relighting ballet and opera in repertoire and on tour, and relighting for broadcast. This has seen him work closely with lighting designers John B Read, Michael Hulls, Lucy Carter and Etienne Boucher (for Robert Lepage). He is co-author of *The Handbook of Stage Lighting* and has written a series of lighting lectures for RADA.

DICK BIRD 129

Dick studied at Goldsmiths' College and has worked as a stage and costume designer in opera, theatre and dance since 1998, including *The Pearl Fishers* for the English National Opera; *Le Donneur de Bain* for Théâtre Marigny; *Beatrice et Benedict* for the Opéra Comique; *La Grande Magie* for the Comédie Francaise; *The Firebird* and Carl Davies' ballet of *Aladdin* for the New National Theatre Ballet, Tokyo; *Un Segreto d'Importanza* at the Teatro Communale di Bologna; *The Gambler* and *Il Trittico* at Opera Zuid, Maastricht; and El Burlador De Sevilla at Teatro Abadia, Madrid.

In the UK and Ireland, designs include *Snegurochka* at Wexford Festival Opera; Complicite's *Light*; Jonathan Kent's production of *King Lear* at the Crucible; *Il Re Pastore* for Garsington Opera; *The Canterville Ghost* with the English National Ballet; *The Walls*, *Owen Meany* and *The Night Season* at the National Theatre; and *Harvest* at the Royal Court Theatre. He designed *Swimming with Sharks* at the Vaudeville Theatre; *The Enchanted Pig, How Much Is Your Iron?* and *Monkey* at the Young Vic; and Shakespeare's Globe productions of *Othello* and *As You Like It*.

JANET BIRD 123

Originally from Cardiff, Janet completed an art foundation at University of Wales Institute, Cardiff, before studying theatre design at Nottingham Trent as an undergraduate, then an MA in Scenography at Wimbledon School of Art. Often working in comedy, her design preoccupations are concerned with actors' journeys within designed spaces and creating positive actor-audience spatial relationships. She lives and works in Kennington, London.

Recent design credits include: *The Merry Wives of Windsor* at Shakespeare's Globe, which has also been redesigned for proscenium spaces for a US and UK tour.

Other UK tours include: *The History Boys* (originating at West Yorkshire Playhouse); *Enjoy* (BTR and Gielgud); *Single Spies* (BTR); *Alphabetical Order* (originating at Hampstead); *The Adventures of Woundman and Shirley* (with Chris Goode for Queer up North).

Music theatre includes: *The Rocky Horror Show* (Ambassador Theatre Group); *Tell Me on a Sunday* (originating at Northampton); costumes for *Mahabharata* (originating at Sadler's Wells).

Repertory Theatre work includes: *The Beauty Queen of Leenane* (Edinburgh Lyceum); *A Doll's House* (Exeter); *A Small Family Business* (Watford).

JOHN BISHOP 65

John is an award-winning international lighting designer who has, over a 25 year period, created original lighting designs for more than 150 operas, ballets and shows for many major companies, including English National Opera, Welsh National Opera, Den Norske Opera, Opera Zuid, Buxton Festival, Music Theatre Wales, Northern Ballet Theatre, Ukraine National Ballet, Teatro Lirico Nacional (Madrid), Teatro Alfa (São Paulo) and Madinat Theatre (Dubai).

John has frequently collaborated with many distinguished directors and designers, including Keith Warner, Stephen Langridge, Stephen Lawless, Stephen Medcalf, Daniel Slater, Aidan Lang, Mike Ashman, Giles Havergal, Michael Barry, Maria Björnson, Russell Craig, Lez Brotherstone, Francis O'Connor, Bernard Culshaw, George Souglides, Leslie Travers and Dan Potra.

Many of John's lighting designs have been acclaimed by the critics:

"Altogether it was a stylish presentation. In some major opera houses one would be glad to find the story illustrated by designs as effective as those of Bernard Culshaw, or as strikingly well lit as these were by John Bishop."

"...the sets are animated by John Bishop's virtuoso lighting plot, telling in its casting of facial shadow, spectacular in creating a portentously blood-red sky, or for that matter, a final conflagration."

"...made one long for a barer stage and more of John Bishop's atmospheric lighting."

John enjoys his work immensely.

ANNA BLISS SCULLY 122

Anna is a theatre designer at Wimbledon School of Art and with the National Youth Theatre of Wales.

Designs for theatre include: *The Country, The Shawl, Victory, Disappeared* (Arcola); *Do We Look Like Refugees?* (NT Studio/Rustaveli Theatre/Beyond Borders); *I Was a Beautiful Day* (Tron Theatre, Finborough), *Girlfriends, Lost and Found* (Trinity College of Music), *The Heidi Chronicles* (East 15); *Practice* (Royal Shakespeare Company); *Sixteen* (SPID); *The Tin Horizon* (Theatre 503); *The Exquisite Corpse, Will Eno Shorts, Friction, Bash, Riddance* (True/Fiction); *Ours, The Zoo* (Finborough Theatre); *Over the Edge, Tales of Mystery and Madness* (Bristol Old Vic); *The Container* (Creative Partnerships); *Cruising* (Bush Theatre); *Showstopper* (Theatre Royal Bury St Edmunds); *The Merchant of Venice* (Orange Tree Theatre); *A Midsummer Night's Dream* (Young Vic); *A Chorus of Disapproval* (Guildhall School of Music and Drama); *Buzz, The Morals of Modern Day Myths* (Sherman Cymru); *The Soldier* (Edinburgh Festival, RADA).

As costume designer: *Vaudevillains* (Les Enfants Terribles); *Monster* (Royal Opera House/Escape Artists); *Jacob Jacobson* (Bloomsbury Theatre). Associate designs include Melly Still's *Cinderella* (Lyric Hammersmith/Warwick Arts Centre). Designs for opera include *Alban* by John Mole & Tom Wiggall (St Alban's the Martyr, Holborn).

Anna also works as a dramaturge, and is joint artistic director of True/Fiction Theatre, a company specialising in experimental visual storytelling.

HAZEL BLUE 111

Originally from South Africa, where she graduated in Fine Arts, Hazel also graduated with a BA Technical and Production Arts from the Royal Scottish Academy of Music and Drama in 2007, specialising in Design. She designed the Jack Bruce Wall for the RSAMD café bar and was Scenic Art Tutor for 2008. Hazel is now a freelance set and costume designer.

Hazel's set and costume designs include Nonsense Room Productions; The Arches Theatre Company: *Herbal Remedies* and *They Make These Noises* (The Kelman Season); *Translations* (Citizens Theatre) and *Bailegangaire* (The Irish Season, 2007/8). The Tron Theatre Company: *The Drawer Boy* (2008); Birds of Paradise Theatre Company: *Offshore* (2008); RSAMD: *King Lear* and *Julius Caesar* (2009); The Arches: *Little Red Riding Hood* (2009); Birds of Paradise Theatre Company: *Clutter Keeps Company* (2010); RSAMD: *Hamlet* and *The Winter's Tale* (2010).

Hazel had two set models selected for The World Stage Design Exhibition in Seoul, Korea, 2009. Her set design for *The Selfish Giant*, in collaboration with students from the RSAMD, was selected to participate in the Showcase competition in Seoul.

Hazel is currently working on set and costume design for *Sea and Land and Sky* by Abigail Docherty for the Tron Theatre, Glasgow.

MARIE BLUNCK 22

Marie Blunck designs explorative performances using new technologies. She has devised interactive installations and designed numerous plays and short films with directors Yael Shavit and Zeb Lamb. As part of Indian Runner Production, she co-devised and designed *Trailer*, which received the New Discovery Prize at the International Mime Festival 2006 in Périgueux, France. In 2008 she collaborated with Slung Low on *Small Worlds* for the Liverpool City of Culture Festival and *Helium* at The Barbican Pit, winner of the 2008 Oxford Samuel Beckett Theatre Trust Award. She recently worked with spoken-word artist Polarbear on *Return*. This and *Small Worlds* toured nationally throughout 2010. Marie studied at Central Saint Martins College of Art and Slade School of Art and lectures at Central Saint Martins, Wimbledon College of Art and Goldsmith's University.

MIKE BRITTON 108

Mike studied theatre design at Wimbledon School of Art. He started his career as an assistant working for leading designers on productions in the UK, Europe and America. Since 2001 he has designed just over 50 productions including *The Late Middle Classes* for the Donmar; *Antony and Cleopatra*, *A Midsummer Night's Dream* and *Coriolanus* for Shakespeare's Globe; *The Vertical Hour* and the premier of *That Face* for Royal Court (also West End); *Statement of Regret* for the National; *Period of Adjustment* for the Almeida; *Glass Eels* and *Comfort Me with Apples* for Hampstead; *Nakamitsu* for the Gate; *Pericles* and *The Winter's Tale* for the RSC; *Rudolf*, a musical for Raimund Theatre Vienna; *The Tales of Ballycumber* and *Three Sisters* for the Abbey Theatre, Dublin.

Designs for regional theatres have taken him to Salisbury, Birmingham, Manchester, West Yorkshire, Liverpool, Plymouth and Sheffield. Mike has won the TMA Best Design Award for *The Lady from the Sea* at Birmingham Rep and the Manchester Evening Post Best Design Award for *Henry V* at The Royal Exchange Theatre Manchester.

JOHN BROOKING 92

John trained at Wimbledon School of Art and has worked throughout the UK as a set and costume designer.

For three years John was Head of Design at the Central School of Speech and Drama. He also worked at Alton Towers for nine years as a costume designer, creating the parade, magic shows and various ice shows including *Peter Rabbit On Ice*.

For the Stafford Festival Shakespeare Open Air Productions: the set for *Macbeth* and set and costumes for *The Comedy of Errors*, *Romeo and Juliet*, *A Midsummer Night's Dream*, *Much Ado About Nothing* and *Hamlet*. Other recent productions include *Celtic Heartbeat*, *A Slice of Saturday Night* and *Neil Simon Trilogy* for Cunard, and he has been production designer for the *Lichfield Mysteries* on the last three occasions.

Recently John has designed for *Dick Whittington* at the Regent Theatre, Hanley, and for other pantomimes up and down the country.

For the Lichfield Garrick Studio John has worked on *Fur Coat and No Knickers*, *Ladies Day*, *The Entertainer* and *The Blue Room*.

PAUL BROWN 31

Born in the Vale of Glamorgan, Wales, Paul trained under Percy Harris at Motley. Designs for opera include *Aïda* (Bregenz Festpiele); *Die Gezeichneten* (Teatro Massimo, Palermo); *The Fairy Queen*, *Lulu*, *The Turn of The Screw* and *Don Giovanni* (Glyndebourne Festival Opera); *Mitridate*, *Re di Ponto*, *Falstaff*, *Tosca*, *I Masnadieri*, *The Midsummer Marriage* (Covent Garden); *King Arthur* (Chatelet); *Lady Macbeth of Mtsensk*, *Moses und Aron* (Met., New York); *Die Zauberflöte* (Salzburg); *Peter Grimes*, *Parsifal* (Bastille); *Don Carlos* (Sydney); *Rigoletto* (Madrid); *Thaïs* (Chicago); *Katya Kabanova*, *Lucio Silla*, *The Tempest*, *The Marriage of Figaro* (Santa Fe); *l'Incoronazione di Poppea* (Bologna); *La Traviata*, *Anna Bolena* (Verona); *Mephistopheles* (Amsterdam); *The Magic Flute* (Bolshoi); *Die Frau ohne Schatten*, *Elektra* (Mariinsky); *He Had It Coming*, *Fidelio*, (BOC); *Tannhäuser* (San Francisco).

Theatre credits include *As You Desire Me*, *The Country Wife*, *The Sea*, *Marguerite* (West End); *The Tempest*, *Naked*, *Richard II*, *Coriolanus*, *King Lear*, *Platonov* (Almeida); *The False Servant*, *Oedipus* (National Theatre); *Hamlet* (Tokyo); *Giselle* (La Scala); *Man of La Mancha* (Broadway). Films include *Angels and Insects* and *Up at the Villa*.

PAUL BURGESS 64

Paul trained at Motley following a degree in English at Oxford. As a director-designer he led devising on *A Place at the Table* (Camden People's Theatre), *Selfish* (Arches, Glasgow, and CPT), *Out of Nothing* (Junction, Cambridge), all for the designer-led Daedalus Theatre Company, which he co-runs).

He led devising on *Rang* (National College of Arts, Pakistan) and has jointly led projects in the UK and Siberia for Scale Project. As a designer, work includes *Pandora*, *The Only Girl in the World* and *Peer Gynt* (all at Arcola); *Reykjavík* and *Black Stuff* (both for Shams); *Triptych* (Southwark Playhouse); *Our Country's Good* (Watermill, Newbury), *On the Rocks* (Hampstead); *Jonah and Otto* (Royal Exchange Theatre, Manchester); *Tom Fool* (Glasgow Citizens' and The Bush); *Flush*, *Other Hands* and *Shoreditch Madonna* (all at Soho); *The Most Humane Way to Kill a Lobster* and *Cancer Time* (both Theatre 503); and *Much Ado About Nothing* (Shakespeare's Globe), as well as work for numerous other venues in London. He has also worked in New York, Vienna and Ghana. His teaching work has taken him to various universities in the UK, as well as NCA in Pakistan, and he is frequently involved with youth arts work.

DAVID BURROWS 61

David has principally collaborated with three directors: Phil Young, Alkis Kritikos and David Graham-Young of Contemporary Stage Company.

Productions designed for Phil Young include: *Crystal Clear* (Wyndhams Theatre), *Les Miroirs Brisés* (French Institute), *The Train Years* (MOMI), *Knickers* (Lyric Hammersmith), *Blood Brothers* (Heilbronn, Germany) and *Tonight: Lola Blau* (Old Red Lion, Islington). Work with director Alkis Kritikos has included: *Miss Julie* (Sir Richard Steel, London), *The Collector* (Portlands Playhouse, London), the British première of Beckett's *Rough for Theatre 1* and *2* (Theatro Technis), *Tartuffe* (National Theatre of Cyprus) and the musical *All Cloned Up*. He designed *The Dinner* by Leah Vitali in Larnaka, and the world première of Vitali's play *Roast Beef* was produced at the Riverside Studios in June 2004. Most recently he designed the Glam Rock musical *BlokBusta*, by Mike Bennett, at the Players Theatre, London.

He has designed five productions for David Graham-Young's Contemporary Stage Company: *A Summer's Day* by Slawomir Mrozek (British première), *Ghosts* (Ibsen), *Mr Paul* by Tankred Dorst (British première), *Mystery of the Rose Bouquet* by Manuel Puig and *The Tunnel of Obsession* by Ernesto Sabato, for the Warehouse Theatre, Croydon.

David has also developed a website detailing the life and work of the designer and teacher Richard Negri, with galleries of his designs supported by many audio clips from interviews with his collaborators: www.richardnegri.co.uk.

ISABELLA BYWATER 106

Isabella has designed sets and costumes for over 50 productions for theatre and opera in the UK and abroad, and has collaborated with, among others, Nicholas Hytner, Deborah Warner, Keith Warner, Francisco Negrin, Robert Carsen, Stephen Medcalf and Jonathan Miller. Recent productions include *L'Elisir d'Amore* at the London Coliseum and New York City Opera, *Jenufa* and *La Traviata* at Glimmerglass Opera, *Eugene Onegin* at Santa Fe and Seattle Opera, *Fidelio* at Aarhus Musikhuset, *Der Rosenkavalier* at the New National Theatre Tokyo and *Don Pasquale* at the Royal Opera House Covent Garden.

She is currently designing *Aida* for the Royal Albert Hall in London.

NERISSA CARGILL THOMPSON 67

Nerissa studied theatre design at Nottingham Trent University. Since graduating in 1995, she has been based in Manchester, working as a freelance set and costume designer for both theatre and film; and as a community artist facilitating projects and workshops in a variety of visual arts, often working alongside drama, music or dance workers to bring a visual element to a performance based project or workshop. Nerissa is Director of Design for Aqueous Humour, a street theatre company specialising in Buffon clown and mask work. Nerissa works closely with the Artistic Director to develop projects, and is in charge of design for all the professional shows and community projects. www.aqueoushumour.com

Designs for theatre and film include shows and projects for British Youth Film Academy, Arden School of Theatre, Mersey TV, Proud & Loud, DIY Theatre Company, Paleface Pictures, The Lowry, Activ8, TIPP, Bury Met and four years as Head of Design for Manchester Youth Theatre.

Work as a scenic artist and prop maker includes shows for the Royal Northern College of Music; Footlights Theatre School; The Lowry; Bolton Octagon; Library Theatre, Manchester and Swan Theatre, Worcester.

Nerissa also teaches workshops in theatre design, prop making, costumes, masks, puppets, sculpture, visual arts, banners and flags for all age groups and abilities.

EMMA CHILD 42

Since graduating from Rose Bruford College, Emma has worked with a vast range of performance styles including carnival, opera, ballet, community theatre and outdoor theatre projects. She has designed and made costumes, sets and props for productions around the world. Emma has designed extensively for children's theatre, including *The Wizard of Oz*, *Crazy For You* and *Honk!* for Wycombe Swan Youth Theatre; *Pinnochio* and *Dimension High* (Bigfoot Arts Education); *Colour the World* (Shed@thePark); *Zak and Zara's Space Adventure* (Perform).

Other experience includes designing for *The Cunning Little Vixen* (Woodhouse Sounds Opera, Surrey); *Patio/Porch* (The Raven Theatre Company, Above The Stag, Victoria); *Homestead* (costume design, Shady Dolls Theatre Company, Theatre Museum, Covent Garden); *African Gothic* (Old Fitzroy Theatre, Sydney); *Blasted* and *Skylight* (New Theatre, Sydney). She has assisted Peter Farmer and Jo Woodcroft.

CORDELIA CHISHOLM 90

Cordelia studied English literature at Cambridge University before training on the Motley Theatre Design Course.

Opera designs include *Carmen* (Scottish Opera); *Hansel and Gretel* (Opera North); *Alessando* (RCM); *Phaedra*, *Ariadne Auf Naxos* and *Cosi Fan Tutte* (RSAMD); *Falstaff* (Diva Opera); *Cavalleria Rusticana* and *Pagliacci*, *The Pearl Fishers*, *Turandot*, *Herodiade* and *Nabucco* (Dorset Opera); *The Marriage of Figaro* and *Peter Grimes* (Surrey Opera); *The Tales of Hoffmann* (Guildford Opera).

Theatre designs include: *Kurt and Sid* (Trafalgar Studios); *Shadow Language* (Theatre 503); *100° Fahrenheit* (Southwark Playhouse); *The Dubya Trilogy* (New Players Theatre); *Touched* (Rada); *Hamelyn Heights* (Young Vic Studio); *Incarcerator* (Old Red Lion); *The Winter's Tale* (Creation Theatre Company); *an Axe For The Frozen Sea* (Bedlam Theatre Company); *Dateless Wonder* (Arts Depot and tour); *Masks and Faces* (Finborough).

Costume designs include: *Orlando* and *La Scala di Seta* (Independent Opera at Sadlers Wells); *Taboos* and *Talk About the Passion* (New End Theatre); *Twelfth Night* (Creation Theatre Company); and *The Wedding* (Southwark Playhouse).

FIONA-MARIE CHIVERS   43

Fiona was a professional dancer before studying theatre design at Rose Bruford and Saint Martins. A Linbury award in 1997 has led to many interesting commissions. Her own performance background means she is passionate about high energy theatre which aims to push boundaries, and open performance to a wider audience.

She has an increasing interest in the value of theatre as a powerful educational tool and aims to continue developing her work in education and community theatre.

DAVID COCKAYNE   49

David trained in theatre design at Birmingham College of Art on a course which included a substantial amount of fine art.

His recent work has been for music theatre: opera, dance and ballet, including Duchy Ballet's new productions of *The Mermaid of Zennor*, *The Nutcracker* and *Tristan and Isolde*. Royal Northern College of Music operas include *La Cenerentola*, awarded Best Opera Production 2005 by Manchester Evening News, *The Rake's Progress* and *Don Giovanni*. He has also designed in Boston in the US and in Moscow.

At the mac (formerly Midlands Arts Centre), Birmingham, *King*, a musical on the life of Martin Luther King; *Satyagraha* and *The Wall*. He has also worked for periods at Manchester Library Theatre Company, and the old Birmingham Repertory Theatre. Freelance design includes Greenwich Theatre, Leicester Haymarket Theatre Studio, the Traverse, Leeds Playhouse and Sheffield Crucible.

He has taught theatre design at Nottingham Trent University, and also at University of Central England. An external examiner for various courses, David is currently Visiting Professor at University of the Arts London. He has represented the UK at a number of OISTAT conferences overseas.

A past adviser to the Arts Council and to East Midlands Arts; and has exhibited with the Society of British Theatre Designers since the 1970s. He continues to design, to write articles and to paint, serves as a member of Equity's Council and the Theatre Designers Committee.

DAVID COLLIS   49

Having initially trained as a potter and textile designer, David eventually joined the Motley course and was awarded an Arts Council Design Bursary. This sent him to the Royal Lyceum Theatre in Edinburgh to work alongside their resident designer for a year. As a result, he was asked to stay on as Assistant Designer, which he did for three years before moving on to Nottingham Playhouse as Head of Design. During this period he had also been designing several operas at English National Opera and, on leaving Nottingham, joined them as Head of Design.

Having spent over 12 years as a resident designer, he decided, on leaving ENO, to go freelance.

SUE CONDIE   125

Sue trained at Middlesex Poly (Foundation) and The Nottingham Trent University, BA(Hons), Theatre Design.

For the first four years she worked with a host of touring companies designing for a variety of spaces. Sue then became Associate Resident Designer at The New Victoria Theatre, Staffordshire, where designs included *Ghosts*, *Private Lives*, *Oliver Twist*, *The Hound of the Baskervilles*, *Overture*, *Beauty and the Beast*, *Insignificance* and *Aladdin* (costumes).

She returned as a freelance designer on *Billy Liar* (for the Stephen Joseph Theatre, Scarborough), *Sweeney Todd*, *Outside Edge*, *Dealer's Choice* and *Don Giovanni*.

Other freelance designs include *Sizwe Banzi is Dead*, *A Christmas Carol*, *A Midsummer Night's Dream*, *The Mikado* and *The Snow Queen* (SJT); *Sleeping Beauty* and *Robin Hood* (Salisbury Playhouse); *Noises Off*, *East Is East*, *Corpse* and *Roughyeds* (Oldham Coliseum); *Insignificance*, *Return To The Forbidden Planet* and *Alice* (Harrogate Theatre); *Three Minute Heroes*, *Dick Whittington* and *Aladdin* (Belgrade Theatre, Coventry); *Murder By Misadventure* and *I'll Remember You* (The Mill at Sonning); *Bleak House*, (Old Town Theatre Company); *Sleeping Beauty*, *Aladdin* and *Twelfth Night* (Cheltenham Everyman); *Mother Country* and *A Chaste Maid in Cheapside* (New Vic, Bristol); *When the Lights Went Out*, *The Higher Ground* and *The Amazing and Preposterous Constance Smedley* (Stroud Theatre Company); *The Just So Stories*, *Jabberwocky*, *Sixth Sense* and *Beginning with Blobs* for Kazzum.

In 2000 Sue set up Stroud Theatre Company with director/actor Chris Garner, promoting innovative new writing. www.stroudtheatrecompany.co.uk

Sue is a visiting tutor at The Bristol Old Vic Theatre School, Central Saint Martins and Staffordshire University. She also works regularly as an artist in schools, particularly with young people and special educational needs, creating installations and large textile banners for site-specific projects and performances.

For more details on Sue's work visit her website: www.suecondie.co.uk

PATRICK CONNELLAN   118

Recent design credits include *Copenhagen*, directed by James Dacre, and *Alphabetical Order*, directed by Gwenda Hughes for the New Vic Theatre; *Ghosts* and *All My Sons*, directed by David Thacker for Bolton Octagon Theatre; *One Night in November* and *The Rink*, directed by Hamish Glen for the Belgrade Theatre, Coventry; *Amongst Friends*, *Life After Scandal* (also Plymouth), *Taking Care of Baby*, *Osama The Hero/A Single Act*, *Nathan the Wise*, *When the Night Begins* and *The Maths Tutor*, all directed by Anthony Clark for Hampstead Theatre; *Blame*, directed by Deborah Bruce for Sphinx Theatre Company.

Other design credits include *Edward III* (RSC/West End); *A Passionate Woman*, *Misery* (West End); *The Slight Witch*, *Saint Joan*, *Julius Caesar* (Birmingham Rep); *Into the Woods* (Derby Playhouse).

Directing credits include *Silent Anger*, a verbatim play for Reveal Theatre; *Abigail's Party* (also as designer) for the New Vic Theatre; *Popcorn* (also as designer) for Bolton Octagon; *This Lime Tree Bower* (Edinburgh Festival) and *A Midsummer Night's Dream* (also as designer) for the Belgrade Theatre, Coventry.

Patrick has previously won the Linbury Prize for Theatre Design. He was a member of the Gold Medal-winning team at the Prague Quadrennial in 1995. He is a Senior Lecturer and Programme Leader in Theatre Design at Nottingham Trent University.

SIMON CORDER   116

Simon has had a diverse career: he joined the circus as a ring boy upon leaving school in 1978, going on to learn his craft as a technician in touring theatre and opera. He designed lighting, projections and environments with Lumiere & Son from 1982–92.

Opera lighting includes productions internationally for La Scala, Milan; LA Opera; Teatro Lirico di Cagliari; Teatro Colon, Buenos Aires; and Opéra de Marseille. Simon has designed lighting for many opera productions in Britain, and scenery as well on several occasions.

Dance productions include stage and lighting for The Featherstonehaughs and The Cholmondeleys since 1994, and several site-specific pieces with Steven Koplowitz in Britain and Germany.

Theatre lighting includes productions for the National Theatre and Royal Court. His work has appeared several times in the West End, and he was nominated for an Olivier Award in 2004.

Simon has designed and lit films with choreographer Lea Anderson: *Double Take* (Cholmondeleys, 2005); *Speed Ramp* (Arts Council, 2002); *Mirrorman* (BBC, 2000). In 2005 he made the stage lighting for *Riot at the Rite*, a feature-length BBC drama directed by Andy Wilson.

In 1995 Simon created lighting for the Night Safari attraction in Singapore, first night-time zoo in the world, since visited by over 10 million people. He is currently working for Artis Zoo, Amsterdam.

Simon makes his own installation and art works, including fluorescent pieces *Bough 1* (London, 2004); *Bough 2* (Glasgow, 2006); and *Winter Garden* (Durham, 2009). *Standing Still* (2002) was a night walk through the ancient oaks of Sherwood Forest. *Cascade* (2006) was a site-specific event in and around the Cascade at The Alnwick Garden.

RUSSELL CRAIG   68

Russell initially trained and worked in New Zealand. Since arriving in Britain in 1974 he has designed extensively both here and abroad.

British theatre companies he has designed for include Royal Shakespeare Company and various regional companies in Sheffield, Manchester, Salisbury, Newcastle, Chichester and in London at Greenwich, Watford, Young Vic, Unicorn Children's Theatre and the Royal Court Youth Theatre.

Russell's most notable plays include *The Taming of the Shrew* (RSC); *The Rivals* (Royal Exchange, Manchester); *The Recruiting Officer*, *Much Ado About Nothing* and *Lovers* (Royal Lyceum, Edinburgh); *Therese Raquin* (Communicado, Edinburgh); *Huckleberry Fin* (Greenwich, London); and *Cinderella* (Unicorn, London).

Major opera companies that Russell has worked for in the UK include English National Opera, Scottish Opera, Opera North, Welsh National Opera, Sadlers Wells and D'Oyly Carte. Abroad he has worked in Ireland, Netherlands, Germany, Switzerland, Italy, Canada and in the USA.

Notable opera productions he has worked on include *Ariadne auf Naxos* and *The Rape of Lucretia* (ENO); *The Magic Flute* and *Boris Godunov* (Opera North); *Le Comte Ory* and *The Barber of Seville* (WNO), *La Bohème* (Glyndebourne, touring); *Hansel and Gretel* (Grand Theatre, Geneva); and *L'Elisir d'Amore* (La Monnaie, Brussels).

Musicals Russell has worked on include *Bitter Sweet* (Sadlers Wells); *Show Boat* (RSC, Opera North, London Palladium); *My Fair Lady* (Minneapolis, Houston); *Guys and Dolls* (Edinburgh Royal Lyceum); and *Beauty and the Beast* (Chipping Norton).

In 1983 he represented Britain at the Prague Quadrennial with *Cosi Fan Tutte* (Opera North) and *Eight Songs for a Mad King* (Edinburgh Festival).

Russell also has wide teaching and lecturing experience and is an accomplished prop maker.

GREER CRAWLEY   12

Senior lecturer in Spatial Design, design for film, television and theatre, and exhibition design, Buckinghamshire New University, UK. Visiting lecturer, MA Scenography, Central School of Speech & Drama. Practising designer, curator and researcher, Doctoral programme in scenography at the University of the Arts, Zurich, and the University of Vienna. Editor for *Blue Pages*, the quarterly journal of the Society of British Theatre Designers.

CHARLIE CRIDLAN 75

Charlie trained at Bristol Old Vic Theatre School under the tutelage of Penny Fit and Andrea Montag and received the John Elvery Prize for Theatre Design. Based in a beautiful Victorian studio in London, she works all over the country and in Europe.

A continued love of new writing has led her to work on many new pieces over recent years, which include *Letting in Air* (world premiere for Box of Tricks Theatre); *Getting Here* and *Cuckoo Teapot* for Eastern Angles, touring East Anglia. She was privileged to work with Alan Dossor on a new play by Ernest Hall, *Liar's Market*; also *Once Upon a Time at the Adelphi* by Phil Wilmot. Both plays have been nominated for the off-West End awards in Best New Play and Best Design categories.

She was Associate Designer at English Touring Theatre for Stephen Unwin and has worked prolifically with Director Nicholai La Barrie at Oval House Theatre, increasing the profile of the Youth Arts Work there, designing site-specific work in local parks and pioneering the STEP programme in Southwark schools (now in its fourth year and part of the National Curriculum). She was resident designer at Chelsea Young People's Theatre.

Charlie has done production design on films for HTV Bristol, Channel 4 and Brownian Motion Pictures, and been a stylist for Endemol/Living TV. She also designs exhibitions and events, Clients include ?What If!, Wavelength, The Roundhouse, Truman Brewery and Charles Dickens's Museum, London.

JUDITH CROFT 109

Judith studied theatre design at Bristol Old Vic Theatre School, then worked at Northampton Theatre Royal, before moving to Chester Gateway Theatre as Associate Designer. She then worked as Head of Design at the Oldham Coliseum and the Library Theatre in Manchester. She has had a long association with the Library Theatre Company, working particularly with directors Chris Honer and Roger Haines on a wide variety of projects, including *Translations*, *My Night with Reg*, *Someone to Watch Over Me* and *Waiting for Godot*, all winners of Best Production award from the Manchester Evening News.

She has designed for musicals and opera, including *Company*, *Assassins* and *Goodnight Mr Tom* for the Library, *Leader of the Pack* for Ipswich and Clwyd Theatre Cymru and *Falstaff* for the Royal Northern College of Music, which won Best Production of an Opera award, also from the Manchester Evening News.

Touring work includes *The Borrowers* and, in the West End, *Laughter on the 23rd Floor* at the Queen's Theatre, followed by a national tour.

Judith designed the Chester Mystery Plays in 2008 and has worked on other small-scale and community projects such as *Home for Christmas* for Theatre in the Quarter, a new theatre company based in Chester.

She has designed a long series of rock and roll pantomimes for Clwyd Theatr Cymru, working with director and writer Pete Rowe.

BOB CROWLEY 53

Bob Crowley has designed over 20 productions for the National Theatre including, most recently, *The Habit of Art*, *The Power of Yes*, *Phèdre*, *Every Good Boy Deserves Favour*, *Gethsemane* and *Fram* (which he co-directed with Tony Harrison); *The History Boys* (Broadway, Tony Award), plus more than 25 productions for the Royal Shakespeare Company, including *Les Liaisons Dangereuses* and *The Plantagenets*, for which he won an Olivier Award.

Other credits include: *Pavane* and *Anastasia* (Royal Ballet); *Don Carlos* and *La Traviata* (ROH); *The Magic Flute* (ENO); *The Cunning Little Vixen* (Châtelet); *The Coast of Utopia* and *Carousel* (Lincoln Center Theater, New York – Tony Award for both); *The Seagull* (Public Theater New York); Paul Simon's *The Capeman*; *The Sweet Smell of Success*; Disney's *Aida* (Broadway – Tony Award for the latter); and *Tarzan* for Disney, which he also directed (Broadway, Germany and Netherlands); *Mary Poppins* (Prince Edward Theatre, UK tour and Broadway – Tony Award); and *The Year of Magical Thinking* (Broadway and National Theatre).

His film work includes *Othello*, *Tales of Hollywood*, *Suddenly Last Summer*, directed by Richard Eyre, plus costume design for the film of *The Crucible*.

He is a recipient of the Royal Designer for Industry Award and in March was presented with the 2009 Robert LB Tobin Award for Lifetime Achievement in Theatrical Design at the TDF/Irene Sharaff Awards in New York.

SEAN CROWLEY 57

Sean studied theatre design at Wimbledon School of Art. After graduating in 1985 he worked across the design spectrum in theatre, dance, opera and television.

In 1993 he left London and returned to Wales to live in Swansea with his wife and four children, and over the past 17 years has designed over 130 productions for companies including Sherman Theatre, Cardiff; Grand Theatre, Swansea; Sgript Cymru; Theatr Na n'Óg; Hampstead Theatre, London; Wales Theatre Company; Theatr Genedlaethol; the Hamburger Kammerspiele Theater and the Danish Royal Opera and Komödie Theater Berlin.

Whilst still maintaining a very active career as a designer, Sean has led a dedicated team in helping to make the Theatre Design course at the Royal Welsh College of Music and Drama, recognised nationally as a force in design training. Sean became a full time lecturer in theatre design in 1998, Head of Design in 1999 and in 2008 he became Director of Drama. In 2010 he also became an Associate Director of the Torch Theatre, with whom he has designed over 30 productions.

Sean was Chair of the Association of Theatre Design Courses for nine years, organising the UK National Schools exhibit in 2003. He has been the schools' representative on the Linbury Prize committee and, as a Vice Chair of the OISTAT Education Commission, he was Project Leader for the Prague Quadrennial Scenofest in 2007.

GABRIELLA CSANYI-WILLS 24

Gabriella is a British-born Hungarian. Educated at the French Lycée, she has a degree in Humanities from the Open University and a degree in Theatre Studies from Central School of Speech and Drama. She has consistently worked in theatre, opera and dance and is at present dividing her time between England and Switzerland. She is working on a series of paintings for an exhibition, as well as an exciting multimedia dance project for choreographer Liz Lea, involving history, projection and narrative.

ALDONA CUNNINGHAM 28

Designer and Lecturer in Scenography, Central School of Speech and Drama, Aldona, a recipient of the Art Foundation Fellowship, trained in Theatre Design at Central Saint Martins.

Her design work ranges from designing operas, plays, adaptations and devised productions in a range of settings, including for the Young Vic, Scottish Opera, Leicester Haymarket, English Touring Opera, Royal Court Upstairs and other independent theatre companies.

Her long-term collaboration with Julia Bardsley also led to working in the realms of installation, film, photography and performance art.

Recent publications: Chapter 10, *Space and Truth/Raum und Wahrheit*, second in the series *Monitoring Scenography 02*, edited by Thea Brejzek, Wolfgang Greisenegger and Lawrence Wallen. Published by Zürich University of the Arts.

ANNE CURRY 46

Anne has a degree in Theatre Design; she completed postgraduate study at the Slade School of Fine Art and has an MA in Education and Professional Development.

In 1977 she received a Royal Society of Arts Bursary for her designs, which funded her research into Renaissance drawing and painting in Italy. She received the Jacobs Memorial Medal for her research report.

In 1982 she was awarded an Arts Council Theatre Design Bursary. She has since worked as both resident and freelance designer. In 1986 she designed set and costumes for *Dreams of San Francisco* at the Bush Theatre, which won the Thames Television Award for Best Production.

In 1997 Anne designed the costumes for *The Boys in the Band*, which transferred from the King's Head to the Aldwych. She has exhibited costume designs in private galleries and the Society of British Theatre Designers UK exhibitions, including the Prague Quadrennial (1999), the Theatre Museum and the National Theatre in Tokyo (2001). Her work was represented in the World Stage Design Catalogue (2005).

Anne is a freelance designer and Senior Lecturer in Costume Design and Interpretation at Nottingham Trent University. She also lectures extensively in drawing and costume design at various higher education institutes in the UK.

CHARLES CUSICK SMITH 102

Charles studied at Glasgow School of Art and took a Post Graduate course at The Slade School of Art in London. He was resident designer with the Library Theatre in Manchester from 1982–86.

Since then he has been freelance, designing for all major rep theatres in the UK and designing internationally for opera and (mainly) ballet.

He designed the European premiers of Sondheim's *Follies* and *Pacific Overtures*; *Sweeney Todd* (Best Production 1990, TMA); the European premiere of *Ladies' Night* in 1989; Boyzone's Something Else tour, 1997; and *Rock Around The Dock* rock extravaganza, Granada TV.

International designs for opera and ballet includes *Giselle* (English National Ballet); *Romeo and Juliet*, *The Nutcracker*, *Cavalleria Rusticana/Pagliacchi* (Estonia); *Romeo and Juliet* (Indianapolis Ballet International); *Nabucco*, *Aida*, *Don Carlos*, *The Wall* (rock ballet), *Otello*, *Der Rosenkavalier*, *Cavalleria Rusticana/Pagliacchi* (Germany); *Il Trovatore* (Hong Kong); and, recently, *Spartacus* (Hong Kong Ballet, choreographed by Irek Mukhamedov).

Recent ballets have been *The Three Musketeers* (Northern Ballet Theatre and Estonia); *The Nutcracker* (Slovenia); *Giselle* (Greece); *Casse-Noisette* and *Alice in Wonderland* (France); and *Pinocchio* (Germany).

Charles was twice awarded for his designs in the UK: Best Designer, Theatre Management of Great Britain in 1993, and Best Designer, the Evening News Award in 1986.

PHIL R DANIELS 80

Phil is a theatre designer and fine artist. He trained in theatre design at the Bristol Old Vic Theatre School. Since graduating in 1983, he has designed shows for leading repertory theatres across the country, for national tours and the West End. Some of his theatre designs have been acquired for the permanent collection of the V&A Museum. In 1987 he set up the design company Upstage Designs with fellow theatre designer Charles Cusick Smith. In addition to designing individually they also collaborate on theatre projects across the world, including opera, ballet, musicals, pantomimes and rock concerts.

His illustration work has been included in the Best of European Illustration and the Association of British Illustrators annuals. He has exhibited his fine art extensively, with work shortlisted for the National Portrait Gallery's BP Portrait Award and included in the Sunday Times Watercolour Competition, and he has been commissioned to design and paint artwork for the fire curtains of two Frank Matcham theatres, the Cheltenham Everyman and, most recently, Theatre Royal Newcastle.

Recent premiers include set designs for *Giselle* for Irek Mukhamedov (Athens); *My Fair Lady* (Germany); *Guys and Dolls* (UK); and the three most recent York Theatre Royal pantomimes, including Berwick Kaler's 30th anniversary. Current projects include premiers of *Alice in Wonderland* for the Ballet du Capitole de Toulouse, and *Pinocchio* in Germany.

BECKY DAVIES 84

Becky graduated from The Royal Welsh College of Music and Drama in 2007 with first class honours in Theatre Design. In the same year she won The Lord Williams Memorial Prize for Design and was shortlisted in The Linbury Biennial Prize for Stage Design. Based in Cardiff, she has been designing site-specific, outdoor, small-scale and touring theatre. Her most recent designs include *Romeo and Juliet* (Taking Flight Theatre), *Piaf* (Fluellen Theatre) and *Second Sight – Oedipus/Antigone* (Sherman Youth Theatre and Acting Out). Other companies include Welsh National Opera MAX, Theatr Iolo and Spectacle Theatre, in addition to assistant work for Welsh National Youth Opera and BBC Wales. Alongside her career in theatre design she has continued her research into the devising of design-led performance through the Sherman's New Artist Development Scheme and Cardiff School of Art and Design Masters Programme.

CARL DAVIES 23

Carl trained at the Royal Welsh College of Music and Drama, graduating in 2004. He was a finalist in the prestigious Linbury Biennial Prize for Stage Design 2005.

Recent designs include *The Bacchae* (Nuffield Theatre, Southampton); *Exams Are Getting Easier* (Birmingham REP); *To and Fro* (Oxford Playhouse); *The Jungle Book, A Midsummer Night's Dream, Robin Hood* (The Castle Theatre, Wellingborough); *Candide, The Calling of Maisy Day* (Welsh National Youth Opera); *Dangerous Liaisons, She Stoops to Conquer, Moll Flanders, The Importance of Being Earnest, Canterbury Tales* (Mappa Mundi); *It Will All Be Over By Christmas, Cyrano de Bergerac, Bankrupt Bride, Big Bad Wolf, Action to the Word, Beyond Words, Read a Million Words, Me a Giant* (Theatr Na n'Óg); *Wardrobe Diaries* (Citrus Arts, Wales); *Il Viaggio, La Casa Sull' Aqua di Flora Mariani, Bebele, Pedro Paramo is Dead* (Elan, Italy); *Miss Brown to You, Gulliver* (Hijinx, Wales); *A Christmas Carol, Pinocchio, Little Hope, Javier Maria and Me, Koan, A Midsummer Night's Dream, The Twits* (The Point, Eastleigh); *The Marriage of Anansewa* (Theatre Royal, Plymouth); *Immortal 2 & 3* (NoFit State Circus); *Kes, The Borrowers, Stig of the Dump, The Adventures of Alice in Wonderland* (The Courtyard Theatre, Hereford); *Carry on Down the River, Golden Valley* (New Theatre Works); *Guys and Dolls* (Sherman Theatre, Cardiff).

NAOMI DAWSON 52

Naomi trained at Wimbledon School of Art and Kunstacademie, Maastricht. Since graduating she has worked predominantly in theatre, with a particular interest in new writing, both in the UK and abroad.

Some recent theatre design work includes: *The Gods Weep* (RSC, Hampstead Theatre); *The Glass Menagerie* (Shared Experience); *The Typist* (broadcast live on Sky Arts); *Krieg der Bilder* (Staatstheater Mainz); *Rutherford and Son* (Northern Stage); *Three More Sleepless Nights* (Lyttelton, National Theatre); *The Container* (Young Vic); *King Pelican; Speed Death of The Radiant Child* (Drum Theatre, Plymouth); *Amgen: Broken* (Sherman Cymru); *If That's All There Is* (Lyric); *State of Emergency* (Gate); *...Sisters* (Gate/Headlong); and *Phaedra's Love* (Barbican Pit and Bristol Old Vic).

She is also part of artists' collective SpRoUt, recently exhibiting in Galerija SC, Zagreb, creating an installation for the exhibition *Under Construction – Staging the Future*, which looked at the nature of collaboration, of 'staged' spaces and links between the past and the future.

Current projects include *Love and Money* by Dennis Kelly, to be performed in the Stadsteater, Malmö, and a version of Kafka's *Amerika* for the Staatstheater, Mainz.

Examples of her work can be seen at: www.naomidawson.com

CHRIS DE WILDE 110

Chris has designed 14 musicals and operas for director Vernon Mound, including *Candide* and *Sweeney Todd* (Värmlandsoperan, Karlstad, Sweden); *Nine* (Malmö Musikteater, Sweden); *Il Trovatore* (Tbilisi Opera & Ballet Theatre, Georgia, and Dalhalla Festival, Sweden); *I Wanna Hold Your Hand* and *Oh What a Night* (Colorline Cruise Ship Fantasy); *Geppetto in Spring*, a new musical by Conor Mitchell (Jacobsonteatern, Gothenburg University, Sweden); and a community youth production of *Crazy For You* with a cast of 250, in which 60 chorus girls emerged from a limousine. He also collaborates regularly with Krazy Kat Theatre Company, creating sign language-integrated theatre for children, such as *A Tempest, Goldilocks and How Many Bears?, Petrushka and the Mysterious Magician, Clownderella* and *The Very Magic Flute*.

Further designs include *Cyberjam* (Queen's Theatre) and *Nixon's Nixon* (Comedy Theatre) in the West End; *Crossings* (Julie McNamara Productions at the Cochrane Theatre, London, DaDa Festival Liverpool and tour); *Oy Vey – It's Ida Levin* (Cape Town, South Africa); *Straker Sings Brel* (King's Head, London); *Queer Counsel* (Croydon Warehouse and tour); *Ceremony of Carols/Winter Words* (Streetwise Opera at New College Chapel, Oxford); *The Winter's Tale* (Youth Music Theatre at the Yvonne Arnaud Theatre, Guildford); five showcase productions for Musical Voices at Greenwich Theatre; and a full scale production of *The Cunning Little Vixen* in a barn in Berkshire.

HARRIET DE WINTON 30

Harriet trained at Bristol Old Vic Theatre School.

Theatre credits include *A Midsummer Night's Dream, The Tempest, Antony and Cleopatra, Julius Caesar* (Shakespeare at the Tobacco Factory); *Uncle Vanya* (Bristol Old Vic and Galway International Art Festival); *Vanity Fair* (Bristol Old Vic Studio); *The Canterbury Tales, Titus Andronicus* (Nuffield Theatre); *The Tale of Lady Stardust* (Soho Theatre, Edinburgh Fringe 2009); *A Month in the Country* (Tobacco Factory); *The Blue Room* (Alma Tavern); *Twelfth Night* (Redgrave Theatre); *The Prisoner* (Edinburgh Fringe 2009, shortlisted for Amnesty International's Freedom of Expression Award); *Fefu and Her Friends, Cloud Nine, Titus Andronicus, Dealer's Choice* (The Workshop Theatre).

Film credits include *Then, Voyager, Rojin* and *First Time*. Harriet is creative editor of *Cloth* magazine.

MATT DEELY 35, 70

Matt studied theatre design at Motley. He assisted designer Carl Tomms on *India Ink* (Aldwych) and *Three Tall Women* (Albery). He then worked with designer Stefanos Lazaridis on over 20 operas, most notably *Lohengrin* (Bayreuth Festival); *Faust* (Munich); *Macbeth* (Zurich); *A Midsummer Night's Dream* (Venice); *Greek Passion, Woyzeck* and Wagner's *Ring Cycle* at the Royal Opera House; *Turn of The Screw* (Brussels, and the Italian Season, ENO, 2000).

He has continued to collaborate with other designers, designing Beethoven's *Symphony No. 9* and *Romeo and Juliet* with Yolanda Sonnabend, K-Ballet, Tokyo. Other designs include *2Graves* (Arts Theatre); *Pas, Pas Moi, Va-et-Vient* (Théâtre National Populaire, Lyon); *Petra Von Kant* (Southwark Playhouse); *Ali to Karim* (USA tour, with Kimie Nakano); two Royal Opera House education projects: *Sun and Heir*, with Lisa Lillywhite and Lucy Griffith, and *Voices of The Future* with Becs Andrews. Recently he designed *to the Stars and Beyond* (Splash 2010, Royal Festival Hall). Matt teaches part time on the Motley Theatre Design Course.

STEVE DENTON 33

Steve studied architecture in the UK and Sweden before moving into theatre design. He has designed for a wide variety of performance styles from small scale touring to large site-specific productions. He has designed dance, opera, theatre and musicals for companies across the UK, and his work has toured internationally, including Cuba, Russia and the Tokyo International Festival.

He has exhibited his designs, drawings and painting in galleries across the UK, and in 2007 he was selected to represent the UK at the Prague Quadrennial, subsequently exhibiting his work at the Victoria and Albert Museum.

Steve has taught and designed for several UK colleges, and currently holds a part time lecturing post at the Royal Welsh College of Music and Drama.

KELLI DES JARLAIS 33

Kelli has designed for drama, dance, musical theatre, new work and opera. She has worked across the US, in the UK, Hong Kong and Korea. She was invited to collaborate in the Showcase Exhibit at World Stage Design 2009 in Seoul, and was part of the team awarded World's Best Design Team.

Recent work includes *Titus Andronicus* (Bard in the Botanics, 2010); *Le Nozze di Figaro* (Royal Scottish Academy of Music and Drama); *First Lady Suite* (Fringe, 2009); *Faustus* (On the Verge, 2009); costume design for *Radio, Le Spectacle* (Into the New, 2010); and co-designer for *Jerry Springer, The Opera* (Fringe, 2009). Recent assistant design work includes *Chérubin* (Guidhall); *Il Pastor Fido* (Royal College); *Les Contes d'Hoffmann* (RSAMD); *Fleeting Moments* (HKAPA); and *The Tempest* (RSAMD). She also participated as a visual collaborator with Scottish Ballet in their choreographic workshop in the spring of 2010. Kelli graduated from the RSAMD with a degree in set and costume design.

ES DEVLIN 38

Es trained in music at the Royal Academy of Music as a teenager, English literature at Bristol University, foundation at Central Saint Martins and stage design at the Motley Theatre Design Course.

Es's career began at the Octagon Theatre, Bolton. She has gone on to design for RNT, RSC, Royal Court, Old and Young Vic, Almeida, and West End and Broadway.

She now designs for most of the major European opera houses, including Barcelona, Amsterdam, Copenhagen, Hamburg, Frankfurt, Royal Opera House, ENO and Glyndebourne; and also for dance, including pieces for Russell Maliphant, Rambert, Northern Ballet Theatre, Sadlers Wells and Cullberg.

In 2005 Kanye West commissioned designs for his world tour. This led to tour designs for Lady Gaga, Muse, Pet Shop Boys, Nitin Sawhney, Take That, Imogen Heap, Jamie Cullum, Shakira and Goldfrapp.

Es's film designs include short films by Mike Figgis and costume design for Sally Potter's film *Rage*. She has also directed films for Nitin Sawhney and Imogen Heap.

Her TV designs include the MTV Europe Music Awards 2010, Pet Shop Boys' performance at the BRIT Awards 2009 and Kanye West's VH1 *Storytellers*.

Es was awarded TPi Stage Designer of the Year Award 2010. Other awards include Olivier Award for Best Costume Design 2006, TMA Award for Best Stage Design 1998 and Linbury Prize for Stage Design 1996.

FOTINI DIMOU 52

Fotini trained at the École des Beaux Arts, Brussels, and the Central School of Art and Design, London.

She has worked extensively as a set and costume designer in the US: in New York, off Broadway and as resident designer at the Alley Theatre, Houston, Texas.

Set and costume designs include *The Duchess of Malfi, The Castle, A Jovial Crew, The School of Night, The Archbishop's Ceiling, The Storm, Fashion* and *Spectaculars* (Royal Shakespeare Company).

Costume design for theatre includes *Julius Caesar* (RSC); *Girl with a Pearl Earring* (Cambridge Arts and Theatre Royal Haymarket); *Romeo and Juliet, Twelfth Night* (Regent's Park Open Air Theatre); *Fram, Therese Raquin, The Seagull* and *Secret Rapture* (National Theatre).

Film and television costume designs include *Skin, Commander, Man and Boy, Ripley's Game, Second Sight* and *The Browning Version*.

She has also designed for opera, ballet and modern dance in the UK as well as in her native Greece and the US.

NICOLA EVE DOBROWOLSKI 39

Nicola graduated with a first class BA(Hons) degree in Theatre Design from Rose Bruford in 2008. She is the Resident Theatre Designer for DumbWise Theatre Company, producing work in Plymouth, and is also the Creative Consultant for the Dos Equis Series, promoting Mexican artists in London.

She has designed in a variety of venues, from respected fringe theatres like The Old Red Lion (*Damages*, 2009, and *Howie the Rookie*, 2009) and The Hen & Chickens (*wekillpimps.com*, 2009), to the beautiful Wilton's Music Hall, Tower Hill (*Hotel Sevilliana*, 2009) and, most recently, in Soho Theatre, (*Strictly Come Scripting*, 2010).

Outdoor shows include *Best Friends and Butterflies*, a children's show for the Hackney Olympic handover in Shoreditch Park (2008), and event design for the *Kuiperfest* festival in Spain (2010). She has mainly been based in London this year, but took *Midnight – When Trumpets Cry* to the Brighton Fringe Festival in June and then on to Gibraltar for the Spring Theatre Festival. She headed to Mexico in November 2010 with *Le Navet Bete* to take part in the Day of the Dead celebrations. In 2011 Nicola will be part of *The Clipperton Project*, a team of eight scientists and artists exploring an uninhabited island off the Mexican coast for seven weeks. Artwork produced will be exhibited and catalogued in a book in late 2011.

ROBIN DON   54

For the Bush Theatre, London, Robin designed the world premieres of Sharman Macdonald's *When I Was a Girl I Used To Scream and Shout* with Dawn French, Celia Imrie, Eleanor David and Geraldine James, and Jonathan Harvey's *Beautiful Thing* with Johnny Lee Miller and Mark Letheren; *Fool For Love* at the Donmar and *Steaming* at the Piccadilly Theatre; *Les Enfants du Paradis* and *Twelfth Night*, directed by John Caird (Royal Shakespeare Company); *A Walk in the Woods* with Sir Alec Guinness (Comedy Theatre); *The Anniversary* with Sheila Hancock (Garrick); *Three Sisters* with Kristin Scott Thomas (Playhouse*)*; and the award-winning *The Winter Guest* with Siân Thomas (Almeida Theatre).

Musicals include the major revival of Richard O'Brien's *The Rocky Horror Show* (Piccadilly) and the premiere of Andrew Lloyd Webber's *Song and Dance* with Wayne Sleep and Marty Webb (Palace); *Ziegfeld*, directed by Joe Layton (Palladium); and for Cameron Macintosh *The Boy Friend* (Old Vic).

Opera and ballet productions include Aldeburgh Festival, Lyric Opera of Chicago, Opera de Lyon, Royal Opera House, San Francisco Opera and Sydney Opera House.

Films: *The Winter Guest*, with Oscar winner Emma Thompson and Phyllida Law (directed by Alan Rickman), award winner at the Venice Film Festival.

Awards: Robin's design for the Almeida Theatre's production of *The Winter Guest* received the 1996 British Theatre Managers' Award for Best Designer.

In the same year the Critics' Circle named Robin Designer of the Year. He was nominated for Evening Standard Design Award 2008 for *Emperor Jones* at the National Theatre.

He was part of the winning team for the Golden Triga at the Prague Quadrennial.

Further details: www.robindon.com

ATLANTA DUFFY   71

Atlanta trained on the Motley Theatre Design Course and at the Lyric Theatre, Hammersmith. Her designs for *The Lion and the Jewel* (Young Genius Season, Barbican Pit, and tour, directed by Chuck Mike) were exhibited at the 2007 Prague Quadrennial. Other designs include *Death and the Maiden* (Muson Centre, Lagos); *Tegonni* (University of Richmond, Virginia); *Women of Owu* (UK tour); *It's Just a Name* (The Door, Birmingham Rep); *Cleo, Camping, Emmanuelle and Dick* (The Octagon, Bolton); *Matchgirls* (Alexandra Theatre, Chichester); *Into The Blue, Come Out Eli* (Time Out best fringe production); *Afterbirth, Sense of Belonging* (Arcola Theatre); *London Cuckolds, Semi Monde* (Guildhall School of Music and Drama); *The Way of the World* (Wilton's Music Hall and Northampton Theatre); *Inside Out* (Clean Break); *Brokenville* (St George's Church); *Villette, Women of Troy, A Month in the Country* (RADA); *Fairy Tales* (Cegrane, Macedonia); *Hansel and Gretel* (Lyric, Hammersmith); *As You Like It* (West Yorkshire Playhouse); *The Basset Table* (Bristol Old Vic); *The Farmer's Bride* (Stephen Joseph Theatre).

Opera includes *Burning Mirrors* (ENO Studio); *Die Gärtnerin Aus Liebe* (Royal Academy of Music); *Apollo and Hyacinth* (Classical Opera Company); *Hugh The Drover, Don Giovanni* (English Touring Opera).

Dance includes collaborations at Chisenhale Dance Space, Waitangi and Yoruba masquerade costumes (Greenwich & Docklands Festival). Atlanta has also curated a number of exhibitions including *The Brokenville Exhibition* (National Theatre).

OLIVIA DU MONCEAU   30

Olivia is a set and costume designer whose work has covered a range of traditional theatre, devised collaborations and promenade site-specific projects.

Theatre work includes *Blood Wedding* (Federico García Lorca), staged at the Liverpool Playhouse; *Bibby Line Story* (Andrew Sherlock); and a tour of *Talking Heads* (Alan Bennett). Olivia has regularly designed with the Manchester Capitol Theatre, which includes *Amadeus* (Peter Shaffer), *On the Razzle* (Tom Stoppard), *The Caucasian Chalk Circle* (Bertolt Brecht), *Erpingham Camp* (Joe Orton), *Albert* (Richard Harris) and *The Gut Girls* (Sarah Daniels).

Site-specifically she has designed for many types of spaces: an abandoned Victorian warehouse filled with pools of water was the setting for *Wall Talks*, a piece of new writing with Cut to the Chase, exploring 200 years of Liverpool immigrant culture. She has worked alongside dreamthinkspeak in the Liverpool Anglican Cathedral, on *One Step Forward, One Step Back*, a Dante-inspired installation journeying through the back corridors of the Liverpool Anglican Cathedral, dealing with modern consumerism and notions of paradise.

She is currently working on Shakespeare's *Romeo and Juliet* in a modern-day setting based in urban Liverpool, staged in the training grounds of Croxteth fire station using HGV vehicles, stacks of shipping containers, transforming outbuildings to look like the Capulet's estate. The concrete backdrop of the fire station will be transformed into markets, nightclubs and tombs.

MATT EDWARDS   82

Matt gained his postgraduate training in theatre design at Motley, scenography training with Diploma and a lecture position at Laban and training on the Design for Film and Television Course at Camberwell and Chelsea Art College.

Recent work for theatre has included *Cigarettes and Chocolate*, *Hang Up* and *Days Like These* by Anthony Minghella, directed by Paul Osborne and Cecily Boys, at the York Theatre Royal Studio in February 2010.

Previous work has included Best Design Award for *Underbelly*, directed by Charlotte Conquest for the London New Play Festival; *Purgatory* by WB Yeats, directed by John Crowley for the National Studios; *The Liberation of Skopje* (Redgrave Productions), directed by Ljubiša Ristić at the Riverside Studios. His installation work has included the Lindberg Lounge at the Royal Festival Hall.

He is also a fully qualified teacher with experience of working with students at postgraduate, graduate, undergraduate, secondary and primary level, including a placement in Ghana with Global Link.

In 2008 he took time out from teaching to design *Beyond Measure* at York Theatre Royal, which reinforced his desire to return to freelance design work combining the wide range of skills he has developed in the interim. He is represented by The Designers Formation for theatre and book illustration, runs workshops for the Creative Partnerships and is studying for an MA in Museum and Exhibition Design.

PAUL EDWARDS   95

Paul studied at the Royal Academy of Dramatic Art, from which he graduated with honours and was made an Associate Member of the Academy.

He has designed stage productions around the world including for the West End and Broadway. His designs for opera include *Tosca* (The Kirov Mariinsky Theatre, St Petersburg); *Lucia di Lammermoor* (Halle Opera); *The Bartered Bride* (Staatstheater, Darmstadt); *Cherubin* (Calgiari); *The Pearl Fishers* (Kazah and Amsterdam); *Die Walküre* (Caracas); *EVA* and *Jacobin* (Wexford); *The Marriage of Figaro* (Dublin); *Die Fledermaus* and *The Coronation of Poppea* (Royal College of Music); *L'Égoïste* (Royal Academy of Music); *The Mikado* (Cardiff), *Orfeo ed Eurdice* (Tel Aviv, Strasbourg, Valladolid, La Coruna); *Otello* (Canadian Opera and Welsh National Opera); *Il mondo della Luna* and *L'Italiana in Algieri* (Garsington); *The Bartered Bride* and *Die Zauberflöte* (Tel Aviv); *Carmen* (Richmond); *La Finite Semplice* (Nice and Paris) and *Il Martrimonia Segreto* and *La Fina Giardiniera* (Paris); *Die Zauberflöte* (Opera Hong Kong, National Opera of China and Norwegian Opera, Oslo).

His future productions include *Sunset Boulevard* (Sweden), *A Little Night Music* (Norwegian Opera, Oslo), *Nabucco* (Staatstheater Darmstadt) and *Carmen* (Saint Louis Opera).

ANNA EFREMOVA   102

Since graduating from the Moscow Art University (named after Stroganoff) in 1998, Anna has worked as an art director and illustrator in international advertising agencies and as a video and graphic designer for broadcasting company Kultura in Moscow.

From 2005 she was involved with a number of opera productions (Helikon Opera Musical theatre) as an artist-decorator and did quite a few concerts and children's performances as a set designer. As a scenographer she did two performances within the frame of the New Drama festival in Moscow, 2008.

Anna completed her Masters course (Theatre: Visual Language of Performance) at Wimbledon College of Art, University of the Arts, London, in 2007.

She has worked as a graphic and scenic designer for event companies, both in London and Moscow.

The project presented for the exhibition is the VE Day concert, Royal Albert Hall, May 2010.

GWYN EIDDIOR PARRY   121

Originally from North Wales, Gwyn now lives in Cardiff, only a short walk through the park from the Royal Welsh College of Music and Drama where he studied theatre design 2003–6. After graduating he mainly worked as an assistant designer and scenic artist, involved on over 25 theatre productions. During this period he mostly worked on designs by designer Sean Crowley, head of drama at RWCMD.

After gaining experience and knowledge as an assistant, in recent years Gwyn has himself been designing with most theatre companies in Wales, working on a variety of different productions for main stage, studio spaces and theatre in education. These companies include Theatr Genedlaethol Cymru, Sherman Cymru, Theatr Bara Caws, Theatr Na n'Ôg and Cwmni'r Frân Wen. In 2009 Gwyn was privileged to design for three plays written by his late grandfather, writer William Samuel Jones, each production produced as a tribute to him: *Bobi a Sami*, *Yr Argae* and *Halibalŵ*.

During the next few years Gwyn hopes to continue to design for a range of different of productions, styles and mediums.

JOHAN ENGELS   47

Johan studied Fine Arts and Design at the University of Pretoria and designed extensively for opera, ballet and theatre in South Africa, where his recent credits include *Boys in the Photograph* by Andrew Lloyd Webber and Ben Elton (The Mandela at Joburg Theatre, 2010); *Show Boat* and *Die Fledermaus*.

Current and recent work: *Die Passagieren* (Bregenz Festival), *Les Troyens* (Deutsche Oper, Berlin) and *Il Trittico* (Lyon), all with David Pountney directing; *Thaïs* (Goteborg Opera, Sweden) and *Beatrice and Benedict* (Chicago Opera Theater), both with dir. Nicola Raab; *Artaxerxes* (Royal Opera House) and *A Midsummer Night's Dream* (Opera North), both with dir. Martin Duncan.

Other collaborations with dir. David Pountney include: *Maskarade* (Bregenz and ROH); *Chorus* (Houston Grand Opera); *Osud* (Vienna State Opera); *Eight Little Greats* (Opera North); Smetana's *The Devil's Wall* (Prague); *Turandot* (Salzburg Festival); *Anything Goes* (Grange Park Opera); *L'Amore dei Tre Re*, Zemlinsky's *Der Kreidekrei*, Johann Strauss's *Simplicius*, Pfitzner's *Die Rose vom Liebesgarten*, *L'Etoile* and *Agrippina* (Zürich); and *Khovanshchina* (Welsh National Opera).

Previous design includes: *Cinderella* (Zurich Ballet); *Beethoven's Fifth* (Vienna State Ballet); *Macbeth* and *Romeo and Juliet* (Opera North); *Otello* (Parma, Monte Carlo, Los Angeles), dir. John Cox; *Don Carlos* (Houston 2012, Welsh National Opera, Canadian Opera), dir. John Caird. Costumes for the Vienna New Year's Day Concert 1998, 1999, 2003, 2004 and 2011.

LIS EVANS 48

Lis trained at Cardiff Art College and the then Trent Polytechnic, graduating in 1987. She then freelanced as a designer, scenic artist and prop maker for various exhibitions, trade shows and theatre companies.

As Head of Design at the New Vic Theatre in Newcastle-under-Lyme, one of the few UK companies retaining such a post, Lis has designed over 80 productions, including *The Cherry Orchard*, *The Tempest*, *Bright and Bold Design*, *Kiss of the Spider Woman*, *Top Girls*, *Cleo*, *Camping*, *Emmanuelle and Dick*, *Lonesome West*, *Moll Flanders*, *Amadeus*, *The Graduate*, *Honeymoon Suite*, *Jamaica Inn*, *Laurel and Hardy*, *Blue/Orange*, *Flamingoland*, *Arabian Nights*, *A Voyage Round My Father*, *Sizwe Banzi is Dead* and *Poor Mrs Pepys*.

Company productions include *The Magic Flute*, *Kitty and Kate*, and *The Mikado* with the Stephen Joseph Theatre, Scarborough; and *Carmen* and *Rafta Rafta* with Bolton Octagon. For Northern Broadsides Lis designed tours of *Vacuum*, *The Tempest*, *Romeo and Juliet* and *The Canterbury Tales*. Lis also works with New Vic Education, and local schools and colleges, designing, leading workshops and mentoring students. Lis has contributed to the National Life Stories audio archive at the British Museum.

Lis would like to pay tribute to the late Peter Cheeseman for seeing her potential and giving her the opportunity 22 years ago to begin a career in theatre.

RICH EVANS 111

Rich studied set and costume design at the Royal Scottish Academy of Music and Drama, graduating with a BA in Technical and Production Arts (Design) in July 2010. He has worked in all genres of performance from drama, dance and opera to new writing, children's theatre and large-scale site-specific projects, both as a designer and an assistant. He also has experience as a costume maker, scenic artist and technician.

Rich recently designed the Scottish Première of *Spring Awakening The Musical* (One Academy Productions, Pleasance Beyond), which played at the Edinburgh Fringe Festival 2010. He also designed *The Seagull* at York Theatre Royal, which was a co-production with the RSAMD in April 2010. Other recent design roles include *The New Year Bar* (Total Theatre) and *Check Mate* (A Seat by the Window Theatre Company).

Rich has worked as an assistant on hugely varied productions including *A Midsummer Night's Dream* (Chickenshed Theatre, designer Graham Hollick), an inclusive production with 180 cast members; *The Hotel* (Invisible Dot, designer Becs Andrews), a large-scale site-specific performance; winner, Fringe First Award 2009; and *Santa's Little Helpers* (Tron Theatre, designer Kirsty McCabe), a piece for three- to six-year-olds developed in rehearsals.

Rich has a keen interest in production design for film, designing *Paperskin* (RSAMD graduation film) and *Cut the Strings*, director Steven Ferguson (Winner, Second In Brief, Kodak Student Commercial Awards).

PETER FARLEY 8

Peter Farley MA is a theatre designer/scenographer and studied at Wimbledon College of Art, where he is now a senior lecturer. In 2006 he was awarded an Arts & Humanities Research Council Promising Researcher Fellowship to explore ways in which current and historic scenographic processes can be documented, archived and disseminated. He has also made written contributions to books and catalogues and has curated many exhibitions. Over the past 10 years his theatre work has been concerned with devising and designing award-winning new work based on classical Renaissance texts. During this time, he has also been an associate designer (in collaboration with Yolanda Sonnabend for the Royal Ballet at the Royal Opera House, Covent Garden) for the re-creation of several works by the late Sir Kenneth MacMillan. He is a committee member of the Society of British Theatre Designers, and curator of the UK National Exhibition of Theatre Design for Performance and the Prague Quadrennial Exhibition of Performance Design & Space 2011. He is honorary treasurer for the Association of Courses in Theatre Design, and chairman of the Nightingale Theatre, Brighton.

RICK FISHER 101

Based in London but originally from the USA, Rick has worked in British theatre for over 30 years, and is currently the chairman of the Association of Lighting Designers. He works extensively all around the world lighting plays, musicals and operas. In 2009 he won the Tony and Drama Desk awards for the Broadway production of *Billy Elliot The Musical*, and in 2008 the Helpmann Award for the Sydney production of *Billy Elliot*. He also received the Theatre Lighting Designer of the Year from Live Design. Previously he received the 2005 World Stage Design Bronze Medal for Lighting Design, 1998 and 1994 Olivier Awards, 1994 Tony, Drama Desk and Critics' Circle awards for *An Inspector Calls*. He has participated in Prague Quadrennial 1995 with Ian MacNeil, showing *An Inspector Calls* and *Machinal*; PQ 1999 with Matthew Bourne's *Swan Lake*; and Prague Quadrennial 2003 with *Woyzeck* (Santa Fe Opera).

HELEN FOWNES-DAVIES 46

Helen trained at Nottingham Trent University in theatre design and over the past 15 years has worked extensively in theatre. After a six year residency at the Arts in Education Centre in Nottingham, Helen became a freelance designer working on main stage, touring, site-specific projects, dance and theatre in education. She is also a part-time lecturer in theatre design at Nottingham Trent University

Recent theatre credits include: *Up the Duff* (York Theatre Royal); *Garage Band*, *I Have Been Here Before*, *Whisky Galore! The Making of a Fillum*, *Satin 'n' Steel*, and *The Man Who* (Nottingham Playhouse); Steven Berkoff's *On the Waterfront* (costume designer); *Romany Wood* (Theatre Severn, Royal Gala Opening); *Small Worlds* (BRB); *Ballet Changed My Life* (costume re-design, BRB and Channel 4); *Misery* (Harrogate Theatre and Liverpool Royal Court); *Safahr* (BRB); *Cinderella*, *Our Day Out* (Harrogate Theatre); *The Emperor's New Clothes*, *The Snow Queen*, *Arabian Nights* and *The Firebird* (mac Birmingham); *The Kiss*, *The Retirement of Tom Stevens* and *A Who's Who of Flapland* (Lakeside Theatre, Nottingham); *Cinderella's Sisters* (Red Earth Theatre); *Those Magnificent Men – New Perspectives*, *Women on the Verge of HRT* (Nick Brooke Ltd); *Booty Call* (Big Creative Ideas); *Natural Breaks and Rhythms* (Northampton Theatre Royal and TWP); *21 Tales* (The Fionnbarr Factory); *The Elves and the Shoemaker* (mac Birmingham).

RICHARD FOXTON 47

Richard trained at Trent Polytechnic, and has been freelance since 1999.

Design work includes *Loot*, *Macbeth*, *Pub Quiz is Life*, *Toast*, *Up on the Roof* and *Under the Whaleback* (Hull Truck); *Kes*, *The Sunshine Boys*, *On the Piste* and *Return to the Forbidden Planet* (Oldham Coliseum); *Up on the Roof*, *Noises Off*, *Vincent in Brixton* and *The Price* (New Wolsey Theatre, Ipswich); *Blue/Orange*, *The Country Wife* and *Big Night Out* (Palace Theatre, Watford); *Brassed Off* (Sheffield Theatres national tour); *Office Suite* (Bath Theatre Royal national tour); *All My Sons* and *Neville's Island* (York Theatre Royal); *Death of a Salesman* and *Things We Do For Love* (Library Theatre, Manchester); *Eight Miles High* (Liverpool Royal Court); *Equus*, *Macbeth* and *Dead Funny* (Salisbury Playhouse); *The Importance of Being Earnest*, *Hector's House* and *Desperate to be Doris* (LipService national tours); and over 50 productions for the Octagon Theatre, Bolton, including *The Crucible*, *The Caretaker*, *Blood Wedding*, *Saved*, *Four Nights in Knaresborough*, *A Midsummer Night's Dream* and *The Pitchfork Disney*. Other theatres include Harrogate Theatre, Contact Theatre, Manchester, Colchester Mercury Theatre, West Yorkshire Playhouse and TAG Theatre Company, Glasgow.

Richard has won five Manchester Evening News design awards (most recently in 2008 for *Oh! What a Lovely War* (Octagon Theatre). He exhibited at Prague Quadrennial 1995 and was a judge of the Linbury Prize in 1997.

LARA FURNISS 27

Lara received a BA(Hons) in Interior Design from Manchester Metro University, and an MFA in Sculptural Installation from The School of the Art Institute of Chicago, and has spent the last 15 years in the UK and USA designing for exhibitions, events, interiors and theatre. During her MFA Lara became resident designer for Chicago's Cook County Theatre Department, where shows included *Clowns Plus Wrestlers*, *Minutes and Seconds* and *Tosca* (in collaboration with Stephanie Nelson). She has since been nominated for an Arts Foundation Fellowship by Simon McBurney, and recently won the Museums and Heritage award for Best Exhibition on a Limited Budget for *The Half: Photographs of Actors by Simon Annand*, at the Theatre Museum (Victoria and Albert Museum), London.

Theatre credits include: *People Without History* (The Performing Garage, New York); *Country of the Blind* and *Powder Keg* (Gate, London); *The Persecution of Arnold Petch* (Red Orchid, Chicago). Design credits include: *Alfred Lunt and Lynn Fontanne: A Life On Stage* (exhibition for Ten Chimneys Foundation, Wisconsin, USA); *The Holocaust Exhibition* (Imperial War Museum, London); *Living Together* (Field Museum of Natural History, Chicago).

Lara is currently a lecturer on the BA(Hons) Theatre, Performance & Event Design course at Birmingham Institute of Art and Design.

OLIVIA GASTON 113

Olivia graduated in 2006 with a first-class honours degree in Design for Film, Television and Theatre from Buckinghamshire Chilterns University College. Previously Olivia trained professionally in musical theatre and classical ballet. On finishing university she worked in a professional repertory theatre in Frinton-on-Sea assisting with scenic art and design and stage management as well as choreographing for *Good Morning, Bill*.

Olivia exhibited her design of *The Birds* at the Prague Quadrennial 2007.

Olivia's designs include *Some Voices* (Alma Tavern Theatre and Oxford Playhouse Studio); *Private Lives* and *A Chorus of Disapproval* (with choreography, The Garrick Playhouse); *Art* (Lauriston Studio Theatre); *Dance Revue* (The Bruntwood Theatre, RNCM). Scenic art includes *Greek* (Lauriston Studio Theatre) and *Cappuccino Girls* (new professional musical world premiere, The Garrick Playhouse). Olivia continues to design and choreograph.

CHRISTOPHER GILES 37

Formerly a principal dancer for Northern Ballet, Chris changed direction professionally and completed a year's Postgraduate Design Diploma at the Royal Welsh College of Music and Drama in 2005, followed by an internship at the Royal Opera House, assisting on the operas *Carmen*, *Lady Macbeth of Mensk*, *L'Heure Espagnole*, *Gianni Schicchi*, *La Fille du Régiment* and *Cyrano* (Birmingham Royal Ballet).

Since graduating Chris has designed both set and costumes for *Glass Canon* and *Hamlet* (Northern Ballet); *Beware of What You Wish For* (short film with Martin Jarvis, Malcolm Tierney and Jane Merrow); *The Rake's Progress* (Welsh National Opera MAX); *Genoveva* and *Camacho's Wedding* (UCO, Bloomsbury Theatre); *The Medium/Ten Belles* (double-bill opera, Sherman Theatre); *Umbilica* (Diversions Dance Company); and designed the costumes for *The Opera Show* (Kilworth House Theatre, US and European tour).

He has also assisted well established designers such as Peter McKintosh on many productions: *Peter Pan* for Birmingham Rep; *John Gabriel Borkman* and *The Cryptogram* for Donmar Warehouse; *Fiddler on the Roof* (for the West End); Antony McDonald, Mark Thompson, Es Devlin, Emma Ryott and director/choreographer David Nixon on *A Midsummer Night's Dream* and *The Nutcracker*.

Chris' next projects include *Bells Are Ringing* (Union Theatre) and *Cleopatra* (Northern Ballet, Grand Theatre Leeds and UK tour).

SOUTRA GILMOUR 130

Theatre includes *Into the Woods* (Open Air Theatre, Regent's Park); *Polar Bears* (Donmar Warehouse); *The Little Dog Laughed* (The Garrick Theatre); *Three Days of Rain* (Apollo Theatre); *The Pride* (Royal Court); *The Tragedy of Thomas Hobbes* (RSC at Wilton's Music Hall); *Piaf* (Donmar Warehouse, The Vaudeville, and Teatro Liceo, Buenos Aires); *The Lover/The Collection* (Comedy Theatre); *Our Friends in The North, Ruby Moon, Son of Man* (Northern Stage); *Last Easter* (Birmingham Rep); *Angels in America* (Headlong, Lyric Hammersmith); *Bad Jazz, A Brief History of Helen of Troy* (ATC); *The Birthday Party* (Sheffield Crucible); *The Caretaker* (Sheffield Crucible, Tricyle); *Petrol Jesus Nightmare #5* (Traverse, Kosovo); *Lovers/War* (Strindberg's Intima Theatre, Stockholm); *Hair, Witness* (Gate); *Baby Doll, Therese Raquin* (Citizens Theatre, Glasgow); *Ghost City* (59e59, New York); *When The World Was Green* (Young Vic); *Modern Dance for Beginners* (Soho Theatre); *Shadow of a Boy* (National Theatre).

ANTONY GORMLEY 32

In a career spanning nearly 40 years, Antony Gormley has made sculpture that explores the relation of the human body to space at large, explicitly in large-scale installations like *Another Place, Domain Field* and *Inside Australia*, and implicitly in works such as *Clearing, Breathing Room* and *Blind Light* where the work becomes a frame through which the viewer becomes the viewed. By using his own existence as a test ground, Antony's work transforms a site of subjective experience into one of collective projection. Increasingly, the artist has taken his practice beyond the gallery, engaging the public in active participation, as in *Clay and the Collective Body* (Helsinki) and the acclaimed *One & Other* commission in London's Trafalgar Square.

Antony's work has been widely exhibited throughout the UK, with solo shows at the Whitechapel, Serpentine, Tate, Hayward Gallery, British Museum and White Cube. His work has been exhibited internationally in one-man and group shows. Major public works include *Angel of the North* (Gateshead), *Another Place* (Crosby Beach, Liverpool), *Event Horizon* (New York, USA) and *Habitat* (Anchorage, USA).

Antony was awarded the Turner Prize in 1994, the South Bank Prize for Visual Art in 1999 and the Bernhard Heiliger Award for Sculpture in 2007. He was made an Officer of the British Empire (OBE) in 1997 and is an Honorary Fellow of the Royal Institute of British Architects, Trinity College, Cambridge, and Jesus College, Cambridge. Antony has been a Royal Academician since 2003 and a British Museum Trustee since 2007.

Antony has collaborated with the choreographer Sidi Larbi Cherkaoui on *Zero Degrees*, 2005, *Sutra*, 2008, and *Babel (Words)*, 2010.

HAYLEY GRINDLE 50

Hayley trained at the Royal Welsh College of Music and Drama where she received the Paul Kimpton prize for innovation.

Hayley's credits include *God in Ruins* (RSC); *Animal Farm* (The Peter Hall Company); *The Nutcracker, Around the World in Eighty Days, His Dark Materials, A Midsummer Night's Dream* and *Blue Room* (Theatre Royal Bath); *My Mother Said I Never Should* and *Peter Pan* (The Dukes, Lancaster); *Travels With My Aunt* (New Wolsey, Ipswich); *King Lear* (BMW Plant); *The Gentlemen's Tea Drinking Society* (Ransom Productions, Belfast); *Two Shakespearian Actors* and *A Midsummer Night's Dream* (Guildhall Drama School); *Amdani* and *Diwrnod Dwynwen* (Sgript Cymru); *Ghetto* and *Great Expectations* (Watford Palace Theatre); *Anthem For Doomed Youth, Scent, Shoa* and *Orpheus* (Nuffield Theatre); *The Mikado* (Welsh National Opera, Youth Opera); *A Day to Remember* (Soho Theatre); *Muscle* (Bristol Old Vic).

Future productions include *Invisible*, a co-production with Transport and The New Wolsey Theatre, *Treasure Island* for Watermill, Newbury, and *Ben Hur* for the Theatre Royal, Bath.

CHRIS GYLEE 42

Chris trained at the Bristol Old Vic Theatre School (2005–6) and was a selected designer on Cheek By Jowl's inaugural Young Director/Designer programme in 2008.

For the Tobacco Factory he has designed *Hamlet, The Taming of the Shrew, Othello* and *Much Ado About Nothing*. Other plays include *Henry V* (Southwark Playhouse); *Colörs* and *Tattoo* (Company of Angels); *Grimms – The Final Chapter* (Trafalgar Studios); *Not Knowing Who We Are* (The Blue Elephant); and designs for Arts Ed, Theatre 503, Bristol Old Vic and The Jermyn Street Theatre.

He has created site-specific designs for *Shooting Rats* (Fanshen); *Oliver Twist* (The Egg/Theatre Royal Bath); *Fanshen* (Theatre Delicatessen); and *Katrina* (The Jericho House as Assistant Costume Designer). Chris is an associate designer with Fairground, for whom he designed *The Red Man, Out of Touch* and *Bonnie and Clyde*. Work with young people and for younger audiences includes tours with Compagnie Animotion and White Horse Theatre, and designs for Sixth Sense Theatre, Broadway Theatre, Barking, and the Waterside Arts Centre. His work as an illustrator and artist includes performance collaborations with the Bristol Jam and Ferment. Projects in development include a new performance piece with live animation, *The Cutting Room*, supported by Theatre Bristol, Bristol Old Vic and the Tobacco Factory. www.chrisgylee.co.uk

ABIGAIL HAMMOND 66

Abigail's dance background included experimental dance at Dartington College of Art in the 1970s and she went on to study dance theatre at the Laban Centre, London, specialising in costume design. Over the past 25 years she has created costumes for over 100 choreographic works.

She was the resident designer for the National Youth Dance Company for 13 years and Tavaziva Dance for six years. Her work with Tavaziva Dance was part of the Society of British Theatre Designers' *Collaborators* exhibition at the V&A Museum in London, 2007–8. Theatre work includes costumes for *The Hobbit* by JRR Tolkien, produced by VFP Ltd, which ran in London's West End and is currently touring again. The designs for *The Hobbit* and an accompanying educational video contributed to the SBTD *2D>3D* exhibition 2002–5 and was selected as part of the UK contribution at the World Stage Design Exhibition in Toronto in 2005.

Abigail has lectured at various higher education institutes, including the Royal Academy of Dance, London College of Fashion, Laban and Croydon College. Her commitment to education includes community projects, with the National Theatre Education Unit, English Heritage, English National Ballet and the Barbican Centre, London.

Abigail is Senior Lecturer in Costume Design at Wimbledon College of Art. Her research focuses on the uniqueness of costume design for dance and she has presented papers at national and international conferences.

SHIZUKA HARIU 51

Shizuka is a Japanese scenographer and architect based in Brussels, London and Sendai.

Her scenography describes the relationship between concrete and imaginary space based on her training as an architect, and acute understanding of architectural environments.

She has been designing for a wide variety of stage productions. Her major work *Sacred Monsters* (choreographer Akram Khan and dancer Sylvie Guillem) has been performed at Sadler's Wells Theatre, La Monnaie Royal Opera House, Théatre des Champs-Elysées, Sydney Opera House, Tokyo Bunka Kaikan and other theatres, with glowing reviews.

Having researched Scenography for Contemporary Dance at Central Saint Martins College Art and Design, London, Shizuka is planning for her first solo exhibition as a PhD researcher at Leeds Metropolitan University. She was awarded a fellowship from the Japanese government Agency for Cultural Affairs from 2002 to 2004 and was also awarded a grant from the POLA Arts Foundation, Japan, in 2005. She obtained a Masters degree in Architecture from Tokyo University of Science in 2000. Since graduating, she worked as an assistant architect at Shoichi Haryu Architects & Associates, Japan, Adjaye Associates, London, and as assistant scenographer for Jan Versweyveld, Belgium, and is now co-director at Shin Hagiwara & Shizuka Hariu Architecture+Scenography. She has obtained awards such as Tokyo Design Centre Award, Mainichi Published DAS Design Award, among others.

DAVID HARRIS 44

Having studied design in the Netherlands, USA and London, David graduated with a first class degree in Design for Performance from Wimbledon College of Art in 2009. He has most recently designed *City*, an international dance collaboration at the Mu Theatre, Budapest; *Doggerland* for the Barons Court Theatre, London; and *Bunk* at The King's Head, London. David has spent much time assisting designers and theatre companies, including Oily Cart and Headlong, as well as working on many site-specific performances. He contributes as a member of the committee for the Society of British Theatre Designers.

KEN HARRISON 92

Trained at the Motley Theatre Design Course. Past work includes designs for Riverside Studios; Lyric Theatre, Belfast; Druid Theatre, Galway; Palace Theatre, Watford; York Theatre Royal; Unicorn Theatre; Mercury Theatre, Colchester; Dundee Rep; King's Theatre, Glasgow; and Northcott Theatre, Exeter.

Designs for national tours include *The 39 Steps, The Ladykillers, Time and the Conways, Travels with My Aunt* and *Mindgame*.

Recent work includes *Travesties, The Hound of The Baskervilles, The Tempest, Our Man in Havana* (Nottingham Playhouse); *Tales from Hollywood, Humble Boy* (Perth Theatre); *Trumpets and Raspberries, The Lion, the Witch and the Wardrobe, The Snow Queen* (Royal Lyceum Theatre, Edinburgh); *Amadeus, Double Indemnity, Kind Hearts and Coronets, The Flowers o'Edinburgh, Whisky Galore: A Musical!* and *an Ideal Husband* (Pitlochry Festival Theatre).

PETER HARRISON 45

Peter trained at the Royal Academy of Dramatic Art, graduating in 1999. His recent lighting designs have included *Ghosts of The Past* for Youth Music Theatre UK (Aberdeen Arts Center); *The Doubtful Guest* for Hoipolloi (Watford Palace, Theatre Royal Plymouth, Traverse Theatre Edinburgh); *Wuthering Heights* for Tamasha Theatre Company (Lyric Hammersmith and tour); and *Snow White* and *Sleeping Beauty* for First Family Entertainment (Richmond Theatre). Other designs have included *The Viewing Room* (The Arts Theatre, London); *Orestes* for Shared Experience (Tricycle Theatre and UK tour); *Too True To Be Good* (Finborough Theatre); *Hallelujah* (Theatre503); *Betwixt!* and *Shadowmaster* (Kings Head Theatre); *Fingerprint* for The Shout (Royal Opera House, Linbury Studio); *Up from the Waste* (Soho Theatre); *Romeo and Juliet* (The New Wolsey, Ipswich); *Once We Were Mothers* (Orange Tree, Richmond); and *Les Miserables* and *Chicago* as part of Pimlico Opera's Prison Project. His dance lighting includes work with The Mikhailovsky Ballet in St Petersburg, members of the Royal Ballet, and pieces for Christopher Bruce, Rafael Bonachela and Michael Popper, as well as lighting productions for Ballet Central, LINK Dance, The Urdang Academy and Intoto Dance Company.

TIM HATLEY 59

Tim trained at Central Saint Martins, London, and was a Linbury Prize commission winner in 1989.

He has worked on a wide variety of projects for theatre, opera and film with companies such as Complicite, Almeida, Donmar Warehouse, RSC, RNT, ENO in the West End and on Broadway.

Theatre includes *The Three Lives of Lucie Cabrol, Stanley, Private Lives, Humble Boy, Rafta Rafta, Monty Python's Spamalot, Shrek the Musical, My Fair Lady, Betty Blue Eyes*.

Film includes *Stage Beauty* (2004), *Closer* (2004) and *Notes on a Scandal* (2006).

Tim has won Drama Desk, Olivier and Tony awards.

FLORENCE HENDRIKS   44

Florence is a London-based Dutch scenographer, having studied BA Design for Performance at Central Saint Martins College of Art, a course which focuses on design theory, reflection and conceptual development. She completed work placements as an assistant designer on a number of productions including placements at the Royal Opera House and Sadler's Wells.

In 2008 she co-founded a dance company, Hensnow Productions, with long-term collaborator Glen Snowden, an established choreographer. They have developed a style of narrative dance which incorporates elements of opera, creating performances which adhere to a classic frame of choreography intertwined with devised, movement-based acting.

Although Hensnow stays her main focus at present, Florence very much enjoys working on other diverse projects, such as short movies and installations, which teach her a great deal about less familiar aspects of performance art and whose energy can be directed into her own work. A recent example would be a short film for the Busaba Eathai chain of restaurants, commissioned by Alan Yau in 2010, which she designed and produced.

ELANOR HIGGINS   112

Elanor is a freelance lighting designer based in Wales. Over the last ten years or so she has lit over 60 shows in a variety of media, from opera, dance, theatre, children's theatre, site-specific spaces and shows for educational companies such as National Youth Theatre of Wales through to lighting bands and book readings for the Hay Festival's international events in Spain.

Her designs have been seen in many countries from Australia to Dubai. She speaks Welsh as a second language and has worked closely with many of Wales' leading Welsh and bi-lingual theatre companies.

Recent lighting designs include *2110/Yn Y Tren*, *Y Gofalwr* (The Caretaker) and *Stick Man* (Theatr Genedlaethol Cymru); *Sweeny Todd* (Scamp); *The Rake's Progress* (WNO MAX); *Opera Scenes* (Royal Welsh College of Music and Drama); *Boxin*, (Kompani Malakhi); *Yr Argae* and *Maes Terfyn* (Sherman Cymru).

Elanor worked closely with the new writing company *Sgript Cymru* over the last six years, lighting 14 shows for them including *Acqua Nero*, *Indian Country*, *Art and Guff* and *Amdani*.

She is a graduate of The Royal Welsh College of Music and Drama, where she works as a part time lecturer in lighting.

Elanor has worked as a full-time lighting technician for Welsh National Opera, The Royal National Theatre and Leicester Haymarket.

ANNA HOURRIERE   84

Anna was born in Germany and grew up in Paris. After a fine art foundation in Paris, she studied Design for Performance in London and graduated in 2008 from Wimbledon School of Art. During her studies she accumulated work experience in various opera houses and theatres, assisting on *Eugene Onegin* (Staatsoper, Unter den Linden, Berlin, 2008), *Sauser Aus Italien* (Salzburger Osterfestspiele, 2007), *Pelléas and Mélisande* (Salzburg Sommer Festspiele, 2006), *Wischen – No Vision* (Neuköllner Oper, Berlin, 2005).

She recently designed set and costumes for *Personal Enemy*, the world premiere performance of a John Osborne lost play (White Bear Theatre, 2009). This work is presented in the SBTD exhibition.

Other design credits include *Friendly Fire* (The Place, Resolution! 2009), *Deux Pas Vers Les Étoiles* (Rosemary Branch, 2008), *Landscape Number Three* (Dance and Design Collaborations 2008, The Place).

In 2009, she exhibited her work on *Going Dark* (in collaboration with Sound and Fury) at the National Theatre, as finalist of the Linbury prize. In January 2010, she won a Royal Opera House Bursary.

Anna is currently working on the Royal Opera House production of *Tannhäuser* with designer Michael Levine.

PAMELA HOWARD   94

Pamela Howard OBE FRSA is Professor Emeritus at the University of the Arts, London, and a practicing director and scenographer especially in contemporary opera and music theatre. In 2008 she was awarded the OBE for Services to Drama. As stage designer she realised over 200 productions in the UK, Europe and USA, and in 1991 at the Tramway, Glasgow, began a series of site-specific works with the late John McGrath. From then, she has been exploring the relationship between architecture and performance, making work in large and small spaces and re-assessing how theatre spaces are used.

In 2005 she directed and designed the Greek premiere of *The Greek Passion* (Bohuslav Martinu/Nikos Kazantsakis) for the Opera of Thessaloniki, staged in the ancient Byzantine citadel and former town prison the Eptapyrgion. In 2006 as Artist in Residence at Carnegie Mellon University, Pittsburgh, USA, *Three Fragments From The Marriage*, an installation and performance piece, was staged at the Miller Gallery of Contemporary Art, serving as the template for the later full production.

In 2009 as Project Designer with Nicholas Kent, director, Tricycle Theatre, Kilburn, London, she created *The Great Game* – 12 newly-commissioned plays about Afghanistan. As director/scenographer for the National Theatre, Janáček Opera, the first professional production in English of *The Marriage*, a comic chamber opera by Bohuslav Martinu/Nikolai Gogol, performed in the historic MozartSal of the Reduta Theatre, Brno, Czech Republic. Pamela is currently directing and designing *The Excursion of Mr Brouček to the Moon* by Leoš Janáček, premiere of the first version (Janáček Opera, National Theatre, Brno).

DAVID HOWE   93

West End lighting design credits include *Sweet Charity* (Haymarket Theatre); *Mrs Warren's Profession* (Comedy Theatre); *Private Lives* (Vaudeville Theatre); *A Christmas Carol* (Arts Theatre); *The Norman Conquests* (Old Vic Theatre); *The Last Five Years* and *Tick Tick Boom* (Duchess Theatre); *Maria Friedman Re-Arranged* (Trafalgar Studios); *Rent* (Duke of York's); *Seven Brides for Seven Brothers* (Haymarket Theatre); *Pageant* (Vaudeville Theatre); *Forbidden Broadway* (Menier Chocolate Factory and Albery Theatre); *The Vivian Ellis Awards* (London Palladium); *Sweet Charity*, *Maria Friedman*, *La Cage Aux Folles*, *Take Flight*, *The Last Five Years* (Menier Chocolate Factory) and *Rags* (Bridewell Theatre).

Broadway credits: *Norman Conquests* (Circle in the Square), *Primo* (Music Box Theatre).

UK national tours of *Oklahoma*, *Little Shop of Horrors*, *Singing in the Rain*, *Seven Brides for Seven Brothers*, *Our House*, *Fiddler on the Roof*, *South Pacific*, *42nd Street*, Disney's *Beauty and the Beast*, *Me and My Girl*, *Carousel* and *The Demon Headmaster*. Also, many regional theatre productions across the UK.

Opera: *Eugene Onegin* (Scottish Opera); *La Bohème*, *Euridice*, *Rossini Double Bill*, *The Rake's Progress*, *The Magic Flute*, *Albert Herring* for British Youth Opera; and *La Serva Padrona* for the Royal Opera House.

International design includes *Fame* (Monaco); *The Full Monty*, *Cabaret* (English Speaking Theatre, Frankfurt); *The Rocky Horror Picture Show* (European tour); *Chicago* (Kula Lumpur, Malaysia); *Woyzeck* (New York); *Stars of The Musicals* (Malaysia); *Sunset Boulevard* (Cork Opera House); and *Jesus Christ Superstar* (tour of Sweden).

MARK HOWLAND   122

Mark studied at Oxford University prior to training in lighting design at RADA. He has worked across all types of live performance, including site-specific and installation, with the majority of projects being for theatre and opera companies.

His style ranges from the most naturalistic to the boldly abstract and he is always keen to explore new methods, new and unusual light sources and the most subtle effects. Mark's work has been seen in tiny studio spaces, large art galleries, proscenium theatres, churches and opera houses.

Previous lighting designs include *The London Merchant*, *Cider With Rosie* and *The Merchant of Venice* (Theatre Royal, Bury St Edmunds); *Carmen* (Dorset Opera); *Pressure Drop* and *On Religion* (On Theatre); *Parallel Electra* (Young Vic); *The Kreutzer Sonata* and *Vanya* (Gate Theatre); *Tête à Tête: The Opera Festival* (Tête à Tête, 2007–9); *Monsters* (Arcola Theatre/Strawberry Vale); *The Barber of Seville* (Armonico Consort); *The Home Place* (Lyric Theatre, Belfast); *A Number* (Salisbury Playhouse); *Topless Mum* (Tobacco Factory); *Haunted* (Only Hope Productions); *Pains of Youth* (Belgrade Theatre); *The Taming of The Shrew* (Watermill Theatre and Old Vic); *Jeff Koons* (ATC); and *Pippi Longstocking* (Dragon Black Productions).

Mark has also been a guest lecturer and tutor for RADA (where guest designs include *The Man of Mode* and *The Last Days of Judas Iscariot*), National Youth Theatre and East 15.

INGRID HU   103

Ingrid trained in scenography in Canada and at Central Saint Martins College of Art and Design, London. Since graduating in 2002 she has been working in theatre and in multidisciplinary design, including with the award-winning Heatherwick Studio.

She works with a wide range of materials and techniques and is particularly interested in the interplay of textures, light and colour. She collaborates closely with directors and performers in developing concepts integral to the narrative. Her designs often involve transformative elements and innovative use of space.

She designs sets and lighting, as well as costumes, and has designed for a variety of performances in the UK and abroad. www.jiachiann.net

RICHARD HUDSON   89

Born in Zimbabwe, Richard trained at Wimbledon School of Art. He has designed operas for Glyndebourne, Covent Garden, The Met, La Scala, Maggio Musicale Florence, English National Opera, Scottish Opera, Kent Opera, Opera North, Wiener Staatsoper, Munich, Chicago, Copenhagen, Athens, Bregenz, Amsterdam, Zurich, Barcelona, Madrid, Brussels, Houston and Washington. He has also designed for the Aldeburgh Festival, Royal Ballet, Royal Shakespeare Company, National Theatre, Royal Court, Almeida and Young Vic. In 1988 he won an Olivier Award for a season of plays at the Old Vic, and for *The Lion King* he received a Tony award in 1998. He is a Royal Designer for Industry (RDI). In 2003 he won the Gold Medal for set design at the Prague Quadrennial, and in 2005 he was given an Honorary Doctorate by the University of Surrey. Recent work includes *Rushes* and *The Goldberg Variations* (Royal Ballet, Covent Garden), *Rigoletto* (Wiener Volksoper), *Armida* (Metropolitan Opera, New York), and *Tamerlano* (Royal Opera, Covent Garden). Future projects include *The Nutcracker* (American Ballet Theatre) and *Romeo and Juliet* (National Ballet of Canada).

BECKY HURST   36

Becky trained on the Motley Theatre Design Course and attained an MA in Communication Design (Illustration) from Central Saint Martins. She is a co-director of Cartoon de Salvo and is their resident designer, for whom she has designed *Pub Rock*, *The Greek*, *The Ratcatcher of Hamelin*, *The Sunflower Plot*, *The Chaingang Gang*, *Ladies and Gentlemen*, *Where am I?*, *Meat and Two Veg* and *Bernie and Clive*. Please see www.cartoondesalvo. com.

She has designed widely across the UK. Designs include *Treasured* (mac, Birmingham); *Kes, Knives In Hens, Electra, Pomegranate* (Manchester Royal Exchange); *Metamorphoses, Alice Through the Looking Glass* and *Punchkin/Enchanter* (London Bubble); *Pinocchio* (York Theatre Royal); *Memory of Water* (Watford Palace Theatre); *The Real Thing* (Northampton Theatre Royal); *Master Harold and the Boys* (Bristol New Vic Studio); *Breaststrokes* (Stella Duffy, BAC), *Measure for Measure* (Cambridge Arts Theatre); *Stoopud F**cken Animals* (Traverse); *Taniko* (the Queen Elizabeth Hall); and *Monogamy* (Riverside Studios).

She has designed productions as a visiting professional for the London Academy of Music and Dramatic Art, Central School of Speech and Drama, Mountview Theatre School, Webber Douglas Academy, Oxford School of Drama and The London Sinfonietta Education Department.

She works widely as a visual artist in education and on creative partnership projects. She also designs for television and works as an illustrator.

www.rebeccahurst.co.uk

KELLY JAGO   43

Kelly strives to design worlds that hold many secrets, revealed gradually to the audience as the stories are told. She is keen to explore performance environments that can have the ability to involve and incorporate the audience, creating an intriguing reality that allows the story to take place.

Kelly trained at Nottingham Trent University, graduating with a first class degree in theatre design. Since graduating she has designed for many companies, most recently working with Red Grit on a new play called *Bittersweet Sunshine* performed in June 2010 as part of the Emerge festival in Leeds. Kelly's other recent design credits include *Under Milk Wood* (Mansfield Palace Theatre); *A Dream Play* (Arts Support Service); *Looking for the Rainbow* (Big Window Theatre Company); *Pericles* (York Theatre Royal); *The Heights* (Stephen Joseph Theatre and National Theatre Connections Project); *The Insect Play* (Thorsby Riding Hall); *Kid's Play* (Stoney Street Theatre); *Burying Your Brother in the Pavement* (National Theatre Connections Project).

Kelly has also worked designing as part of the Aim Higher project with Roundabout Theatre at the Nottingham Playhouse. This role included devising and leading design workshops with young people, culminating in a collaborative set and costume design for performances including *Seven Jewish Children* and *Burglars*.

Kelly particularly enjoys the collaborative process that is required when creating new and interesting theatre, always discovering new people and developing new skills.

www.kellyjago.com

MARTIN JOHNS   124

Having trained at Wimbledon School of Art and the Motley Theatre Design Course, Martin started his career at the Belgrade Theatre, Coventry and became Head of Design for the Tyneside Theatre Company, York Theatre Royal and Leicester Haymarket Theatre. During the latter period he designed the set for the West End production of *Me and My Girl* at the Adelphi and subsequently Berlin, Broadway, Japan, Australia, South Africa and the British and American tours.

Other West End shows include *Master Class* (Old Vic and Wyndham's); *Passion Play* (Wyndham); *West Side Story* (Her Majesty's); *The Hired Man* (Astoria); *The Entertainer* (Shaftesbury); *Brigadoon* (Victoria Palace); *A Piece of my Mind* (Apollo); *The Secret Lives of Cartoons* (Aldwych); *Rolls Hyphen Royce* (Shaftesbury); *Let the Good Stones Roll* (Ambassadors Theatre); *Mack and Mabel* (Piccadilly Theatre) and the set for *The Romans in Britain* (National Theatre).

Since 1999 Martin has been resident designer at the Theatre by the Lake in Keswick, Cumbria.

VICTORIA JOHNSTONE   90

Victoria trained at Rose Bruford College, receiving first class honours in theatre design. She has lived in Scotland, Texas and the Middle East and is now based in south London. Her recent designs for theatre include *Coming Home* by Athol Fugard (dir. Cordelia Monsey, Arcola), *Sense* by Anja Hilling (Company of Angels, Southwark Playhouse), costume design for *Saturday Night* (dir. Tom Littler, Jermyn Street Theatre/Arts Theatre), *Unstated* (Red Room, Southwark Playhouse), *Hotel Medea* (Shunt Vaults), set design for *The Dilemma of a Ghost* by Ama Ata Aidoo (Border Crossings/National Theatre of Ghana), *The Cow Play* by Ed Harris (dir. Andrea Brooks, Nightingale Theatre/regional tour), Heiner Müller's *Hamletmachine* (Imploding Fictions, BAC/international tour), *Vincent River* by Philip Ridley, *A Mother* by Dario Fo and Franca Rame, and Amir Reza Koohestani's *Amid The Clouds* (all BAC). She has also worked as a costume, puppet and prop maker with companies including Punchdrunk, Scarlet Theatre, Soho Theatre and Oily Cart.

Victoria is also a highly skilled model-maker and has often assisted other designers in this capacity, most notably the opera designer and director Tim Hopkins on productions such as *Of Thee I Sing/Let 'em eat Cake* for Opera North and *Give Me Your Blessing For I Go to a Foreign Land* at the Royal Opera House.

MARK JONATHAN   83

Mark has extensive experience as a lighting designer in opera, drama, dance, ballet, musicals and arena productions in all scales and formats both in the UK and worldwide.

His dance designs include contemporary and classical works for The Royal Ballet, including *The Sleeping Beauty*, *Sylvia* and *Cinderella*. At the Birmingham Royal Ballet he is a regular collaborator with the choreographer David Bintley. His many productions there include *Far from the Madding Crowd*, *Beauty and the Beast*, *Cyrano* and *The Sleeping Beauty*. Designs for other ballet companies includes Northern Ballet Theatre, American Ballet Theatre, Berlin Staatsballett, Stuttgarter Ballett, Ballet Capitole de Toulouse, The London Children's Ballet and Japanese National Ballet.

He has designed for Los Angeles Opera, Washington National Opera, Bayerische Staatsoper, Potsdam, Scottish Opera, Vlaamse Opera, Israeli Opera, Strasbourg Opera du Rhin, Spoleto Festival, Glyndebourne, Opera Holland Park and Opera Northern Ireland.

His lighting for drama and musicals has taken him from London's National Theatre, where he was Head of Lighting from 1993–2003, to the West End, Broadway and New York, as well as many of the UK's leading regional theatres including the RSC, Manchester Royal Exchange, Birmingham Rep, Chichester Festival (where he was an associate from 2006–8), Bristol Old Vic, Sheffield Crucible and West Yorkshire Playhouse as well as all of the principal touring houses. His lighting for *Prometheus Bound* in New York was nominated for the Drama Desk award for Outstanding Lighting.

www.markjonathan.com

MAX JONES   118

Max is a graduate of the Royal Welsh College of Music and Drama in Cardiff and was a winner of the Linbury Biennial Prize for Stage Design in 2001. He is also an Associate Artist at Theatr Clwyd.

Previous productions at Theatr Clwyd include *Dancing at Lughnasa* by Brian Friel, *Blackthorn* by Gary Owen, *A Small Family Business* by Alan Aykbourn, *Mary Stuart* by Friedrich Schiller, *Measure for Measure* by William Shakespeare, *Two Princes* by Meredith Barker and *The Grapes of Wrath* by John Steinbeck.

Other productions include *Così Fan Tutte* by Mozart (Welsh National Opera), *Spur of the Moment* by Anya Reiss (Royal Court Theatre), *Party* by Tom Basden (Arts Theatre), *Mad Forest* by Caryl Churchill (JMK Award, BAC), *The Caretaker* by Harold Pinter (Glasgow Citizens Theatre), *Dumb Show* by Jo Penhall (New Vic Theatre, Stoke), *Sweeney Todd* by Sondheim/Wheeler (Welsh National Youth Opera), *Ryan and Ronnie* by Meic Povey (Sgript Cymru) and *Salt Meets Wound* by Tom Morton-Smith (Theatre503).

Max has also worked as a costume assistant for film. Features include *Harry Potter*, *Robin Hood*, *Prince of Persia*, *James Bond: A Quantum of Solace*, *Children of Men*, *Closer*, *Bridget Jones 2*, *Thunderbirds*, *Hippy Hippy Shake* and *Alexander the Great*.

SOPHIE JUMP   39

Sophie designs for theatre and is Associate Director and designer for performance company seven sisters group. The company has become well known for its site-specific work and has toured nationally and internationally. Joint Honorary Secretary of the Society of British Theatre Designers, she is co-editor and designer of the SBTD journal. Her work was selected to represent Britain at the Prague Quadrennial 1999, 2003 and 2007 exhibitions of world theatre design, and her designs were chosen to be part of the Collaborators exhibition at the Victoria and Albert Museum in 2008.

Work includes *Led Easy* (directed by Emma Bernard for Cardboard Citizens); *Mobilis In Mobili* (dir. Bruno Roubicek, Shunt Lounge); *The Winter's Tale* (dir. Neil Caple, Birkenhead Park); *The Bald Prima Donna* (dir. Hanna Berrigan Etcetera Theatre); *Blackbird* and *The Difficult Unicorn* (both directed by Jane Howell at the Southwark Playhouse); *The Tempest* (dir. Nancy Meckler, Shared Experience tour); and *Full Moon*, (dir. Helena Kaut-Howsen).

Sophie's designs for seven sisters group include *Salome* (St Pancras Chambers); *Trainstation* (Kings Cross, Waterloo, nationally and internationally); *Concrete* (Royal National Theatre); *Ballroom* (Royal Festival Hall); *The Forest* (Newlands Corner); and *The Forbidden* (Royal Opera House).

Sophie curated an exhibition at the V&A Museum called *When Marcel Met Motley*, about the collaboration between Motley and the architect Marcel Breuer. She is researching a book about the London Theatre Studio and Old Vic School.

SAKINA KARIMJEE   95

Sakina's design credits include *Hänsel und Gretel* (Royal Academy of Music); *White Peacock*, a play for young people labelled as having profound and multiple learning difficulties (Roundabout, Nottingham Playhouse); *Blood Wedding*, *The Visit*, *Find Me* and *Down in the Dumps* (Nottingham Playhouse Youth Theatre); Gala Event (Royal Albert Hall); *Under the Bed* (Theatre Centre, national tour); *Lyrical MC* (Tamasha Theatre Company, touring to Oval House, Soho Theatre, Half Moon and Unicorn Theatre, London); *Who's Afraid of Virginia Woolf*, *Under the Blue Sky* and *Days of Wine and Roses* (Theatre by the Lake Studio, Keswick); *The Joy of Politics* (Black Sheep Comedy, national tour); *The Golden Voyage of Sinbad* (Sideways Theatre, C Venues, Edinburgh Festival); *Homestead* (Shady Dolls Theatre Company, Theatre Museum, Covent Garden); *A Christmas Carol* (Big Foot Theatre Company, Schools Tour); Junior Embrace Summer Schools (Theatre Royal Bath). As an assistant designer: *Ghosts In The Gallery* (Polka Theatre).

Sakina has also worked as an AutoCAD draughtsperson/ assistant production manager at the Royal Opera House and as a model-maker for the National Theatre. She is a visiting lecturer in AutoCAD at the Bristol Old Vic Theatre School and has taught model-making at Rose Bruford College.

ADELE KEELEY   81

Adele studied costume at Bournemouth and an MA in Theatre Arts at Nottingham Trent University, focusing her studies on the digital platform for costume design communication. A costume practitioner and senior lecturer in costume design at the Arts University College at Bournemouth, Adele continues to practice costume design alongside her teaching commitments.

Adele started her career as costume maker creating work for the English National Opera, Royal Opera House and Salisbury Playhouse. Adele's work as a costume designer includes *Little Shop of Horrors* (Pavilion Theatre, Brighton); *The Serpent Slayer* (Vision Youth Theatre); *Within These Walls* (C-Scape Dance Company, Havant Art Centre); *Tender, La Ronde, Mary Barton* (Arts Ed MA Season, Chiswick); *Mary Barton* (The Studio, Bournemouth); and *Hamlet* (Brownsea Open Air Theatre).

SIMON KENNY 37

Simon trained in set and costume design at the Central School of Speech and Drama.

His designs for theatre include *There's Only One Wayne Matthews* (Sheffield Crucible Studio); new adaptations of the award-winning children's novels *Holes* (New Wimbledon Studio) and *The Machine Gunners* (Polka); *Pedestrian*, a new play for one man and a goldfish, at Bristol Old Vic; *Tales from the Bar of Lost Souls*, a British Council project with Imitating the Dog and the National Theatre of Greece; *Seven Jewish Children* (Hackney Empire); *Gross Indecency* for Duckie; *Michael X* (Tabernacle); Peter Shaffer's *White Liars* (etcetera); revivals of the previously censored *Young Woodley* and *Tea and Sympathy* (Finborough); *The Veiled Screen* and *True or Falsetto?* (Drill Hall, and international tours); and three national and international tours of new plays for British-Asian company Rifco Arts.

Opera includes *The Prodigal Son*, *The Homecoming*, *Háry János* and *Orlando*, all for Ryedale Festival; *A Night at the Opera* (London Palladium and UK tour); and *Carmen* (Hampstead Garden Opera).

He works regularly with drama and theatre production students. Recent projects include *The Rimers of Eldritch*, *Woyzeck* and *Machinal* (Central School of Speech and Drama); *The Madras House* and a new adaptation of *L'Atelier* (RADA); a promenade production of *Watership Down* (Oxford School of Drama at the Botanic Garden, Oxford); and a series of devised education projects for Creative Partnerships.

www.simonkenny.co.uk

KEVIN KNIGHT 50

Kevin trained at the Central Saint Martins School of Arts in London and has worked extensively as a set and costume designer in the United Kingdom and abroad.

He has worked at most of Britain's leading repertory theatres and on numerous West-End productions. He has designed premieres of plays and musicals that have toured throughout Europe and America, where productions have gained international recognition and won numerous awards.

As an international opera designer he has worked for many of the world's leading opera companies. Credits include: *Rusalka*, *The Marriage of Figaro* (Oslo); *Lulu*, *Die Frau ohne Schatten* (Lyric Opera of Chicago); *Tosca* and *Lady Macbeth of Mtsensk* (Canadian Opera Company, Toronto); *Schwanda the Bagpiper* (Augsburg); *Rita* (Royal Opera House); *La Bohème* and *Albert Herring* (Santa Fe Opera); *Pastorale* (world premier, Staatsoper Stuttgart); *Tannhäuser* (La Scala, Milan); *Il Trovatore* (Bologna/Japan/Bilbao); *Il Lombardi* (Florence); *I Capuleti e i Montecchi* (Spoletto Opera Festival, USA); *The Miserly Knight*/*The Floretine Tragedy* (Teatro San Carlos, Lisbon); *Les Contes d'Hoffmann*, *Summer and Smoke*, *The Rape of Lucretia* (Central City Opera Festival, Denver USA); *Death in Venice* (Chicago Opera Theatre, USA); *Die Drei Pintos* and *Mirandolina* (Wexford Opera Festival and Lugo Opera Festival, Italy); *La Finta Gardiniera* (Garsington Opera Festival); *Daphne* and *Ariadne auf Naxos* (Teatro la Fenice, Venice, and Vlaamse Opera, Antwerp); *Königskinder* (Teatro San Carlo, Naples – winner of the Premio Abbiati); *Sweeney Todd* and *Don Giovanni* (Opera North).

He directed and designed the world premier of Naomi Wallace's stage adaptation of *Birdy* for the West-End and American productions (winner, Barrymore Award for outstanding contribution to stage design); *The Truman Capote Talk Show* (winner, Edinburgh Fringe First Award), also produced in London, off Broadway and European tour; and British premiers of the plays *Oktoberfest* and *Webster* in London.

www.kevin-knight.com

RALPH KOLTAI 99

Hungarian by descent, Ralph Koltai CBE RDI served with British Intelligence at the Nuremberg Trials and on War Crimes Interrogation at the end of the Second World War.

He subsequently studied at the Central School of Art and Design in London and became Head of Theatre Design (1965–72). He has since designed some 250 productions of opera, dance, drama and musicals throughout the world.

As director/designer, work includes *The Flying Dutchman* and *La Traviata* (Hong Kong Arts Festival, 1987–90), and *Suddenly Last Summer* (Nottingham). Thirty productions for the Royal Shakespeare Company where he is an Associate designer. Work for the Royal National Theatre includes, amongst others, a notable all-male production of *As You Like It* (1967, and San Francisco/New York, 1975). Over 100 opera productions include the Brecht/Weill music drama *The Rise and Fall of the City of Mahagonny* for Sadlers Wells Opera under the guidance of the legendary Lotte Lenya, the original Jenny in 1928, and a major *Ring Cycle* (1970–81) for the English Opera Company under Reginald Goodall.

Among a string of awards he was made a CBE in 1983 and is a Fellow of the Royal Academy of Performing Arts, Hong Kong, The University of the Arts, London, the Royal Society of Art RDI (Royal Designer of Industry), Rose Bruford College, Kent.

CHLOE LAMFORD 85

Chloe trained in theatre design at Wimbledon School of Art. She won Best Design at the 2007 TMA awards for her design for *Small Miracle* by Neil D'Souza.

Chloe's designs for theatre include *Ghost Story* (Sky Arts Live Drama season), written and directed by Mark Ravenhill; *My Romantic History* (Sheffield Crucible and Bush Theatre); *Joseph K* (Gate Theatre); *Songs from a Hotel Bedroom* (Linbury Studio ROH and tour); *Romeo and Juliet* (Pilot Theatre); *Sus* (Young Vic); *It Felt Empty…* (Clean Break, installation at Arcola's Studio K); *The Kreutzer Sonata* (Gate Theatre); *Everything Must Go!* (Soho Theatre); *This Wide Night* (Soho Theatre and tour); *The Mother Ship*, *How to Tell the Monsters from the Misfits* (Birmingham Rep); *Blithe Spirit* (Watermill Theatre); *The Snow Queen* (Sherman Theatre, Cardiff); *Antigone at Hell's Mouth* (Kneehigh Theatre and NYT); *Silence* (NYT); *Lola* (Trestle Theatre Company); *Small Miracle* (Tricycle Theatre and Mercury Theatre, Colchester); *The Wild Party* (Rosie Kay Dance Company); *The Good Person of Sichuan* (Birmingham), *The Shy Gas Man* (Southwark Playhouse).

Her designs for opera include *The Magic Flute* (English Touring Opera), *War and Peace* (Scottish Opera and RSAMD), *The Cunning Little Vixen* (Royal College of Music) and *La Calisto* for the Early Opera Company. Chloe has also designed various music videos and promos, as well as *The Full Monteverdi*, an opera feature film by Polyphonic Films.

KATE LANE 28

Kate graduated in 2008 from the MA Costume Design for Performance at London College of Fashion, where she gained a Distinction and won the MA Centenary Award for Costume. Previously she studied BA Sculpture at Camberwell College of Art. She designs costume for dance, theatre and live art.

Designs include *Sufi-Zen* (choreographer Gauri Sharma Tripathi, Queen Elizabeth Hall, Southbank Centre and UK tour); *SkinTight* (dir. Stella Duffy, Pleasance, Islington, and Riverside Studios); *Shimmy Shimmy*, Ascendance (choreographer Brook Smiley, Lilian Baylis Studio, Sadlers Wells); *Interfaces* (Late Night at the V&A) and *Black Mirror* (UK tour), with choreograper Marie-Gabrielle Rotie; *Sissy* (short film, dir. Judy Jacob); *Rain Emperor*, site-specific performance (Village Underground); *Clown With Love* (The New Wolsey Studio, Ipswich/The Junction, Cambridge); *Damned Beautiful* (The Place, Pleasance, Edinburgh Fringe and UK tour), with Helix Dance; designs for Drama Centre London include *Hot L Baltimore*, *The Kitchen*, *Figaro Gets Divorced*, *The Wild Duck*, *The Rehearsal*, *Much Ado About Nothing* and *The Winter's Tale*. She designed her first opera, *Carmen*, for Dorset Opera in summer 2010.

MORGAN LARGE 77

Morgan graduated from LIPA in 2003 with a first class degree in theatre and performance design, the Sennheiser Award for Theatre and Performance Design and The Philip Holt Trust Award.

Morgan's West End credits include *Cat on a Hot Tin Roof* (Novello), winner of the 2010 Oliver award for Best Revival; *Flashdance* (Shaftesbury); *Footloose* (Novello/Playhouse and South Africa); *Tick, Tick… Boom!* and *The Last Five Years* (Duchess); *Fame* (Shaftesbury); and *Room on the Broom* (Garrick and worldwide).

Other designs include *The Hostage* (Southwark Playhouse); *Madagascar* (Theatre503); *Anyone Can Whistle* (Jermyn Street Theatre); *Don Giovanni* (Opera East); Tim Firth's *Sign of the Times* (UK tour); *Jolson & Company* (UK tour); *Never Forget* (UK tour); *Fight Face* (Lyric, Hammersmith); *Dov and Ali* (Theatre503); *Three Sides* (45th St Theatre, NY); *Rock* (UK tour); *The Comedy of Errors* (Oval House); *Marlon Brando's Corset* (Yvonne Arnaud and UK tour); *Only the Brave* (George Square).

Morgan's designs for dance include *Planet Wonderful* (Royal Danish Ballet, Copenhagen).

Morgan has also designed the Olivier Awards since 2006, and worked extensively as associate designer to Christopher Oram, and assistant to John Napier.

www.morganlarge.com

MARIE-JEANNE LECCA 55

Marie-Jeanne was born in Bucharest, where she studied at the Beaux Arts Institute. She now live in London and works extensively in opera. Her set and costume designs include *Therese Racquin* (world premiere, Dallas); *Falstaff*, *The Stone Guest*, *Pelléas and Mélisande* (ENO); and *Carmen* (Houston, Seattle, Minnesota). Among her recent costume designs are *Die Frau Ohne Schatten*, *Agrippina* (Opernhaus, Zürich); *Krol Roger* (Bregenzer Festpiele and Barcelona); *Khovanschina* (WNO); *Carmen* (Bolshoi Opera); *The Ring Cycle*, *Woyzeck*, *Greek Passion* (Royal Opera House, joint winner Oliver award); *Julietta*, *The Dwarf* and *Seven Deadly Sins* (Opera North, South Bank Show Award); *Moses and Aron*, *Faust*, *Katya Kabanova* (Bayerische Staatsoper, Munich); *Die Soldaten* (Ruhr Triennale); *Maskarade*, *West Side Story* (Bregenzer Festpiele); *Turandot* (Salzburger Festpiele); *La Juive*, *L'Etoile*, *Peter Grimes*, *Macbeth* (Opernhaus, Zurich); *Jenufa*, *Rienzi* (Wiener Staatsoper); *Salammbo* (Opera National de Paris); *The Turn of the Screw* (La Monnaie, Brussels); *The Magic Flute* (Wiener Volksoper); *The Nose* (De Nederlandse Opera, Amsterdam); *Der Freischütz*, *The Adventures of Mr Brouček* (ENO).

She received the Martinu Foundation Medal for *Juliette* and *The Greek Passion*, and was nominated by Opernwelt magazine as Costume Designer of the Year for *Maskarade*. Her theatre work includes sets and costumes for *As You Like It* and *La Bête Humaine* (Nottingham Playhouse); and costumes for *The Taming of the Shrew* (RSC); and *Napoleon* (West End). For film and TV, *Amahl and the Night Visitors* (BBC Wales, BAFTA nomination.) She was part of the British team that won the Golden Triga at the 2003 Prague Quadrennial.

Current projects are *The Passenger* (Bregenz) and *The Trojans* (Deutsche Oper Berlin).

LEFT LUGGAGE THEATRE 34

Left Luggage Theatre's work responds to the histories, stories, memories and myths connected with and embedded in the places that resonate with human experience. We create narratives from these hidden stories that are told through physical theatre, puppetry, mime, mask, projection and multi-sensory scenography.

Left Luggage Theatre became 2007/08 graduate residents at The Puppet Centre Trust at BAC, London, and have since been commissioned to create bespoke shows for festivals across the UK and for the Brit Awards After Show Party, as well as producing sell-out performances at The Little Angel Theatre and Shunt Lounge in London.

In 2009 Left Luggage Theatre undertook their first major project in Newcastle-upon-Tyne. *Alveus* was performed at world heritage site Segedunum on the banks of the Tyne and was supported by the National Lottery through Arts Council England, North Tyneside Council, Tyne & Wear Museums and Empty Space.

The company members are all first class graduates of Nottingham Trent University's BA(Hons) Theatre Design. Individually they have worked for acclaimed companies such as WildWorks, Punchdrunk, Northern Stage, Unicorn Theatre, Bristol Old Vic, Leicester Theatre Trust, Metro-Boulot-Dodo and Birmingham Opera Company.

Left Luggage Theatre are: Alison Garner, Anna Harding, Kimberley Turner and Verity Quinn.

VERENA LEO 88

Verena initially trained as dressmaker before gaining a degree in theatre design and moving on to studies in architecture. She has designed various dance pieces performed at the Robin Howard Dance Theatre, including *QUaRteT*, choreographed by Marguerite Caruana Galizia, June 2008/January 2009; *Catch My Head*, choreographed by Jessie Brett, January 2009; *Resolution! 09* and *For Living*, choreographed by Neil Hainsworth, March 2008; Dance and Design Collaborations 2008. Other projects include production design for *The Barber's Cut*, a short-film by Mark Bröcking, June–August 2009; *'Til the Petals Fall*, a short film by Natalie Lindiwe Jones, March 2008; and the Nasty Sweets' production *A Faceful of Fists*, *The Thingumywotsit* and *Sparrow Heights*, performed at the Wimbledon Studio Theatre, November 2008, The Hen & Chickens, February 2009, and Greenwich Playhouse, March 2009.

Verena was a Linbury Prize finalist at the National Theatre London, 2009, working with the Birmingham Opera Company on Verdi's *Othello*. Other awards include the third prize at the Enterprise Week Challenge 2008, London College of Fashion; first College Drawing Prize in Theatre 2008, Wimbledon College of Art; and Student of the Year 2005, Foundation degree in Art and Design, Gateshead College.

ADRIAN LINFORD 113

Adrian trained at Wimbledon School of Art and works as a freelance set and costume designer for theatre, film and television.

Theatre work has included *When Five Years Pass*, *The Inkwell*, and *The Shoemaker's Wonderful Wife*; productions of *Art*, *Blithe Spirit* (both in Singapore); *Betrayal*, *Family Voices* and *IPH…* (all Mercury Theatre, Colchester); *The Glass Menagerie*, *Camino Real* and *Blood Wedding* at RADA. He designed *Inside the Firm* and *Up on the Roof* (Queen's Theatre, Hornchurch); and in New York, Ionesco's *The Bald Soprano* and Genet's *The Maids* at the Meisner Theater.

Musicals have included *Peter Pan*, *Poppy*, *Grease* and *Hairspray* (both series for SKY TV); *Assassins* (Pimlico Opera); and *A Twist of Fate*, followed by *They're Playing Our Song*, in Singapore and Manila. Television costume credits include *Wish* (BBC2), *Tea* (MTV/Channel 4) and *Belzoni* (Channel 4 series).

Adrian has designed *Albert Herring* (Aldeburgh Festival); *Così Fan Tutte* and *Nabucco* (Opera West, Scotland); *Orlando* (Cambridge Handel Opera); *Il Seraglio* (English Touring Opera); Judith Weir's *The Vanishing Bridegroom* at RSAMD, Glasgow; *Così Fan Tutte* for Grange Park Opera; and he co-designed *Il Trovatore* at the Bastile Opera in Paris, directed by Francesca Zambello.

Recently working on *The Turn of The Screw* (Macedonian Opera); *The Marriage of Figaro* (Opera Theatre Company, Dublin); productions of *Katya Kabanova* and *Die Fledermaus* for Scottish Opera; and *Orfeo ed Eurydice* for Minnesotta Opera.

JANE LINZ ROBERTS 93

After completing a Foundation course at the Central School of Art and Design, Jane went to Bristol University to read Drama. Later she also completed an MA with Distinction in Film and Television Design at Kingston University.

Jane designs for an eclectic range of companies, mixing large and small spaces, classics and new writing and site-specific and touring productions. Early work included *Lear's Daughters*, a piece devised by Women's Theatre Group which is now performed regularly all over the world. Jane has designed many pieces of new writing and is passionate about contributing as a designer and theatre maker to the creation of new work.

Jane was resident designer at the Sherman Theatre and designed many productions for their main house and studio. She also designed for companies all over Wales including Y Cwmni's *Song from a Forgotten City* and *Double Indemnity* for Theatr Clwyd.

Jane is now based in London. Other theatre includes *The Whisper of Angels' Wings* (Birmingham Rep); *Pacific Overtures* and *Beautiful Thing* (Leicester Haymarket); *Children of The Crown*, *The Silver Sword* and *The Caretaker* (Nottingham Playhouse); *Seeing Without Light* (Theatre Royal Plymouth); and *The Flying Machine* (Unicorn Theatre).

Jane designed the film *September*, which won the BAFTA for Best Short Film in 2008, and award-winning feature documentary *Deep Water*.

Current work includes *Soul Exchange* for the National Theatre of Wales.

SOPHIA LOVELL SMITH 94

Sophia enjoys exploring the architecture of space and what it has to offer the creative process. A recent production took over the whole of St Steven's in Hampstead: an enormous gothic church became a Swiss mountain village for NLC's *The Ice Mountain* (dir. Abigail Morris). Sophia continues to relish the team nature of theatre making and is at present working with seven-year-olds on a design for their outdoor mobile theatre, a structure offering lots of locations. Sophia works with A New Direction as artist in residence in schools and supports the company in their growing links with other countries' school art programmes.

Sophia's work includes working with Unicorn Theatre (*Jemima Puddle Duck and her Friends*); Little Angel Theatre (*Handa's Surprise*, *Jonah and the Whale*); 20 Stories High (*Blackberry Trout Face*); many seasons at Theatre by the Lake, Keswick (including *The Caretaker*, *Hello and Goodbye*, *Speed-the-Plow*); Graeae (*The Flower Girls*, *Blood Wedding*); Tell Tale Hearts (*Space Hoppers*); ENO Baylis Programme, Theatre Centre (*Common Heaven*, *Souls*); M6 (*Peacemaker*); and Trestle (*Chagall*, *Little India*).

Sophia works regularly with Mountview Academy, RADA and West Sussex Youth Theatre, teaching and designing productions. She is at present designing a giant children's playmat for the Royal & Derngate Theatre, Northampton, a show that turns the Derngate stage and auditorium into Flathampton, an interactive town for children and their grown ups.

CLAIRE LYTH 79

After a pre-diploma course at Sutton College of Art, Claire read drama, history and English at Bristol University.

Recent designs include *The Talented Mr Ripley*, adapted by Phyllis Nagy at the Queen's, Hornchurch, and *Ladies Night* for the Royal Court, Liverpool. Some other designs include *Stormforce* at the Riverside Studios in London; *Twelfth Night* for the National Theatre of Norway; *The Winter's Tale* for Chicago's Shakespeare Theater; *The Man Who Thinks He's It* (The Steve Coogan Show, Lyceum, London); *Goodness Gracious Me* (tour); *Macbeth* and *Twelfth Night* (English Shakespeare Company); *Macbeth* (Residenz Theatre, Munich); *Split Second*, *Mad and Her Dad* (Lyric, Hammersmith); *All's Well That Ends Well* (Regent's Park); *Peter Pan* and *The Three Musketeers* (Crucible, Sheffield); *Rigoletto* (tour for WNO); *The Winter's Tale*, *Macbeth* and *Tosca* (Everyman, Liverpool); *Othello* (Ludlow Festival); *My Fair Lady* (Aarhus, Denmark); *Fungus the Bogeyman* (Belgrade Theatre, Coventry); *Archangels Don't Play Pinball* (Bristol Old Vic); *Romeo and Juliet* (Sherman Theatre, Cardiff, and tour – part of the British stand at the Prague Quadrennial Exhibition of Theatre Design in 2001).

Claire is particularly interested in new writing and has designed over 50 premieres, including *Shirley Valentine*. She has also designed 39 Shakespeare productions – not new writing, but always fascinating to work on new interpretations. Her designs have toured all over the world and she has worked in the United States, Hong Kong, Scandinavia, Germany, Vienna and Beirut.

JOHN MacFARLANE 56

John was born in Scotland and studied at the Glasgow School of Art. He received an Arts Council of Great Britain Trainee Designer award and spent some time as resident designer at the Young Vic Theatre in London.

For the first 15 years of his career he worked mainly in dance with many of the major international companies. He collaborated with Jiri Kylian and the Netherlands Dance Theatre (*Songs of a Wayfarer*, *Les Noces*, *Dreamtime*, *L'Enfant et les Sortilèges*, *Piccolo Mondo*, *The Soldier's Tale*, *Forgotten Land* and *Tanzschul*); and with Glen Tetley, *The Fire Bird* (Danish Royal Ballet), *Wiegenlied* (Vienna State Opera), *La Ronde* and *Tagore* (Canadian Royal Ballet), and *Dialogues* (Dance Theatre of Harlem). He has also designed for the classical ballet repertoire: *Swan Lake* in Munich, *Giselle* (Royal Ballet) and *The Nutcracker* (Birmingham Royal Ballet), both with Sir Peter Wright; and *Le Baiser de la Fée* (Birmingham). *The Nutcracker* has been remounted recently by the Australian National Ballet.

Latterly John has focused on opera, where he designs both sets and costumes. He works regularly with the German producer Willy Decker, and with Francesca Zambella, David McVicar and Richard Jones.

With Willy Decker John designed *A Midsummer Night's Dream* (Cologne Opera); *Julius Caesar* (Scottish Opera); *Peter Grimes* (Brussels); *La Clemenza di Tito* (Paris Opera); *Otello* (Brussels); *Falstaff* (Florence); *Boris Gudunov* (Amsterdam); *Bluebeard/ Erwartung* (ROH); and *Idomeneo* (Vienna Opera). With Francesca Zambella he designed *Benvenuto Cellini* (Grand Theatre, Geneva), *The Barber of Seville* (Santa Fe) and *War and Peace* (Paris).

John worked with David McVicar on *Agrippina* (Brussels); *Magic Flute* (ROH) and *Don Giovanni* (Brussels); and *The Rake's Progress* in Copenhagen.

Hansel and Gretel, his first production with Richard Jones for Welsh National Opera, won an Olivier Award and was remounted by the Met in New York at Christmas 2007. Their second production, *The Queen of Spades*, won the Royal Philharmonic Award. They worked together on *Euryanthe* for Glyndebourne Festival Opera; the second part of *The Trojans* for English National Opera; *Lady Macbeth of Mtsensk* and a double bill of *L'Espagnol* and *Gianni Schicchi* for the Royal Opera House.

John's future commitments include *Cinderella* for Birmingham Royal Ballet, *Elektra* for Chicago and *Maria Stuarda* for the Metropolitan Opera, New York.

In addition to his opera and dance work, John exhibits regularly as a painter and print maker in the UK and Europe.

IAN MacNEIL 96

Ian has been designing since 1984. He trained at Croydon School of Art and in New York. He spent seasons at Manchester Library Theatre and Birmingham Rep. In London he has designed for Gate Theatre, Royal Court, Young Vic and the National Theatre. Notable designs include *An Inspector Calls* (Royal Court); *Festen* (Almeida and West End); *Afore Night Comes* and *Vernon God Little* (Young Vic). He has won many awards.

ALEX MARKER 97

Alex is resident designer at the Finborough Theatre, where he has designed over 20 productions. Recent credits include *The Drawer Boy*, *Dream of The Dog* (and transfer to Trafalgar Studios), *Molière, or the League of Hypocrites*, *Death of Long Pig*, *Untitled*, *Plague over England* (and transfer to the Duchess Theatre), *Hangover Square*, *Sons of York*, *Little Madam*, *Eden's Empire*, *The Representative*, *Red Night*, *Lark Rise to Candleford*, *Albert's Boy* and *Hortensia and the Museum of Dreams*.

Alex trained at the Wimbledon School of Art. He has designed productions for many venues ranging from traditional theatre auditoria to a converted mortuary. Recent designs include *The Searcher* (Wilton's Music Hall); *Jus' Like That – A Night Out with Tommy Cooper* (national tour); *The Best of the Little Big Woman* (Leicester Square); *The Real McCoy – Reconnected* (Hackney Empire); *The Viewing Room* (Arts Theatre); *School's Theatre Festival* (Young Vic); *My Real War 1914–?* (Trafalgar Studios and national tour); *Origin: Unknown* (Theatre Royal, Stratford East); *The Pink Bedroom* (Courtyard Theatre); *Cherry Docs* (Kings Head); *King Arthur* (Arcola Theatre); *The Wedding Singer* and *Anything Goes* (Arts Ed); *Cooking with Elvis*, *Gym and Tonic*, *The Opposite Sex* and *Inside Job* (Lyceum Theatre, Crewe); and a charity gala performance of *Sweet Charity* (Theatre Royal, Drury Lane).

Alex is also director of a large youth theatre in West London.

GARANCE MARNEUR 97

Garance studied Fine Art in Paris and went on to graduate in Design for Performance with first class honours from Central Saint Martins in London.

In 2007 she was the overall winner of the prestigious Linbury Biennial Prize for Stage Design held at the National Theatre.

Based in London, Garance works freelance designing set and costume for theatre, dance and opera in the UK and internationally. Most recent work includes a UK tour of *Huck*, *Romeo and Juliet* at Stadttheater Bern (Ballet Switzerland); multi-award-winning *Orphans* at the Traverse in Edinburgh; Birmingham Rep/The Door and Soho Theatre, *Gagarin Way* for Theatre Royal Bath, Ustinov Studio; *Turandot* (winning design of the Linbury Prize for Stage Design) at the Hampstead Theatre; *Romeo and Juliet* at the National Theatre Studio; *Gianni Schicchi*, conducted by Valery Gergiev at the Mariinsky Theatre (Opera St Petersburg); *Dirty Butterfly* at the Young Vic/Clare; and *I Am Falling* at the Gate Theatre and Saddler's Wells/Lilian Baylis (nominated for a South Bank Show Award).

She is currently working on four plays for Greyscale and designing *The Chairs* for Theatre Royal Bath.

THOMASIN MARSHALL 70

Thomasin recently trained at the Motley Theatre Design Course after achieving a first-class honours degree in Theatre Design at Rose Bruford College in 2007. As well as designing, she is a freelance scenic painter and has worked as a creative workshop leader and design mentor employed by youth theatre groups.

Her recent design productions include *Henry IV Part I* (Drum Theatre, Plymouth); *A Voyage to Change the World* (Design Mentor, Barbican Theatre, Plymouth); *The Misanthrope* (Drum Theatre, Plymouth); The Hidden City Festival (various site-specific venues, Part Exchange Company); *One Small Step, One Giant Leap* (site-specific promenade production, assistant designer to Nat Tarrab, Royal William Yard, Plymouth).

LOIS MASKELL 82

Lois trained at The Liverpool Institute for Performing Arts, receiving a first-class honours degree in Theatre and Performance Design. Since then, she has enjoyed an intensive period of diverse work. In 2005, Lois was shortlisted for the Linbury Prize for Stage Design and was a finalist in the BBC Design Vision Competition 2007. Her approach looks at the manifold interpretations of the performance space, realising designs with considered vision and imagination.

Recent collaborations as a freelance designer and scenic artist include dreamthinkspeak, Liverpool Culture Company, FUSE Theatre, Hope Street Ltd, National Museums Liverpool/Find Your Talent, Action Transport Theatre, Royal Exchange Theatre Manchester, COAL Theatre with Told By An Idiot's John Wright, Royal Court Liverpool, Octagon Theatre Bolton, Liverpool Everyman and Playhouse, Lakeland Opera and work on the BBC Comedy series *The Mighty Boosh*.

GARY McCANN 98

Originally from County Armagh, Northern Ireland, Gary trained at Nottingham Trent University.

Recent design work includes *33 Variations* (Volkstheater, Vienna); *La Voix Humaine* and *L'Heure Espagnole* (Nationale Reisopera, Netherlands); *The Girl in the Yellow Dress* (Market Theatre, Johannesburg, and Stadsteater, Stockholm); *Così Fan Tutte* (Schönbrunn Palace, Vienna); *Norma* (National Opera of Moldova); *Così Fan Tutte* (Royal Academy of Music); *Fidelio* (Garsington Opera); *Motherland* (Live Theatre and UK tour); *Grimm Tales* (Library Theatre, Manchester); *Guys and Dolls* (Theater Bielefeld, Germany) *Im Zeichen der Kunst* (Volkstheater, Vienna); *A Northern Odyssey* and *Motherland* (Live Theatre, Newcastle); and *The Pitmen Painters* at the Lyttelton, National Theatre and the Friedman Theatre, Broadway.

Other design work includes *There's Something About Simmy* (Theatre Royal Stratford East, national tour); *Me and Cilla*, *Top Girls* (Live Theatre, Newcastle); *Home by Now* (Baltic Gallery, Gateshead); *Iron* (Northern Stage); *Thieves' Carnival*, *Broken Glass* (Watermill Theatre, Newbury); *Hurricane* (Arts Theatre London, 59th St Theatre, New York); *Protestants* (Soho Theatre); *Much Ado About Nothing*, *The Glass Menagerie*, *The Man of Mode*, *Twelfth Night*, *Iphigeneia* (Lyric Theatre, Belfast); *Song of the Western Men* (Chichester Festival Theatre); *L'Elisir d'Amour*, *The Magic Flute*, *La Bohème*, *The Barber of Seville*, *La Fille du Régiment* (Swansea City Opera); and *Promised Land* (Canterbury Festival).

Gary is lecturer in design with the drama department at the University of Kent.

HOLLY McCARTHY 54

Holly graduated from the Royal Welsh College of Music and Drama with a BA(Hons) in Theatre Design in 2005; and the Cardiff New Theatre Award for innovation in puppetry for *Wide Awake and Dreaming*.

Some of her professional design credits include, as set and costume designer: *Frost Nixon* (dir. Michael Bogdanov, The Hamburger Kammerspiele); *The House of Bernarda Alba* and *The Trojan Women* (Theatr Pena); *Swbryd Yn Y Nos*, *Warrior Square* and *Hazey Jane* (all new plays for Theatre Iolo, T.I.E tours).

As costume designer: *The Thorn Birds, A Musical*, co-designed with David Emanuel (Wales Theatre Company); *For You*, written by Ian McEwan and Michael Berkeley, and *Letters of a Love Betrayed*, by Eleanor Alberga and Donald Sturrock (Music Theatre Wales).

Holly has assisted for companies such as the BBC (*Torchwood*), Bath Theatre Royal and Tobacco Factory. She has also worked as a dresser for companies such as Welsh National Opera, Matthew Bourne and for Cameron Mackintosh (most recently on the opening of the *Les Miserables* 2009 UK tour). She has also recently worked as a tutor at RWCMD in puppetry and has been coordinating the third year design exhibition. This year she has also been a design lecturer and a tutor in model-making for the University of Aberystwyth. Holly is incredibly proud to have worked as part of the Scenofest team at the 2007 Prague Quadrennial Exhibition.

LAURA McEWEN 100

Laura has a first class degree in theatre design from Nottingham Trent University. She has designed for numerous companies including York Theatre Royal, Nottingham Playhouse, Southwark Playhouse, Sheffield Crucible, Polka Theatre, Red Earth Theatre, Unicorn Theatre, Oxfordshire Theatre Company, Lakeside Arts Centre, Pilot Theatre and the English National Opera Bayliss Programme. Her most recent work includes *A Day in the Death of Joe Egg* (Nottingham Playhouse), *Skitterbang Island* (Polka Theatre) and *Bomber's Moon* (Lakeside Arts Centre). She enjoys designing for a range of spaces and this has included studios, main stages, parks, community centres, school halls, classrooms and site-specific environments. In 2005 Laura won the Manchester Evening News Design Award for *Beautiful Thing* (Pilot Theatre Company, Bolton Octagon). As well as designing, she frequently works as a creative workshop leader, employed by theatre-in-education companies, youth theatres, galleries, schools and community groups. She has designed the Unicorn Theatre's summer programme of education work for the last four years and, most recently, directed a 10-week course in theatre design for Clean Break theatre company.

Laura has a specific interest in new and devised work and is associate director of Red Earth Theatre Company.

www.lauramcewen.co.uk

IONA McLEISH 120

Since graduating in theatre design at Wimbledon School of Art, Iona has enjoyed an extensive self-employed career as a designer for theatre. These range from productions such as *Women of Troy* (Olivier Theatre RNT); *For the Love of a Nightingale*, by Timberlake Wertenbaker (RSC Barbican); *India Song*, with Annie Castledine and Annabel Arden (Theatr Clwyd); through to middle scale and fringe, notably *Arturo Ui*, with Simon Callow (Half Moon Theatre), *Pal Joey*, with Dennis Lawson and Siân Phillips (New Half Moon and The Albery Theatre); *The Merchant of Venice*, directed by Michael Attenborough (Young Vic); and *Savannah Bay* (BAC and tour with Foco Novo). She received the London Theatre Award for Best Design with *Heresies* by Deborah Levy (RSC, Barbican). Iona has also been engaged as costume designer on various films and TV programmes. In recent years, design work has included *Heldenplatz* (Arcola Theatre Studio One), *Yours Abundantly, From Zimbabwe* (Oval House Theatre) and *Orla's Song*, a short film (Hoffman Productions).

Complementing and throughout her design career she also enjoyed her work as a lecturer in design for performance at a range of colleges and art schools.

She is Joint Honorary Secretary of the Society of British Theatre Designers.

PREMA MEHTA 101

Prema graduated from Guildhall School of Music and Drama, London. She works as a freelance lighting designer for dance and theatre.

Her recent drama lighting designs include *The Great Extension* (Theatre Royal Stratford East), *The Snow Queen* (Derby Playhouse), *The Massacre* (Theatre Royal, Bury St. Edmunds), Propeller season (Gate Theatre, London), *Knock Against My Heart*, in collaboration with Nós Do Morro (Unicorn Theatre and UK tour), *Year 10* (Mettre en Scène, Rennes, and Théâtre National de Strasbourg) and *The Electric Hills* (Liverpool Everyman).

Dance and music lighting designs include The Puppini Sisters (Bloomsbury Theatre), *Swingin' in Mid Dream* (Albany Theatre), *Dance Ihayami* (tour), *The Ring Cycle* (Derby Dance), *Trail* (national tour), *Spill* (Düsseldorf, Germany), *Flat Feet* (South Bank Centre), *Fine Line* (The Place, London), *Parallels* (Lilian Baylis, Sadler's Wells) and *The Penguin Café* (Cochrane Theatre).

www.premamehta.com

FRED MELLER 61

Fred is a freelance international scenographer and theatre designer and a senior lecturer at Central Saint Martins College of Art and Design, University of the Arts, London. She was educated at the University of Ulster and The Royal Welsh College of Music and Drama.

Fred received an Arts Council design bursary in scenography. Design work has included the Royal Shakespeare Company, Cardboard Citizens, Almeida, Gate Theatre, Royal National Theatre Studio, Watermill Theatre, Nuffield Theatre, Royal Court Theatre, Young Vic, Kaos and Grid Iron. The synthesis of the 'live' and recorded, performer and image is realised in spaces often other than theatre buildings: designing for spaces that include an old hospital, jam factory, a mortuary, a disused brothel, labyrinthine Victorian town hall cellars, a supermarket distribution complex and the biggest potting shed in Europe. She has created a broad and diverse range of work also for traditional theatre buildings.

Fred has exhibited at The Prague Quadrennial in 1999 and 2003, winning the Golden Triga and was selected to exhibit at World Stage Design in Toronto, 2005, and in the Society of British Theatre Designers exhibitions. Her work is part of the V&A Museum permanent collection. Other awards include The Jerwood Design Award and a Year of the Artist award.

MIRANDA MELVILLE 45

Miranda studied theatre design at the Motley Theatre Design Course with Percy Harris.

She has designed extensively for theatre, opera, film and dance, while continuing fine art and, more recently, sculpture and installation. This includes co-designing a gold medal-winning garden at Chelsea Flower Show, and a large earthwork for Westonbirt International Garden Festival.

Her designs for opera and music theatre led to her designing the film biography of Handel, *Honour, Profit and Pleasure*, and Benjamin Britten's opera *Owen Wingrave*, which he wrote especially for TV.

After a period of working solely in film she returned to theatre design as a result of designing a number of dance films, including *Cross Channel* with The Cholmondeleys and The Featherstonehaughs, and *Outside In* with Candoco. She designed predominantly for dance and multi-disciplinary companies, notably Yolanda Snaith Theatre Dance and V-TOL Dance Company, with whom she collaborated on their large education projects and designed many productions. She also designed the *Move-Me Booth*, an interactive video/dance booth, for Goat and Ricochet Dance Company.

She has collaborated with Bobby Baker, designing *How to Live*, and continues to work with Electric Voice Theatre, for whom she designed the opera film *Scipio's Dream* by Judith Weir, Vinao's opera *Rashomon* for the Almeida, and *Ircam*, *Bagdad Monologues* and Lovat's *The City Weeps*.

Previous designs for Volcano includes their production of *Private Lives*.

MADELEINE MILLAR 87

Madeleine trained at Trent Polytechnic, Nottingham and has a BA(Hons) in Theatre Design. She has been working as a set and costume designer for over 25 years, mostly in touring theatre, youth theatre, theatre in education and opera. Since 2001 she has also been designing for TV and film (for example, four series of *Last of the Summer Wine*). Two of the 15 or so short films for which she was costume designer – *Goodbye Mr Snuggles* and *Private Life* – are winning awards all over the world. She is also currently designing *The Bartered Bride* for Surrey Opera. Madeleine has also exhibited sculpture at galleries such as the Christchurch Mansion and Wolsey Art Gallery, Ipswich, and Piece Hall, Halifax.

www.mmillar.freeuk.com

ANNE MINORS PERFORMANCE CONSULTANTS 55

Anne Minors Performance Consultants are fast becoming world leaders in spaces that look beautiful, operate smoothly and sound excellent. With completed projects in Central Asia, North America, Canada and the Middle East as well as in the UK. We are devoted to creating the best conditions for presenting and enjoying performances.

Since 1996 the practice has been briefing, planning and equipping performance spaces, working with directors, performers and architects to explore and extend the boundaries of performance architecture. We do not deal in formulaic solutions but create concepts for performance spaces from the ingredients unique to each project, its client and location.

AMPC believe in the triumvirate of architect, performance consultant and acoustician working together to design facilities with the best possible acoustics, sightlines, technical facilities and ambience. Past projects include the Royal Opera House redevelopment and Linbury Studio, Covent Garden (Dixon Jones and BDP, architects); Koerner Hall, Royal Conservatory of Music, Toronto (KPMB, architects); Palace of Peace and Reconciliation, Kazakhstan (Foster + Partners); The Egg Children's Theatre, Bath (Haworth Tompkins); the Barbican Theatre refurbishment and a prize-winning competition for the Abu Dhabi Performing Arts Centre (Zaha Hadid, architects). AMPC also designed the seating system for the Roundhouse in Camden and were instrumental in developing the 1,000 seat thrust template for the Royal Shakespeare Company.

BECKY MINTO 124

Becky trained in theatre design at Royal Welsh College of Music and Drama and in interior design at Liverpool College. She has worked across Scotland as a set and costume designer for companies including National Theatre Scotland, the Royal Lyceum, Grid Iron, Visible Fictions, Vanishing Point, Wee Stories, Perth Rep, Borderline, 7:84, The Byre, Tag and Citizens Theatre. She has designed a wide range of productions for main-house shows, site-specific and large outdoor spectacles and small- to large-scale tours. She was nominated for Best Design for *Lost Ones;* costume design (*Vanishing Point*, 2005); Manchester Evening News Awards 2006 (*Drenched*, Boilerhouse) and for Critics Awards for Theatre in Scotland 2008 (*The Emperor's New Kilt*, Wee Stories). Apart from traditional theatre spaces, she has designed productions and installations in a forest, a disused tyre factory, a boathouse in Norway, Barony Bar, Edinburgh, and converted a 4m × 4m office into a Japanese tea room at the Assembly Rooms.

Outside of theatre she works as a freelance design mentor at Royal Scottish Academy of Music and Drama and teaches set design on the performance costume degree course at Edinburgh College of Art. Upcoming projects include *Cargo* (Iron-Oxide/Edinburgh Mela); *Playback*, a site-specific production for Ankur Productions; and designer for *Walk the Planks*, a production for the opening ceremony of the European Capital of Culture, Turku, Finland, in 2011.

NICK MORAN 76

Nick has worked professionally in the performance industries as a lighting designer and programmer, lighting engineer and production manager for over 25 years. He has been working in higher education since 2003 and continues to practice as a designer.

A representative selection of recent professional credits includes *The Masked Ball* (G Verdi and A Somma), English National Opera (London Coliseum, 2003): *Bullie's House* (T Keneally) for Border Crossings (Phoenix, Leicester, and ACE Tour, 2004); setting and lighting design for *Love is a Dog Called Hell* (Bukowski), WienFest (MuseumsQuartier, Vienna, 2005); *Music Lessons* and *The Wedding Party*, a double bill for CSSD (2007); *Dilemma of a Ghost* (Ama Ata Aidoo) for Border Crossings, 2007 (Africa Centre, Soho, and ACE Tour); set, projection and lighting design for *It Must Be Madness*, a devised musical for CSSD (Embassy Studio, 2008); set design for *Oliver's Army* (2009) and lighting design for *Keeping the Faith* (2010), both written and directed by Fiona Laird (Webber Douglas Studio for CSSD); lighting design for *Re-Orientations* (Soho Theatre, September, 2010), directed by Michael Walling and devised by the company for Border Crossings.

Nick is the author of *Performance Lighting Design* (A&C Black, London, 2007) and a regular contributor to FOCUS, the journal of the Association of Lighting Designers. He is a member of the executive of the Association of Lighting Designers (ALD), and was the co-convenor of the scenography working group of The Theatre & Performance Research Association (TaPRA), 2007–10.

CATHERINE MORGAN 108

Catherine graduated from Nottingham Trent University with a first class honours degree in theatre design. While there, she collaboratively devised and designed shows including *The Pit and the Pendulum* (Waverly Studio Theatre) and *Counting Footsteps*, which was showcased at the International Festival *Test!* in Croatia. Design credits include *Verona Road* (St Saviour's Church); *Love, Lies and London* (Southwark Playhouse); *What Shall We Tell Caroline?* (White Bear Theatre); *Macbeth* and *Hobson's Choice* (Broadway Theatre Catford); *The Ostrich and the Dolphin* (national tour, including the Royal Institution); and *Mercury Fur* (Hertford Bop Cellar, Oxford). She worked as a design assistant on *The Hotel*, directed by acclaimed comedian Mark Watson (Edinburgh Fringe). For Punchdrunk she worked as a design assistant on *The Clod and The Pebble* (a secret show in a shop off Carnaby Street) and as a scenic artist on *Masque of the Red Death* (Battersea Arts Centre). She has acted as an assistant designer to Helen Goddard on productions including *The Spanish Tragedy* (Arcola Theatre).

MARTIN MORLEY 64

Martin trained at Wimbledon School of Art, 1963–66. He first worked as a design assistant at the Royal Lyceum Theatre, Edinburgh. While there, designed three productions.

From 1969–72 Martin was head of design at the Liverpool Playhouse, designing a wide range of plays from Shakespeare to Bond. There followed a lengthy period as designer for Cwmni Theatr Cymru (1973–84). With them he learnt the skills of designing touring productions for a wide range of venues. The repertoire was mainly Welsh and ranged from contemporary writing to translations of European classics. It was a very stimulating period.

In 1985 Martin went freelance and started to design for TV, which now dominates his output – notably *Hedd Wyn* (BAFTA Cymru 1993 with Jane Roberts for Best Design) and a string of drama series for S4C. During this period he designed several productions for Theatr Gwynedd, Bangor, including *Pwy Sy'n Sal* (a Molière double bill), directed by Graham Laker and Firenza Guidi (exhibited in Time + Space); *Dyn Hysbys* (*The Faith Healer*) by Brian Friel, directed by Siân Summers (exhibited in Time + Space and the 1999 Prague Quadrennial); and in 1999 *Amadeus*, directed by Graham Laker. This was exhibited in the 2D>3D exhibition in Sheffield.

For Theatr Genedlaethol Cymru Martin designed *Hen Rebel* in 2005 (exhibited at Collaborators) and *Cysgod y Cryman* in 2007.

In 2008 he designed the set for *Llyfr Mawr y Plant*, the exhibit in Transformation and Revelation (a joint production between Theatr Bara Caws, Theatr Gwynedd and Galeri).

PETER MUMFORD 117

Peter studied stage design at the Central School of Art under Ralph Koltai. He was a founder member of mixed media theatre group Moving Being, designing sets, projections and lighting (1969–78). During the 1980s he was a founder member of Second Stride Dance Company (Siobhan Davies, Richard Alston and Ian Spink). Many contemporary dance works with Rambert Dance, London Contemporary Dance Theatre, the Royal Ballet, and the Siobhan Davies Company. In the late 80s he formed Dancelines Productions, a TV and film production company specialising in dance and music productions, commissioning many new pieces for television.

Most recently: *Carmen, Madame Butterfly, Peter Grimes*, 125th Gala (Metropolitan Opera, New York); *A Streetcar Named Desire* (Guthrie Theater Minneapolis); *Drunk Enough to Say I Love You* (also The Public Theater, NYC), *Cock, Dying City* (also set design) and *The Seagull* (also Broadway), *Sucker Punch* (Royal Court); *The Misanthrope, Prick Up Your Ears* (Comedy Theatre, London); *A View from the Bridge* (Duke of York's); *Pictures From an Exhibition* (Young Vic); *Parlour Song, Cloud Nine* (Almeida); *All's Well That Ends Well, The Reporter, The Hothouse, Exiles* (National Theatre); *A Midsummer Night's Dream, Miss Julie* (The Rose); *Petrushka*, and set design for *Carmen* (Scottish Ballet); *Faust, Elegy For Young Lovers, Punch and Judy, Bluebeard's Castle* (English National Opera); *Prima Donna* (MIF); *Take Five, E=mc²* (BRB); *Siegfried, Götterdämmerung, Fidelio, Two Widows, Don Giovanni* (Scottish Opera); *Eugene Onegin, The Bartered Bride* (Royal Opera House).

Peter directed and designed the European premiere of *Earth and the Great Weather* (John Luther-Adams), Almeida Opera, 2000; and *The Man with the Wind at his Heels* (Kevin Volans); co-directed, designed sets and lighting for *L'Heure Espagnole* and *L'enfant et Les Sortileges*, Opera Zuid. Set/lighting design includes *Un Ballo in Maschera* for Vilnius Festival and *32 Cryptograms*, Scottish Ballet (Ashley Page), and *Peter Pan* for Northern Ballet Theatre.

2003 Olivier Award for *Bacchai* and 1995 Olivier Award for Dance.

www.petermumford.info

RUARI MURCHISON 120

Ruari has designed productions in Helsinki (Finland), Washington DC (USA), The Stratford Festival (Canada), Stuttgart (Germany), Luzern (Switzerland), Haarlem (Holland), Elsinore (Denmark) and many regional theatres in the United Kingdom.

Recent design credits include *Mappa Mundi, Frozen, The Waiting Room* and *The Red Balloon* (National Theatre); *Titus Andronicus* (Royal Shakespeare Company); *Othello* (Trafalgar Studios); *The Solid Gold Cadillac* (Garrick); *A Busy Day* (Lyric Theatre); *Peggy Sue Got Married* (Shaftsbury Theatre); *The Snowman* (Peacock Theatre); *Toyer* (Arts); *The Three Sisters On Hope Street, The Glass Room* and *Gone to LA* (Hampstead Theatre); *Henry IV Parts I & II* (Washington Shakespeare Company, USA); *West Side Story* and *The Sound of Music* (Stratford Festival, Canada); *Hamlet* (Elsinore, Denmark); *Pravda, The Critic* and *The Real Inspector Hound* (Chichester); *Macbeth, Medea, The Lion, the Witch and the Wardrobe* and *The Secret Garden* (West Yorkshire Playhouse); *An Enemy of the People* (Theatr Clwyd); *Arthur and George, Cling to Me Like Ivy, Uncle Vanya, A Doll's House*, the David Hare trilogy *Racing Demon, Absence of War* and *Murmuring Judges* (TMA Best Design nomination, 2003), *The Tempest, Macbeth, Hamlet* and *His Dark Materials* (Birmingham Repertory Theatre); *Intemperance* and *Tartuffe* (Everyman and Playhouse Theatres, Liverpool); *Copenhagen* and *Alfie* (Palace Theatre, Watford).

Opera credits include *Der Freischütz* (Finnish National Opera); *Peter Grimes, Così Fan Tutte* (Luzerner Opera); *La Cenerentola, Il Barbiere di Siviglia* (Garsington); *l'Italiana in Algeri* (Buxton); *Les Pelerins de la Mecque, ZaZa* (Wexford).

Ballet credits include *Bruise Blood* (Shobana Jeyasingh Dance Company); *Landschaft und Erinnerung* (Stuttgart Ballet, Germany); and *The Protecting Veil* (Birmingham Royal Ballet).

CONOR MURPHY 109

Conor trained at Wimbledon School of Art and later gained an MA in scenography in Utrecht, Holland.

His opera designs include *The Magic Flute* (Korean National Opera); *Salome* (Montpellier and Korean National Opera); *Powder Her Face* (Royal Opera House Linbury Theatre); *Wake* and *The Turn of the Screw* (Nationale Reisopera); *The Rake's Progress* (Angers-Nantes); *The Rape of Lucretia* (Flanders Opera); *Susannah* (Wexford); *Greek* (Queen Elizabeth Hall); *The Country of the Blind* (Aldeburgh); *The Lighthouse* (Neue Oper Wien); *The Marriage of Figaro* (Grange Park); *La Bohème* (Augsburg); *Un Ballo in Maschera* (Opera Zuid, Holland), *Facing Goya* by Michael Nyman (tour of Spain and Italy) and *Die Versicherung* (Darmstadt). He has also designed sets for *Olav Tryggvasson* (Norwegian Opera); *The Flying Dutchman* (Opera Zuid) and *Il Trovatore* (ENO).

Designs for dance include *The Four Seasons* (Birmingham Royal Ballet); *Giselle, A Midsummer Night's Dream* and *Carmen* (Donlon Dance Company); and *Attempting Beauty* (Munich).

Theatre includes *Hoors* (Traverse); *The Birthday Party* (Bristol Old Vic); *The Resistible Rise of Arturo Ui, The Crucible, Woman and Scarecrow* and *The Rivals* (Abbey Theatre); *Life is a Dream, Attempts on Her Life* and *Dream of Autumn* (Rough Magic, Dublin); *The Real Thing* (Gate, Dublin); *Major Barbara, The Playboy of the Western World* and *Sex, Chips and Rock 'n' Roll* (Royal Exchange); *Salome* (Riverside Studios); *Measure for Measure* (English Touring Theatre); *Summer Begins* (Donmar); and *The Decameron* (Gate Theatre).

MIRIAM NABARRO 74

Miriam is a London-based artist, scenographer and photographer. She trained at the European Scenography Centres (Central Saint Martins, London; HKU, Utrecht; and DAMU, Prague), and holds degrees in English literature from Edinburgh University and in political science from SOAS, University of London. Between 1999 and 2004 she worked extensively as an aid worker, running creative arts programmes for children affected by conflict in DRC, Sudan, Eritrea, Kosova and Georgia. She continues to work as a visiting artist for the British Council in Syria and Georgia. Her current work includes *Palace of the End* for the Royal Exchange and Traverse Theatre (winner of the Amnesty International Freedom of Speech Award 2009); *The Great Game: Afghanistan* (with Pamela Howard) for Tricycle Theatre/US tour; *Dr Korczak's Example* (Royal Exchange, Best Studio Production 2008), and is informed by her commitment to illuminating political themes with theatrical integrity. Other recent work includes *The Winter's Tale* (Headlong/Schtanhaus), *The Snow Queen* for Polka Theatre, and several Shakespeare productions for young people at the National Theatre. She is particularly interested in new writing, site-specific work and developing long-term working relationships with directors, writers and composers, as well as developing her own artistic practice. As an artist and printmaker, she exhibits regularly in the UK and internationally. In 2010, Miriam opened her first solo photographic exhibition, *SE1 9PX: Hidden Corners*, at the National Theatre.

KIMIE NAKANO 130

Kimie studied literature in Tokyo, theatre costume at ENSATT in Paris and theatre design at Wimbledon School of Art in London. She gained design assisting experience at Opera de Paris in France and Saito Kinen Festival in Japan 1997–99. She also assisted on costume for film, including *8½ Women* by Peter Greenaway.

She designed the award-winning *Yabu no Naka* (a modern Noh/Kyogen play), directed by Mansai Nomura, in Japan Art Festival, 1999; and the collaboration with Megumi Nakamura's *Sandflower* received the Gold award in the Maastricht Festival 2000 in Holland.

International work as a designer includes *Ali to Karim*, directed by Hafiz Karmali (USA tour, 2008); *Pas, Pas Moi, Va et Vient* for a Beckett celebration at Theatre National Populaire (Lyon, 2006); *The Oslo Experiment* (Stratos, Oslo, 2007, and in UK); *2Graves* (Arts Theatre and Edinburgh Festival, 2006). She continues to work in various media such as film, video, animation, installation and illustration, and has designed for the short film *Basho* (2008).

Directorial credits in UK include *Snow*, a workshop with three blind singers (ENO studio); *8:15* for the Rambert Dance Company; and a collaboration with Eda Megumi, *Sandflower*, in Den Haag.

She strives to create intercultural projects for the stage, workshops and films, to promote world cultures.

www.kimienakano.com

DODY NASH 112

With a background in classical music, ballet and fine art, Dody's education included foundation (Central Saint Martins), English/history of art (York University), design (Motley) and assisting designers for ENO. Much of her work is music-based design for opera, dance and installation. She also creates spaces for the general public: *The Sonic Garden* was created in 2008 for the London Festival of Architecture. Dody is recognised internationally for the *Listening Shell* sound sculpture (South Bank Centre/London Sinfonietta, 2004). This was for a major installation about Berio for which Dody was also creative director. This led to developing technically innovative designs with DuPont, which were exhibited at Royal Festival Hall, 100% Design, A Grand Design (V&A), Designer Days (Paris) and featured in the international design press. Designs for *The Merry Widow* (Scottish Opera, 2008) also received critical acclaim.

Recent work includes projects with ROH Development, Jette Parker Young Artists (ROH), *Swanhunter* (Opera North), and *Orfeo ed Euridice* (Classical Opera Company). Dody is a dance addict: she sees, designs and writes about it, and occasionally commissions, devises and performs. She is Visiting Practitioner at Central Saint Martins (MA Innovation Design) and has devised projects with young people for ENO, ROH, Opera North, Glyndebourne and for the Royal Designers for Industry's renowned summer school. Her work is archived as a resource for the Sorrell Foundation's Joinedupdesign programme.

PIP NASH 128

Pip trained at Dartington College of Arts and on the Motley Theatre Design Course. Her work as a designer over nearly 30 years has encompassed new writing, repertory, devised and community theatre, and theatre and dance in education. Recently she has been mostly involved in participatory and site-specific theatre projects, intergenerational performance, installations and exploring performance work in galleries, non-theatre and outdoor settings.

Pip is interested in the ways in which creativity, particularly of theatre design practice, interacts with theatre that deals with social engagement. To what extent is the theatre designer an artist, facilitator, initiator or participant within theatre making, that is focused on an inclusive and collaborative process, rather than particular outcomes.

Pip works as a freelance designer, workshop leader, and as lecturer at Rose Bruford College.

PIPPA NISSEN 26

Pippa has worked extensively as a theatre designer and as an architect. She is director in the practice Pippa Nissen Studio which she formed in January 2010. Previously she was partner in the award-winning Nissen Adams architecture practice.

Current and recent theatre work includes film and design work for *The Way to the Sea* (Aldeburgh Festival, with director Netia Jones); film work for Teatro Di Varese concerts at the Queen Elizabeth Hall and Royal Festival Hall, with Cathie Boyd; *Elephant and Castle* for Aldeburgh Music, dir. Tim Hopkins; *Paper Nautilus* (Theatre Cryptic, dir. Cathy Boyd); and a film for *Nothing Like The Sun*, settings of Shakespeare sonnets, with composer Gavin Bryars for Opera North Projects.

Pippa previously collaborated with Cathy Boyd on *A Midsummer Night's Dream* for the RSAMD in Glasgow.

Other work includes *Transfigured Night* and *Forest Murmurs* (Opera North); *The Rake's Progress* (Hannover); *Mare Nostrum* and *Eugene Onegin* (Basel); *Kantan/Damask Drum* (Almeida Opera and Aldeburgh Festival), all with dir. Tim Hopkins; *Breaking the Code* (Northampton), dir. Philip Wilson; *The Boy Who Left Home* and *Faust* (ATC), dir. Nick Philippou; *Normal Programming Will Resume Shortly*, live video projects and *Eugene Onegin* (Clonter Opera and Buxton Festival), both with director Netia Jones.

Pippa Nissen Studio works on different scale projects including theatre, architecture, exhibition and film work. Recent exhibition work includes the *Telling Tales* exhibition at the V&A, and she is working on *Once Upon a Wartime*, a children's war stories exhibition for the Imperial War Museum. In 2005 Pippa exhibited (at the Prague Biennale) a film looking at the relationship of architecture and theatre. Recent projects include: winning the international competition in 2005 for a new theatre in Gdansk, Poland, and the refurbishment of the Gate Theatre, London. In 2005 Pippa was selected for the *40 Under 40* exhibition at the V&A, which toured the country. She also art directed the film *Love for Sale*, directed by Carey Born. Pippa also runs a diploma unit for architecture students at Kingston University.

TIMOTHY O'BRIEN 98

Timothy was born in India and educated at Cambridge and the Yale Drama School. From the 50s he worked in television and West End theatre before being invited by Peter Hall to be an associate artist of the RSC in 1966.

He has collaborated crucially with the directors John Barton, Peter Hall, David Jones, Harold Prince, Terry Hands, Elijah Moshinsky, Hans Werner Henze, Gotz Friedrich, Maximilian Schell, Harold Pinter and Graham Vick.

Early on, there was talk of his designing *The Ring*. Fortunately, this came to nothing. Late in his career, he was invited by Graham Vick to work on *The Ring* in Lisbon, by which time he understood better that experience transforms you and that designing in the theatre is alchemy, giving life and new meaning to spaces and materials.

He was involved in the birth of the Society of British Theatre Designers and in British participations at the Prague Quadrennial, beginning with the first in 1976. He was chairman of the SBTD 1983–91; elected a Royal Designer for Industry in 1991 and was Master of the Faculty of RDIs 1999–2001. Some of his designs survive in the Robert Tobin Collection in San Antonio, Texas.

FRANCIS O'CONNOR 114

Francis trained at Wimbledon School of Art. He has designed operas, plays and musicals in the UK and around the world.

Collaborating with directors, performers and technicians is the best part of the job!

GUY O'DONNELL 80

Guy trained at the Royal Welsh College of Music and Drama and qualified in 1996.

He has designed for Theatr Na n'Óg, Spectacle Theatre, Hijinx Theatre, Sherman Theatre and Theatr Genedlaethol Cymru.

Guy is also an arts development officer for Bridgend County Borough Council.

CHRISTOPHER ORAM 128

For the Donmar: *Passion, Red* (also New York – Critics' Circle Award, Tony Award); *Hamlet* (also New York); *Madame de Sade, Twelfth Night, Ivanov, Othello, Parade* (also Los Angeles); *Frost/Nixon* (also Gielgud, New York and US tour); *Guys and Dolls* (Piccadilly); *Don Juan in Soho, Grand Hotel, Henry IV, World Music, Caligula* (Evening Standard Award), *The Vortex, Privates on Parade, Merrily We Roll Along, Passion Play, Good* and *The Bullet*.

Theatre includes *Backbeat* (Citizens Theatre, Glasgow); *A View from the Bridge* (Duke of York's); *King Lear/The Seagull* (RSC); *Evita* (Adelphi); *Macbeth, The Jew of Malta, The Embalmer* (Almeida); *Danton's Death, Stuff Happens, Marriage Play/Finding the Sun, Summerfolk, Power* – Olivier Award (National Theatre); *Oleanna* (Garrick); *Loyal Women, Fucking Games* (Royal Court); *The Caretaker, All My Sons* (Bristol Old Vic). For Sheffield Crucible: *Suddenly Last Summer* (also Albery – Critics' Circle Award), *The Tempest* (also Old Vic), *Richard III, Don Juan, Edward II, The Country Wife, Six Degrees of Separation* and *As You Like It* (also Lyric Hammersmith).

Film: *The Magic Flute*.

Opera: *Billy Budd* (Glyndebourne) and *Madam Butterfly* (Houston).

BEK PALMER 62

Bek trained in theatre design at LIPA and, later, post graduate theatre design at Royal Welsh College of Music and Drama.

She has designed various productions encompassing main stage, touring, community theatre, youth theatre, educational projects, drama, opera and children's theatre. Previous set and costume designs include *A Midsummer Night's Dream* (British Touring Shakespeare); *The Provoked Wife* (The Courtyard Theatre); the opera *Cendrillon* (Sherman Theatre, Cardiff); *Dr Korczak's Example* (Birmingham Young Rep Company); *Godfather Death* (Warhorse Theatreworks); *My Mother Told Me Not to Stare* (Theatre Hullabaloo and Action Transport); and *The Night Pirates* (Theatre Hullabaloo). She specialises in designing and making puppets, some of which have recently featured in *A Christmas Carol* (Greenwich Playhouse), *Sweeney Todd* (Finger in the Pie Productions) and *High Muck-a-Muck* and *Cobbo* (Theatre Alibi).

Bek has an interest in immersive performance for unusual spaces, that she has developed by working on a couple of Punchdrunk's projects, most recently as a member of the design team for *The Duchess of Malfi*, a collaboration with ENO. Other work includes prop-making for theme parks and corporate events and wardrobe mistress for pantomimes and onboard production shows on the Cunard fleet of ships.

JOANNA PARKER   28

Designer and senior lecturer in scenography at the Central School of Speech & Drama – course leader, MA Scenography.

Joanna trained at London Contemporary Dance School and was a recipient of an Arts Council design bursary. Theatre designs include work for Lightwork, Complicite, West Yorkshire Playhouse, Salisbury Playhouse, The Gate, Young Vic and Hampstead Theatre; opera designs for the Royal Opera House, English Touring Opera, Opera Theatre Company, Dublin, and Scottish Opera; dance designs for The Cholmondeleys, Shobana Jeyasingh Dance Company, London Contemporary Dance Theatre and other independent dance companies.

Current research: inter-textual design; improvisational processes within performance design/choreography; theatre architecture and its interface with the scenographic object.

ROMA PATEL   23

Roma is multidisciplinary theatre maker. Her work explores the potentiality of various media from scenography to virtual reality, video projections, art installations and interactive exhibitions. She comes from a traditional scenography background, but the increase in access to digital technology has had a profound impact on her work.

Roma's work has also been exhibited internationally at the Prague Quadrennial, International Exhibition of Scenography and Theatre Architecture in 2007, where her designs were part of both the British and Irish exhibitions. Her digital interactive work of *The Tempest* was seen at the V&A Museum at a national exhibition for theatre design, *Collaborators*, in 2008. Since the exhibition ended in August 2008, the piece has been acquired by V&A as part of their permanent collection.

She trained at Wimbledon College of Art (set design for stage and screen) and went on to complete an MA in scenography (1999) at Birmingham Institute of Art and Design. She has designed digital installations, stage sets and projections for companies in UK, Ireland and Netherlands since 1998.

Her recent theatre work includes *Knock Against Your Heart* (2008) and *Romeo in the City* (2007) for the Theatre Centre; a large-scale site-specific production of *The Tempest* on a pond in Cork (2006); and *The Merchant of Venice* (2005). Since 2005 she has been teaching at Nottingham Trent University.

MICHAEL PAVELKA   57

Michael trained at Wimbledon School of Art.

He designed Lindsay Anderson's *The Fishing Trip* and *Holiday* (Old Vic); with Edward Hall and Propeller Theatre Company, world tours of *Henry V, Rose Rage (Henry VI)* at the Theatre Royal Haymarket and Chicago Shakespeare Theatre, transferring to New York (Best Costume Design nomination, Chicago's Jeff Awards); *The Taming of the Shrew* (RSC's Complete Works) with *Twelfth Night* (Old Vic). He won TMA Best Set Design 2009 for *The Merchant of Venice*.

Library Theatre, Manchester, productions include *The Life of Galileo* (Best Design, MEN Awards); *Measure for Measure, The Resistible Rise of Arturo Ui, The Caucasian Chalk Circle, Angels in America, Oliver Twist,* and *The Good Soul of Szechuan.*

Dance: *Revelations* (QEH) and *Off the Wall* (South Bank Centre) with Liam Steel, and *Stan Won't Dance.*

International work includes *Twelfth Night* (Seattle Repertory Company) and *Death of a Salesman* (Gate, Dublin), both with David Esbjornson. He designed the first African language *Mother Courage and Her Children* (National Theatre Uganda, USA and RSA).

Other West End productions include *The Constant Wife, How the Other Half Loves, Other People's Money, Leonardo, Blues in the Night* (also Dublin, New York and Tokyo), *Absurd Person Singular, Macbeth, A Midsummer Night's Dream* and *A Few Good Men.*

RSC productions include *The Odyssey, Two Gentlemen of Verona, Henry V* and *Julius Caesar*; and for the National Theatre (Olivier), *Edmond* with Kenneth Branagh.

JOHN PAWSON   69

John's work focuses on ways of approaching fundamental problems of space, proportion, light and materials. Often labelled as 'minimalist', he is known for his rigorous process of design.

Projects have spanned a wide range of scales and building typologies, ranging from private houses to Calvin Klein's flagship store in Manhattan and airport lounges for Cathay Pacific in Hong Kong, to a condominium for Ian Schrager on New York's Gramercy Park, sets for ballet and the interior of a 50 metre yacht.

Recognition includes RIBA awards for the Sackler Crossing at the Royal Botanic Gardens, Kew, and the Frate Sole International Prize for Sacred Architecture for the new Cistercian monastery of Our Lady of Novy Dvur in Bohemia.

In June 2010 John won an international competition to transform London's Grade II-listed former Commonwealth Institute building as the new home of the Design Museum.

Exhibitions on his work include *Plain Space*, held at the Design Museum in 2010–11, for which he created a site-specific installation.

Publications include *John Pawson Plain Space, Minimum, John Pawson: Leçons du Thoronet, John Pawson Works.*

His collaboration with Wayne McGregor, *Chroma*, received the Critics' Circle National Dance Award for Best Choreography and the Laurence Olivier Award for Best New Dance Production. In 2011 he designed the set for a new work by Wayne McGregor for the Paris Opera Ballet, *L'Anatomie de la Sensation*, inspired by the work of Francis Bacon, with music by Mark Anthony Turnage.

XRISTINA PENNA   114

Xristina has been working internationally as a designer for theatre and performance, as an art director and performance maker.

Currently she is the artistic director of the aswespeakproject creating mixed media and installation work: creator/designer with associate artist Julieta Kilgelmann for *I Know This… I Do This All the Time (I Don't Like It Though)*, an interactive performance installation (Shunt Vaults and Area 10, London, 2009; Byzantine Museum, Athens, 2009; Benaki Museum of Modern Art, Athens, 2010, as part of *Locus Solus* by Outofthebox Intermedia).

Site-specific designer for *Black Tonic* by The Other Way Works, Manchester, 2008.

Designer/associate artist for *A Kiss from the Last Red Squirrel* by Elyssa Livergant and *Rough Memory* (Camden People's Theatre and Shunt Vaults, 2008; Spill Festival, 2009).

Art director in film for *Revolution* by Kate Moyse (London, 2007).

Founding member of Poemstomyotherself, a collective of visual and theatre artists: artistic director/designer for *Holes* by Gabriella Svenningsen (Round Chapel, London, 2007).

Event designer for *Metropolis* by Future Cinema (Fabric, London, 2006).

Stage designer for *One Bird's Only Voice* by George Papadopoulos, director Melina Mascha (Experimental Stage of the National Theatre Greece, Athens, 2003).

Xristina has an MA in scenography from Central Saint Martins College of Art and Design with financial support from the Alexander Onassis Foundation, and a BA from the School of Drama, Aristotle University, Thessaloniki, Greece.
www.xristinapenna.com

CELIA PERKINS   115

Celia trained in theatre design at Croydon College and the Slade School of Fine Art, graduating in 1990. She became assistant scenic artist at the Manchester Library Theatre, then joined the Oldham Coliseum in 1993 as design assistant, becoming head of design until 2002. Whilst resident at the Coliseum she designed over 30 productions, ranging from traditional pantomimes to musicals, straight plays and comedies.

Celia is now a freelance designer, designing the annual Oldham Coliseum Pantomime, dance pieces and theatre productions in the North West.

TOM PIPER   58

Originally planning to be a biologist, Tom graduated from Trinity College, Cambridge, before training in theatre design at the Slade School of Art. He was then lucky to be able to assist on Peter Brook's production of *The Tempest* before beginning to work in fringe and regional theatre. His collaboration with Michael Boyd began in the early 90s with pantos at the Tron Theatre, Glasgow, followed by a production of *Macbeth*, which brought them to the attention of the Royal Shakespeare Company. He has since designed over 30 productions at the RSC, including the epic eight-play *Histories* cycle, which won the Olivier Award for Best Costume Design. As associate designer for the company, he has been heavily involved in the design of the temporary courtyard theatre and the new Royal Shakespeare Theatre, and is proud to have set up a trainee designer scheme to give young designers their first chance to experience large-scale work. He also works freelance for numerous theatres such as the Abbey Dublin, Traverse, Dundee Rep and recently on the Bridge Project productions of *As You Like It* and *The Tempest*. As a relief from all the Shakespeare he is currently planning world domination with *Zorro the Musical*. He is married with five children, all girls.

POST WORKS   115

Post Works is a multidisciplinary art and design collective founded by Matthew Butcher and Melissa Appleton in 2008. Post Works operates across the fields of art, architecture and performance. Recent projects include the set design for Rosemary Butcher's *Episodes of Flight*, performed at the Riverside Studios, London; and a futurological tour of *Nottingham's Monuments of the Near Future*, commissioned by Nottingham Contemporary. Upcoming projects include a collaboration with Daria Martin and Rosemary Butcher, *Lapped Translated Lines*, a live performance and film installation for Sadler's Wells (autumn 2010) and *Writtle Calling*, a radio station and performance space to be installed at Writtle College, Essex in autumn 2010. Post Works are also currently collaborating with artist Pablo Bronstein on a forthcoming book on neo-Georgian architecture to be published by Koenig Publications in early 2011. Their work has been published in *Blueprint, The Architects' Journal* and *Icon* magazine. Both Matthew Butcher and Melissa Appleton lecturer in architecture at the Bartlett School, Architectural Association and Nottingham University.

REBECCA PRIDE   116

Rebecca is a scenographer (formerly known as Rebecca Janaway) with over 20 years experience designing both set and costumes for major theatres, nationally and internationally. Trained in theatre design at the Slade, her work includes *Three Steps to Heaven*, dir. Clifford Milner (Watford Palace Theatre); *Love Me Slender*, dir. Marina Calderone (Perth Theatre and national tour); *Northanger Abbey, Snow White, Tess of the D'Urbervilles, Dick Whittington, Aladdin, Pumpboys and Dinettes, The Talk of the Steamie, Cold Sweat, Daisy Pulls it Off,* all dir. Marina Calderone (The Queens Theatre, Hornchurch); *The Long Mirror, What the Butler Saw,* also *Habeas Corpus,* dir. Marina Calderone (Theatr Clwyd).

Recent work as a designer includes productions of Brecht's *The Threepenny Opera*, Lope de Vegas' *Fuente Ovejuna!*, Schnitzler's *La Ronde*, Abi Morgan's *Tender* and Andrew Louden's *Mary Barton* (an adaptation of Mary Gaskell's novel).

Rebecca is currently course leader for BA(Hons) Costume with Performance Design at The Arts University College in Bournemouth. Alongside her work as a theatre practitioner Rebecca is engaged in research into effective teaching methodologies for designers. This work formed the body of her PGCE thesis on the idea of developing 'designer thinking' among student scenographers. The idea of creating 'the backstory' for set and costume design (in the manner of Stanislavski's 'method') has also been the focus of considerable research.

VERITY QUINN   36

Verity trained at Nottingham Trent, where she received a first-class honours in theatre design. She works across design, devising and making both site-specific and touring productions, often with puppetry and mask. Verity has worked with Northern Stage, The Sage (Gateshead), Vamos Theatre, Punchdrunk, WildWorks, Magnetic Events and Culture10 and The Empty Space. Verity is also joint artistic director of Left Luggage Theatre.

KATHERINA RADEVA 48

Katherina has been working professionally since 2005 after graduating from theatre design at Wimbledon School of Art. The same year she was a finalist at the Linbury Prize for Stage Design, working with Random Dance. Since then she has been designing for theatre and dance. Recent credits include *Moon Fool – Ill Met by Moonlight*, a Trestle & Moon Fool co-production (national tour); *The Glass Mountain*, a Trestle Theatre production (national tour, Trestle International Residency, Trestle Arts Base and Siobhan Davies Studios); *London Veil* by Horse and Bamboo Theatre (national mid-scale tour); *Fat Christ* (King's Head Theatre, London); *Pig Tales* by Julie McNamara (small-scale national tour); *The Underpants* by Steve Martin (Old Red Lion, London); *Hungry Ghosts* by Lost Dog (The Place, London, and international tour); and *Persona Non Grata* by Carlotta Miceli (The Place, London).

www.katherinaradeva.co.uk

COLIN RICHMOND 99

Colin trained at the Royal Welsh College of Music and Drama, Cardiff; first-class BA(Hons), Lord William's Prize for Achievement in Design, 2002 and 2003).

2003 Linbury Prize finalist and a resident designer as part of the Royal Shakespeare Company's trainee programme, 2004–5.

Colin's credits include *Entertaining Mr Sloane* (costumes); *Touched…* (set); *Ring Round the Moon, Bad Girls – The Musical*, the RSC production of *Breakfast With Mugabe* (all West End); *The Cherry Orchard, Dancing at Lughnasa, A Christmas Carol, Hapgood, The Bolt Hole, 'Low Dat* (Birmingham Rep Theatre); *Twelfth Night, Bad Girls – The Musical, Bollywood Jane, Salonika, Hapgood, Animal Farm, Billy Liar, A Christmas Carol* (West Yorkshire Playhouse); *L'Opera Seria* (Italy); *Hansel and Gretel* (Northampton Theatre Royal); *Play/Not I* (BAC); *Human Rites* (Southwark Playhouse); *Absent Friends* (Oldham Coliseum); *House of the Gods* (MTW/ Royal Opera House 2 and national tour); *Restoration* (Bristol Old Vic, Headlong Theatre); *The Shadow of a Gunman* (Glasgow Citizens); *Sweeney Todd, Europe, Hansel and Gretel* (Dundee Rep); *Suddenly Last Summer* (Theatr Clywd); *Europe* (Barbican); *The May Queen* (Liverpool Everyman); *Amadeus* (The Crucible, Sheffield); *All the Fun of the Fair* (Number One, national tour); *When We Are Married* (West Yorkshire Playhouse/Liverpool Playhouse); *La Bohème* (Holland Park); *The Lady In the Van* (Salisbury Playhouse); *Letters of a Love Betrayed* (Royal Opera House 2); *The Caucasian Chalk Circle* (Shared Experience); and *The Three Musketeers* (English Touring Theatre, Belgrade, and Traverse).

Television credits include *Doctor Who* (BBC Wales).

MALCOLM RIPPETH 127

Theatre includes *Brief Encounter* (Kneehigh, West End, Broadway, UK and US tours); *Six Characters in Search of an Author, Calendar Girls* (West End, UK and Australian tours); *Don John, Cymbeline* (Kneehigh/RSC); *The Red Shoes, Nights At the Circus* (Kneehigh); *The Devil Inside Him* (National Theatre Wales); *His Dark Materials* (Birmingham Rep and tour); *Edward Gant's Amazing Feats of Loneliness, Faustus* (Headlong); *Dark Side of Buffoon* (Coventry Belgrade); *The Grouch, Homage to Catalonia* (West Yorkshire Playhouse); *Hamlet, Mother Courage* (English Touring Theatre); *The Bloody Chamber, The Little Prince* (Northern Stage); *Confessions of a Justified Sinner, Copenhagen* (Edinburgh Royal Lyceum); *Kafka's Dick* (Watford Palace); *Cyrano de Bergerac* (Bristol Old Vic); *Monkey!* (Dundee Rep); *Tutti Frutti* (National Theatre of Scotland); *Dumb Show, The Winslow Boy* (Rose Kingston); *Spur of the Moment, Kin* (Royal Court).

Dance and opera includes *The Philosophers' Stone, Armida* (Garsington Opera); *Seven Deadly Sins* (WNO/Diversions Dance); *Designer Body, MaEternal, Blood, Sweat and Tears* (balletLORENT); and *Carmen Jones* (Royal Festival Hall).

Malcolm won the 2009 Theatregoers' Choice Award for Best Lighting Designer for *Brief Encounter* and *Six Characters in Search of an Author*, and a Village Voice OBIE Award as part of the design team for *Brief Encounter* at St. Ann's Warehouse, New York.

JOHN RISEBERO 83

John trained in theatre design at Central Saint Martins College of Art and Design, graduating with a first class degree.

He founded the theatre company Antic Disposition with director Ben Horslen in 2005. For the company he has co-directed and designed *Much Ado About Nothing, The Lion, the Witch and the Wardrobe, Richard III, A Christmas Carol* (St Stephen's, Hampstead); *Romeo and Juliet* (Jermyn Street/Teatr Elblągu, Poland); *The Importance of Being Earnest* (Jermyn Street/Festival Shakespeare du Quercy); *A Midsummer Night's Dream, Twelfth Night, Romeo and Juliet* (Festival Shakespeare du Quercy/ Cochrane); and *The Shakespeare Revue* (New End/UK tour).

Other design credits include *Megan Mullally and Supreme Music Program* (Vaudeville); *Christmas in New York* (Prince of Wales/Lyric); *Marilyn and Ella* (Apollo); *Alan Cumming: I Bought a Blue Car Today* (Vaudeville); *Closer* (ADC, Cambridge); *Golden Boy* (Yvonne Arnaud/UK tour); *The Barber of Seville* (Linbury Studio, Royal Opera House); *The Lover* (White Bear); *Evelina, Johnny Simple* (Pentameters); *Waking Up Suddenly* and *Heroes* (Blue Elephant).

Alongside his own design work, John has worked on numerous plays, musicals and operas as assistant designer, including productions in the West End, for the National Theatre, Glyndebourne, the Royal Opera, Birmingham Rep, Bill Kenwright and New Adventures, amongst many others.

John's design for *Closer* was part of the award-winning British exhibit at the Prague Quadrennial International Exhibition of Stage Design 2003.

www.johnrisebero.com

FRANCISCO RODRIGUEZ-WEIL 131

After obtaining a degree in architecture, Francisco completed the post graduate course in set and costumes design at the Bristol Old Vic Theatre School, graduating with distinction in 2000. Since then, he has worked in numerous productions in the UK and abroad ranging from dance, musical theatre, straight theatre and opera.

Some of his most loved designs include *Watercolours* (national tour); *Who Killed Mr Drum?* (Riverside Studios); *Alice in Wonderland* (national tour, Netherlands); *Robin Hood* (National Theatre, London); *The Beggar's Opera* (Welsh National Opera, touring show); *When We Are Married* (Bristol Old Vic); and *The School for Scandal* (Redgrave Theatre), among many others.

www.theatre-design.com

KATHRINE SANDYS 131

Kathrine is a practitioner, academic and doctoral researcher at Goldsmiths, University of London, working across live performance and the visual and audio arts. She predominantly uses space, sound, light and illusion in live performance, gallery installation and site-specific events. Commissions and collaborations nationally and internationally include *Vintage* at Goodwood; Opera North; Liverpool International Biennial of Contemporary Art; Harare International Festival of Arts; Royal Liverpool Philharmonic Orchestra; Tate Gallery; FACT; Stephen Berkoff; Prague Festival Ballet; Video Positive; The People Show; Realworld Records; Oxford Stage Company; Hemingway Design; New York ICFF; Glaxo Neurological Centre; and Liverpool Everyman Theatre. In 2002 she created the light environment for the award-winning *52 Degrees South* – opening presentation of the Imperial War Museum North.

At higher education level, her teaching includes design for both the purpose-built and non-purpose-built space, with emphasis on how the environment starts to inform our experience of the work through light, sound and structure.

She has directed devised work with performing and non-performing students in the UK and USA, blurring the perception of conventional performance and production roles. These have included filling a white cube space with soil for *Static*, and devised response works for *Striptease, The New York Avant-Garde, Philadelphia Street Stories*, Kurt Weill's *The Seven Deadly Sins* and the closing ceremony for *Liverpool, European Capital of Culture 2008*.

HANSJÖRG SCHMIDT 75

Hansjörg is a lighting designer and programme director of lighting design at Rose Bruford College. He graduated with a BA (first-class honours) in drama and theatre arts from Goldsmiths College, University of London and an MSc Built Environment: Light and Lighting from the Bartlett School, University College London.

Hansjörg particularly enjoys developing new work, often non text-based, in unusual spaces. He has built strong relationships with a handful of theatre makers and companies, such as Clod Ensemble, David Harradine and Sound&Fury.

Recent theatre designs in London: *The Forest* (Fevered Sleep); *Kursk* (Young Vic); *Under Glass* (Clod Ensemble); *Wedding Day at the Cro-Magnons* (Soho Theatre); *Red Ladies* (Clod Ensemble); *Camera Obscura* and *Going Off* (BAC); *The Taming of the Shrew* and *Performances* (Wilton's Music Hall); and *Saucy Jack and the Space Vixens* (West End).

Regional and touring: *Journey's End* (Mercury Theatre, Colchester); *Northanger Abbey* (Salisbury Playhouse); *Hospitalworks* (Theatre-Rites, London and Theater der Welt, Stuttgart). Other projects: Fortress exhibition at the Tower of London, collections by Jessica Ogden and Miki Fukai for London Fashion Week, The Beautiful Octopus Club and Unplugged for Heart 'n' Soul.

www.hansjorgschmidt.com

JOANNA SCOTCHER 25

Joanna completed a graduate design apprenticeship with the Royal Shakespeare Company in 2007. She received the York Prize for Theatre Design and was commissioned to design *Patient Number One* and the original site-specific version of *The Railway Children* at The National Railway Museum. Her work has specialised in promenade and site-responsive design, spaces from the epic to the intimate, including *Counted?* (County Hall Debating Chamber and West Yorkshire Playhouse); *The Caravan* (The Royal Court Theatre, Sloane Square); *The Roundhouse History: The Roundhouse and Economy* (Battersea Arts Centre, with Look Left Look Right Company). Her design for *Platform* (Old Vic New Voices), opened at the Old Vic Tunnels, Waterloo, in the winter of 2010, while *The Railway Children* (Waterloo) is extended to run into 2011. Her other design work includes *Inches Apart* (Old Vic New Voices Award at Theatre503); *Cardboard Dad* (Sherman Cymru Theatre); *Rattle and Roll, Open Clasp* (live theatre and UK tour); *Wagstaffe* (Mercury Theatre); *Paradise* (Sheffield Crucible Theatre); *The Spidermen* (National Theatre, Cottesloe); *Wired* (The Kings Head Theatre); *Blooded* (New Perspectives Theatre Company); and costumes for *Don Juan Comes Back From the War* (The Belgrade Theatre). Joanna is committed to producing exciting new performance design.

NETTIE SCRIVEN 78

Nettie is a theatre designer whose experience spans a wide range of theatre spaces, including main stages, studio theatres, art galleries, arts and community centres, and schools. She represented the UK at the Prague Quadrennial in 1999 with *Best of Friends* (Komedia) and selected to exhibit *Dragon Breath* at the Collaborators: UK Design for Performance 2003–7 at the V&A Museum in 2007.

Productions include *His Dark Materials* (The Curve); *Journey to the River Sea* (Unicorn Theatre and Theatre Centre); *The Secret Garden* (Nottingham Playhouse); *The Snow Spider, Aesop's Fables* (Sherman Theatre); *Plague of Innocence* (1988 Best Young People's Production); *The Lost Child* (Sheffield Crucible); *Hamlet* (Contact Theatre); *One for Sorrow* (Hijinx Theatre). Her most recent productions include a national tour of *Loving April*, by Giles Croft, for Oxfordshire Touring Company (2010) and *Broken Hearted*, by Lucy Gannon, for Derby Theatre (2010).

She is co-founder and director of Dragon Breath Theatre, which creates epic, visual theatre for young people, with professional artists working alongside scientists, teachers and young people. Most recently *Cosmos* (2009), a collaboration with Curve Leicester, brought the wonders of astronomy to very young children through immersive theatre. Short listing for awards includes ACE/THES Excellence & Innovation (2007); ACE/Brain Way/Theatre Centre Young People's Writing 2005, 2008 and 2010; and Nottingham Creative Business Awards 2010.

FABRICE SERAFINO   66

Fabrice's theatre experience includes 15 years as a dancer in different renowned companies throughout Europe. In September 2004, he retired from dancing and attended the Motley Theatre Design Course. Since then, he has been successfully working as a set and costume designer.

Fabrice has designed some productions for the Almeida Theatre, the Nuffield Theatre in Southampton, the Stephen Joseph Theatre in Scarborough, LAMDA, the Theatre Royal Stratford East, the Norwich Playhouse, Theatre503, Southwark Playhouse, the Oval House, the Linbury Studio, Royal Opera House, Rambert Dance Company, Protein Dance and Bare Bones Dance Company, among many others.

www.fabriceserafino.com

ASHLEY SHAIRP   34

Ashley trained in theatre design at Trent Polytechnic, Nottingham. His first professional design job was with Michael Boyd at The Tron, Glasgow, in 1986. He was the associate designer at The Dukes, Lancaster, where designs included When I Was a Girl I Used To Scream and Shout, Look Back In Anger, several pantomimes and the outdoor promenades The Adventures of King Arthur and Twelfth Night.

Freelance work includes designs all over the country, with sustained working relationships with Everyman, Liverpool, Ludus Dance Company, Cheltenham Everyman, Bolton Octagon and director Ian Forrest.

He designed Angels in America at Unity, Liverpool, and at the same address devised, designed and performed a puppet performance, Front Window, with partner Sam Heath. An exhibit based on this show was shown as part of the design exhibition Collaborators in Nottingham and at the V&A. Recent design work includes A Midsummer Night's Dream for Bolton Octagon with David Thacker.

He is the course leader for theatre and performance design at The Liverpool Institute for Performing Arts (LIPA).

RAJHA SHAKIRY   119

Rajha was born in Iraq and educated in England. After an honours degree in mathematics and five years in marketing, she re-trained in theatre design, graduating from Wimbledon School of Art in 2003. Rajha has since worked as a freelance theatre designer, with extensive experience in small, middle and touring productions.

Her stage and costume designs have included Muhammad Ali and Me (Oval House Theatre, London); Safe, Feeble Minds and Angina Monologues (for Spare Tyre at Tara Arts, the Albany and Rich Mix); Krunch (Talawa and National Arts Festival, South Africa); Lincoln Road and The Lion and the Unicorn (Eastern Angles); Speak (Theatre Royal Stratford East, London, and LIFT Festival); Moj of the Antarctic, an African Odyssey (Lyric Studio Hammersmith, Oval House Theatre and a British Council tour of Southern Africa); A Night at the Theatre (touring for Theatre Royal, Bury St Edmunds); Visible (Cardboard Citizens at Contact Theatre, Manchester, Everyman, Liverpool and Soho Theatre, London); Goblin Market (Sydmonton Festival and Southwark Playhouse); King, The Wall, Changes and Love Wars (Cardboard Citizens); Don Giovanni and Le Nozze di Figaro operas (Beauforthuis, Holland). Rajha has recently performed as a member of the Skills Ensemble in Philip Glass's Satyagraha (Improbable and English National Opera, London Coliseum).

www.rajhashakiry.co.uk

NICKY SHAW   119

Nicky trained at West Sussex and West Surrey colleges of art and design.

Work includes, for opera, Alcina and The Coronation of Poppea (OTC); Iolanta (Opera Holland Park); the sets for The World's Stage Gala, Royal Opera House; The Bartered Bride and Don Giovanni (Mid Wales Opera); Songs of Li Po, Phaedra and Savitri (Aldeburgh Festival); The Cunning Little Vixen and Semele (Queen Elizabeth Hall, and as costume designer); The Rape of Lucretia, Il Viaggio a Reims, Il Prigioniero/Volo di Notte and La Cenerentola (all for Frankfurt Opera); La Cenerentola (Opera Zuid); Medea (Reisopera); Macbeth (Theatre Royal de la Monnaie, Brussels); the world premiere of Scoring a Century (Birmingham Conservatoire).

For theatre: Picasso's Women (Seoul Arts Festival); Some People I Know (Teatergarasjen, Bergen); The Lifeblood and Broken Journey (Hen & Chickens); Anyroad (Bridewell); Take the Fire (Lyric Studio, Hammersmith); The Power of Darkness (Orange Tree); The Revenger's Tragedy (The Orange Tree Room); La Nuit de Valognes and Woyzeck (The Other Place, RSC).

The musicals: The Fantasticks (Duchess Theatre, costumes); the world premiere of Dancing Shadows (Seoul, South Korea, winner of five Korean Musical Awards, including Best Musical); and Eating Raoul (Bridewell).

For film and television: The Assessments (short film, art director/costume designer); The Score (BBC 2, studio set and title sequence); The Empress (Channel 4, associate set designer to artist Bruce McLean).

Nicky has also worked as a design consultant to fashion designer and businessman Jasper Conran.

JULIET SHILLINGFORD   129

Juliet trained at Ravensbourne and Croydon colleges of art, obtaining a degree in fine art, specialising in sculpture, and a diploma in theatre design. She was awarded an Arts Council bursary and since then has designed over 90 professional productions ranging from small scale tours to large musicals.

Most recently she designed The Lieutenant of Inishmore and The Long Road (Curve, Leicester); also The Pillowman, which was the first production in the Curve studio space after it opened in 2008. She has a long association with the Nuffield Theatre, Southampton, and its artistic director Patrick Sandford, working on a number of new plays and classic texts; most recently She Stoops to Conquer, The House of Bernada Alba, Betrayal, Playboy of the Western World and Peeler, a new play commissioned by the Hampshire Police Force. Recent productions for New Perspectives are Faith Healer, Gawain and the Green Knight and The Hired Man, which also formed part of the 2008 Brits Off-Broadway Festival at 59E59 in New York. Current projects for autumn 2010 are Dolly, a new musical for New Perspectives, and Translations and Molly Sweeney for Curve, Leicester.

Juliet has exhibited with the SBTD several times: her design for School For Wives was chosen to form part of the British entry for Prague Quadrennial 2007 which, together with the model for Don Quixote, formed part of Collaborators: UK Design for Performance at the V&A, 2007–8.

RACHAEL A SMITH   35

Prior to studying at Bristol Old Vic Theatre School Rachael worked at BAC where, alongside design, she gained experience as a producer, production manager, assistant director and performer. The first show she designed there, an Audience With Adrienne, went on to be nominated for a Total Theatre Award.

Rachael developed a passion for intimate and interactive performance through working with Kazuko Hohki (Oh Doh, Chelsea Theatre) and site-sympathetic company Punchdrunk (Faust, Red Death, Tunnel 228) and transformed BAC's attic space into a bedroom for Bedtime Stories.

She enjoys the challenge of designing for both non-theatre and theatre spaces, and uses her experience of one to inform the other, through consideration of the audience's role, level of participation and distortion of expectation. While believing in pursuing a bold aesthetic, she always aims to remain true to the text.

Since graduating her design work includes What Every Woman Knows (Finborough Theatre); the musical Bernada Alba (Blackheath Halls); Faces in the Window (a tour devised by the 50+ group at the Arcola Theatre); and Iago (Edinburgh Festival, winner of Fringe Review Third Outstanding Theatre Award).

She assisted Ultz for Falstaff at Glyndebourne and was assistant designer for The Lost World at Bristol Old Vic, where she also designed and co-produced the Bristol Shakespeare Project.

With Coney, a collaborative company that fuses theatre and pervasive gaming, she co-created and designed adventures at the Science Museum, BAC, Tate Britain and a nationwide schools project.

Rachael is a National Theatre design associate and part of the Young Vic Genesis Project.

YOLANDA SONNABEND   35, 70

Yolanda studied painting and theatre design at the Slade School of Fine Art. Her many credits include, for The Royal Ballet, A Blue Rose (Peter Wright); L'Invitation au Voyage (Michael Corder); for Kenneth MacMillian, Symphony, Rituals, Valley of Shadows, Requiem, Playground, Different Drummer and My Brother, My Sisters (BRB); Anthony Dowell's Swan Lake and costumes for Natalia Makarova's La Bayadere. She has designed The Nutcracker (Strasbourg); Cinderella (Lisbon); Five Ruckert Songs for Rambert Dance Company; Swan Lake (K-Ballet Tokyo) and recently design collaborations with Leslie Travers on Le Corsaire and The Nutcracker; and with Matt Deely on Beethoven's Symphony No.9 and Romeo and Juliet, all for K-Ballet Tokyo. Her theatre design includes Camino Real and Anthony and Cleopatra for the RSC. She lectured at the Slade School's theatre department and was made a Fellow of UCL. Her paintings have been exhibited, having had solo exhibitions at the Whitechapel and Serpentine galleries, and her portraits are represented at the National Portrait Gallery.

GEORGE SOUGLIDES   91

Born in Cyprus and educated in Greece and England, George studied 3D design at Kingston University and theatre design at the Motley Theatre Design Course. He has designed internationally for theatre and opera. In Europe he has worked at the Bregenz Festival (Offenbach's Barbe Bleue); Salzburg Festival and Rome Opera (Otello); the Malmö Opera (Salome); the Greek National Opera (Serse, Orphée et Euridice, Elisir D'Amore, Il Prigioniero and the world premiere of The Possessed); Nationale Reisopera in The Netherlands (Arianna in Creta, Der Freischütz); and at many important British venues: Grange Park Opera (Maria Stuarda, The Marriage of Figaro, The Barber of Seville); the Aldeburgh Festival (A Midsummer Night's Dream); the Buxton Festival (Semele); and Scottish Opera (Aida, Così Fan Tutte). In the United States his work has appeared at the Lyric Opera of Chicago (La Damnation de Faust) and Chicago Opera Theater (the acclaimed production of The Flowering Tree by John Adams). His theatre work has been seen at the Epidaurus Festival (Peace and The Acharnians by Aristophanes); the National Theatre of Northern Greece (Le Bourgeois Gentillhomme, Arcadia); the Gate Theatre, London (Lady Aoi by Mishima); Ilisia Theatre, Athens (The Misunderstanding); the Curve Theatre (The Light in the Piazza); and most recently at the Chichester Festival (42nd Street). In June 2010 he had a solo exhibition of his work at the Mediatheque in Uzes, France (Le Fil d'Arianne).

He was a member of the Greek design team at the Prague Quadrennial of scenography in 2007 and was also part of the exhibition of British theatre design at the Victoria & Albert Museum.

MICHAEL SPENCER 58

Michael has been designing in the professional theatre for over 20 years since graduating from the Wimbledon School of Art in 1983. The range of his work incorporates community theatre, commercial touring, repertory theatre – featuring a long collaboration with director Andrew Manley – and opera. Highlights include an infamous *Marriage of Figaro* for the Welsh National Opera and three British premieres of David Mamet adaptations of Chekhov plays: *The Cherry Orchard, Uncle Vanya* and *Three Sisters*.

In 1991 he returned to the Wimbledon School of Art to become the first person in the UK to receive an MA in Theatre Design, which then became the catalyst for a teaching career alongside continuing professional practice. He has been course director of what is now the BA Performance Design & Practice course (formally BA Theatre Design) at Central Saint Martins College of Art and Design for the past decade, over which time the course has broadened its remit to reflect both expanding applications of the discipline and a changing student agenda, incorporating interdisciplinary practices.

Michael's own practice reflects this shift. Recent commissions include a site specific *Attempts on Her Life* (Crimp) at a disused gas utilities building in Colorado Springs, and the design and performance of a pure maths paper, *The Anatomy of Integers and Permutations*, for the Institute of Advanced Study at Princeton University.

He has presented at two USITT conferences and was a UK representative at the recent OISTAT symposium in Moscow, as well as giving a presentation of his devised performance *Variation, Verification and Vindication* at the recent Prague Quadrennial 2011 Expanding Scenography symposium in Riga, Latvia.

As a member of the executive committee of the Associated Courses in Theatre Design (ACTD) Michael has been heavily involved in two recent ACTD conferences and the UK schools exhibit for the last three PQs. He has written articles for the ACTD's *Sightline* magazine, SBTD's *Blue Pages* and BBC *Vision* magazine.

HAYLEY SPICER 79

Hayley originally studied fashion design at the University of Gloucestershire and was a manager of a costumiers for several years before studying postgraduate theatre design at the Royal Welsh College of Music and Drama, graduating in 2002. Since then she has worked on a number of shows as a set and costume designer, costume supervisor, and costume- and prop-maker. Design work includes *The Firebird* and *Big Sister, Little Brother* (Oxford Touring Theatre Company and Pride of Place Festival); *The Dawn Treader, Skellig, The Government Inspector, Our Day Out, Shirley Valentine, We'll Meet Again, The Silver Sword*, and *The Rotten Plot* (Everyman Theatre, Cheltenham); and *Our Country's Good, The Little Mermaid and Other Stories* (Salisbury Playhouse). As well as designing, Hayley works as a freelance workshop leader for schools and youth groups, teaching arts activities. She also trained as a make-up artist and works around the country as a make-up artist and teacher.

ZOE SQUIRE 123

Zoe graduated from Bristol Old Vic Theatre School in 2008 in set and costume design and has previous experience in set- and prop-making for theatre and films. She is the co-artistic director/ designer for Pins and Needles Productions.

Other design credits include *Sun Trap* (Gala Theatre); *Tartuffe* (Circomedia); *A Month in the Country, The Elves and the Shoemaker* (Tobacco Factory); *A Clockwork Orange* (Alma Tavern); The Shakespeare Project; *The Lost World: The Impossible Play* (Bristol Old Vic Theatre); *James and the Giant Peach, The Witches* and *Beasts and Beauties* (The Egg, Theatre Royal Bath). Zoe has also designed for companies in both the UK and Germany, including Travelling Light Theatre Company, White Horse Theatre Company and Gromito Theatre Company. She has worked on several feature films including Fox Films' latest, *Fantastic Mr Fox*, and *Hush* (WarpX), and designed both music videos and mainstream commercials.

Zoe was selected to represent the UK for the 2009 Next Generation Programme at the Augbik Mal Festival of Theatre in Berlin and is a member of the Young Vic Genesis designer project.

BEN STONES 60

Ben trained in stage design at Central Saint Martins College of Art and Design and went on to win a Linbury Prize commission to design *Paradise Lost* for Rupert Goold.

Designs include *Creditors, Kiss of the Spider Woman* (Donmar Warehouse); *Beautiful Thing* (Sound Theatre, Leicester Square); *When Five Years Pass* (Arcola Theatre); *Humble Boy, Paradise Lost, Someone Who'll Watch Over Me, Just Between Ourselves* (Theatre Royal, Northampton); *Paradise Lost* (Headlong Theatre); *The Arab Israeli Cookbook* (Tricycle Theatre); *The Mighty Boosh, Mitchell & Webb Live!* (Phil McIntyre national tour); *The Vegemite Tales* (The Venue, Leicester Square); *The Herbal Bed, The Real Thing* (Salisbury Playhouse); *A Taste of Honey, Salt* (Royal Exchange, Manchester); *Romeo and Juliet* (Shakespeare's Globe); *My Mother Said I Never Should* (Watford Palace Theatre); *My Dad's a Birdman* (Sheffield Crucible); *Speaking in Tongues* (Duke of Yorks, West End); *Ingredient X* (Royal Court Theatre Upstairs); *No Idea* (Improbable Theatre, Young Vic); *Doctor Faustus* (Royal Exchange); *Lower Ninth* (Donmar Trafalgar Season); *An Enemy of the People* (Sheffield Crucible); and *Creditors* (Harvey Theatre, Bam, New York).

AMANDA STOODLEY 71

Amanda trained at LIPA and graduated in 2009 with a first class honours degree in theatre and performance design. She previously studied and worked in illustration, graphic and interior design.

Credits through LIPA include costume design for *Kindertransport* (Unity Theatre, Liverpool); set design for *Angels in America, Part One: Millennium Approaches* and co-costume design for Edward Bond's *Lear*. She worked as design assistant to Liz Ascroft for *Three Sisters* (Royal Exchange Theatre, Manchester) and *Faith Healer* (Sydney Festival) and also created puppets and props with Jo Pocock and at Robert Allsopp & Associates.

Latest projects at the Royal Exchange Theatre include co-designer for *Pub*, designer/curator for *Making an Exhibition of Ourselves* (At Home), assistant designer for *Blithe Spirit* and costume assistant for *1984*.

Other recent work includes design for the Everyword Festival's *Wish You Were Here* (Liverpool Everyman); co-design with Kevin Pollard for Spike Theatre's *Top of the World* (on tour); design assistant to Liz Ascroft for *Lucia di Lammermoor* (Grand Opera Houston) and *Canary* (Liverpool Playhouse); design assistant to Morgan Large for *Cat on a Hot Tin Roof* (Novello Theatre); and design assistant to Becs Andrews for Ballet Bern's *Momo* (Stadttheater, Bern).

Amanda is currently designing the *Four Corners* exhibition at Bluecoat Arts Centre, Liverpool, and *Winterlong*, a new play by Andrew Sheridan directed by Sarah Frankcom, for the Royal Exchange Studio.

NANCY SURMAN 88

Nancy's recent work includes *The Corstorphine Road Nativity* (adapted from *The Flint Street Nativity* by Tim Firth for the Festival Theatre, Edinburgh); *The Daughter-in-Law* and *Dangerous Corner* (New Vic Theatre, Stoke-on-Trent); an outdoor production of *Animal Farm* (The Old Prison Yard, Oxford); and *Can't Pay? Won't Pay!* (Oldham Coliseum).

She designed the world premieres of *Get Ken Barlow* (Watford Palace Theatre); *The Swing of Things* (Stephan Joseph Theatre, Scarborough) and *A Stinging Sea* (Glasgow Citizens Theatre); also the stage premieres of Hanif Kureishi's *The Buddha of Suburbia* and *My Beautiful Laundrette* (SNAP Theatre Company).

Her touring work includes major national tours of *Dad's Army* and *'Allo 'Allo* (Calibre Productions); *Aspects of Love* and *Noel and Gertie* (Gordon Craig Theatre, Stevenage); a Far East tour of Noel Coward's *Private Lives*; and tours of *The Road to Hell* and *Johnny Watkins Walks on Water* (Birmingham Repertory Theatre).

Other productions include designs for *Indian Ink, To Kill a Mockingbird, The Waters of the Moon, The Duchess of Malfi, The Rivals* and *The Winter's Tale* (Salisbury Playhouse); *The Accrington Pals* (Dukes Theatre, Lancaster); *Private Lives* (Bolton Octagon); and *The Final Appearance of Miss Mamie Stuart* (Torch Theatre, Milford Haven).

Nancy designed Maxim Gorky's *Barbarians* (Salisbury Playhouse), for which she was nominated for the TMA Best Designer award 2003.

TAKIS 100

Takis studied stage design at the National University of Arts in Bucharest, the Royal Academy of Dramatic Art and is currently finishing his practice-based PhD at London College of Fashion.

During his studies he has assisted at the Royal Opera House, the opera festival of Rome, the Greek National Opera and the Megaron-Athens Concert Hall.

His work has been seen in around 60 productions worldwide in various indoor and outdoor venues. He is designer in residence for HighTide, which recently produced the very successful *Stovepipe* in collaboration with the National Theatre, and *Ditch* with Old Vic. He is also the artistic director of his own company, called Artluxe, which produces installation and performance art.

Theatre includes *Ditch* (Old Vic/HighTide); *Lidless* (HighTide and Edinburgh Festival); *The Early Bird* (Finborough Theatre/Project Art Centre, Dublin); *Signs of a Star-Shaped Diva* (Theatre Royal Stratford East and national tour); *Stovepipe* (National Theatre/ HighTide); *The Marriage Bed* (Hong Kong/New York); *Invasion* (Soho Theatre); *I Caught Crabs in Walberswick* (Bush Theatre and Edinburgh Festival); *Scenes from the Big Picture* (RADA); *Crazy Lady* (Drill Hall and Contact Theatre, Manchester).

Installations include *Forgotten Peacock* (Design Museum/ The Brunswick); *Goldfish* (Paris Fashion Week); mythological installation *Oedipus* (Bucharest Museum of Contemporary Art); visual performance in *Baroque Spirit* (Venice Carnival).

Music performances include *A Tale of Two Cities* (Theatre Royal, Brighton); Maria Callas: *Vissi d'Arte, Vissi d'Amore* (Barbican); *Choruses* (Epidaurus Festival/Frankfurt Old Opera House); *In the Light of the Night* (Epidaurus Festival); Nikos Skalkotas (Queen Elizabeth Hall).

www.takis.info

SHEREE TAMS 62

Sheree was born in South Wales. She studied art and environmental design in art college, followed by post graduate studies at Motley in London. She has exhibited art installations, video and photography in several solo and group shows. She has worked on a wide range of design projects, differing in scale, budget and content; most recently, devised theatre, site-specific events, a season of theatre for the elderly, theatre for young audiences, theatre-in-education, theatre of the oppressed, music theatre, experimental theatre, exhibition design, dance and opera. A passion for travel and art has taken her all over the world, which contributes to her global design perspective. She has designed productions in the United States, Canada, the UK and continental Europe.

www.shereetams.co.uk

STUART TARGETT 121

Whilst studying biochemistry at Oxford, Stuart was, for four years, the sole student designer at the Oxford Playhouse.

In 1995 Stuart attended Mountview Academy of Theatre Arts, London, on their technical theatre course, where he designed a triple bill of Sam Shepard plays and *The Bitter Tears of Petra Von Kant*.

Stuart went on to work in London's fringe theatre, including designing the world premiere of Nell Dunn's *Babe XXX*. He was then selected for the Motley Theatre Design Course, during which he produced the designs for a devised project for the ENO's Baylis Programme.

Since graduating from Motley, Stuart has worked mainly in the operatic world, designing sets and costumes for productions including *The Marriage of Figaro, The Barber of Seville, Così Fan Tutte, Don Giovanni, Dido and Aeneas, The Wandering Scholar, La Bohème, La Cenerentola, La Voix Humaine, Socrates, Rigoletto, Madam Butterfly, Aida, The Rake's Progress, Trouble in Tahiti, The Bear, Samson, The Pirates of Penzance* and *Iolanthe*. He has also designed for the opera scenes at Birmingham Conservatoire.

Although Stuart's focus has been on opera, he has designed costumes for *The Witch of Edmonton* (Southwark Playhouse), set and costumes for *Hermes the Musical* (Rosemary Branch) and costumes for *Spring Awakening* (Italia Conti). He has also recently been designing and making costumes for the competitive dancesport world.

IAN TEAGUE 78

Ian trained in theatre design at what was then Trent Polytechnic (now Nottingham Trent University), graduating in 1982. Best known for small-scale touring and educational theatre with such companies as Oxfordshire Touring, MakeBelieve Arts and the National Theatre Education Department, his design projects also include main house rep shows, community plays, and site-specific work.

He is a regular guest lecturer at London Metropolitan University. He has also developed and delivered a number of projects in schools and INSET training for teachers with MakeBelieve Arts and The Mousetrap Foundation.

Ian is the chair of the managing committee of the SBTD and represents the society on the board of SkillScene. He is also a member of the Equity Theatre Designers' Committee.

His designs for small-cast productions of Shakespeare formed part of the British Golden Triga-winning entry at PQ2003.

THEATREPLAN 24

Richard Brett, Roger Fox, Peter Ruthven Hall, Dave Ludlam, Clive Odom, John Whitaker, Matt Atwood, Neil Morton, Mathew Smethurst-Evans, Robin Townley, Lizzie Cheeld, Cathy Dulin and Neville Ware.

Theatreplan is a world-renowned specialist consultancy providing advisory and design services to performing arts companies, venue managements, architects, project managers and engineers. We specialise in creating theatres, opera houses and music venues, places for events and education facilities in existing and listed buildings, found spaces and new structures. We offer a wide range of theatre planning and technical design services based on our experience of projects worldwide and our knowledge of future expectations.

Theatreplan's experienced team includes theatre practitioners, architects, technicians and venue managers. Working with clients and architects, we contribute practical detail to every project. From initial concepts to detailed plans and specifications, we deliver a tailored service to ensure well-functioning stages, practical backstage facilities, comfortable auditoria and excellent audience circulation areas.

Recent and current projects include: Copenhagen Operaen; Classical Theatre for Opera and Ballet, Astana; Parco della Musica e della Cultura di Firenze, Nuovo Auditorium; Hampstead Theatre; Dunstable Grove Theatre; Inverness Eden Court Theatres Cinemas and Studios; Genexis Theatre at Singapore's Fusionpolis, Singapore School of the Arts; Belfast Lyric Theatre; Benenden School Theatre; and refurbishment work at the Sydney Opera House, Royal Opera House, Watford Palace Theatre, Leeds Grand Theatre, Barking Broadway Theatre, Kingston College Theatre, Barbican Theatre, Sheffield Crucible Theatre and Studio.
www.theatreplan.co.uk

EMMA THOMPSON 106

Emma graduated from UCE in 2001. Now working as a freelance designer, Emma has worked with small- to mid-scale touring, site-specific and TIE companies, as well as a facilitator for arts projects in schools and educational workshops. Emma has also worked on numerous shows as prop-maker and scenic artist. She became resident designer for macYouth Theatre in 2004.

Recent theatre credits include Singer, Chicken Soup With Barley and Fear and Misery of The Third Reich (macYouth Theatre); Henry V (Maverick Theatre Company); Blood Knot and Days of Hope (Mac Productions); The Devil's Doctor (Shifting Sands Theatre Company); Echoes and Under the Influence (Gazebo TIE).

JOHANNA TOWN 77

Shortlisted for Best Lighting Designer for Speaking In Tongues (WhatsOnStage Awards 2010).

Johanna began her lighting career at the Royal Exchange Theatre in the 1980s and then became resident head of lighting at the Liverpool Playhouse, followed by the Royal Court Theatre, for whom she has designed over 50 productions, including The Kitchen, Rhinoceros, Shopping and Fucking, The Steward of Christendom, My Name Is Rachel Corrie.

Johanna has worked extensively in theatre and opera throughout the world. Her most recent work includes Speaking in Tongues (Duke of York's); Fat Pig (Comedy Theatre); That Face (Sheffield Crucible); Pride and Prejudice (UK tour); For King and Country (UK tour); To Kill a Mocking Bird, The Hounding of David Oluwale (West Yorkshire Playhouse, UK tour); The Tragedy of Thomas Hobbes (RSC); A Raisin in the Sun, The Glass Menagerie, Haunted, All the Ordinary Angels (Royal Exchange); In Praise of Love (Chichester); Les Liaisons Dangereuses, The Herbal Bed (Salisbury Playhouse); Guantanamo (Broadway/West End/Tricycle); Llwyth (Sherman).

For Out of Joint: Dreams of Violence, The Permanent Way, The Overwhelming, O Go My Man and Talking To Terrorists.

Opera credits include Carmen, Kátya Kabanová, Cinderella, The Secret Marriage (Scottish Opera); Phaedra and Ariadne auf Naxos, War and Peace (RSAMD); Giustino (Trinity College of Music); The Marriage of Figaro (Classical Opera Company); Othello, The Marriage of Figaro (Nice Opera House)

MAYOU TRIKERIOTI 65

Mayou is a set and costume designer. In the past ten years she has designed more than 40 productions for a diverse group of directors and spaces, both in Greece and the UK.

In 2004 she also started working as a production and costume designer for film, and has since designed two features and various short films, many of which have won awards in international film festivals.

Mayou has also been teaching stage design for beginners in a private graduate school in Greece, and has had her work exhibited in design exhibitions in Toronto, London, Sheffield, Athens and Prague and included in publications both in Greece and the UK.

She holds a BA(Hons) in drama and theatre studies from the University of Kent and a first class postgraduate diploma in theatre design from the Bristol Old Vic Theatre School.
www.mayoutrikerioti.com

JACQUELINE TROUSDALE 91

Jacqueline grew up in Newcastle-upon-Tyne and gained a degree in fine art at Reading University, then began designing for the stage at the Mercury Theatre Colchester. Designs included A Taste of Honey, Look Back in Anger, Loot and When I Was a Girl I Used to Scream and Shout. Jacqueline joined the Belgrade Theatre Coventry designing productions for the main stage and studio, including Kiss of the Spiderwoman, It's a Girl and Cinderella (costume). She spent two years as resident designer at Oldham Coliseum Theatre. Designs included Romeo and Juliet, and La Ronde, the latter being nominated for a MEN design award.

Jacqueline became freelance. Having two children led her to become interested in children's literature. She has designed many productions for younger audiences and was asked to art direct the theatrical events that took place in the gardens of Buckingham Palace for The Queen's 80th birthday, celebrating the great names in children's literature. Jacqueline's most recent productions for The Birmingham Stage Company have included Skellig, touring to New York in the spring of 2011, Roald Dahl's George's Marvellous Medicine, and stage adaptations of Scholastic's Horrible series, the latest being Horrible Science. This production involved close design collaboration with Amazing Interactives 3D animation company to engage, educate and entertain young audiences through the latest technology.

KATE UNWIN 63

Kate has worked as a freelance set and costume designer for ten years. Highlights include FIB for Metro-Boulot-Dodo, Girls' Night national tour 2010 (Goodnights Entertainment); A Christmas Carol in Wormwood Scrubs Prison (Only Connect); The Book of Everything (National Theatre Connections); The African Company Presents Richard III (Collective Artistes), Godspell number one tour (Oftrot Productions); Animal Farm (Derby Playhouse); Hot Stuff, To Kill a Mockingbird, An Ideal Husband, Macbeth, The Cripple of Inishmaan, all for Leicester Haymarket Theatre, where Kate worked extensively, designing for the main stage, studio and foyer spaces.

Other collaborations include working with disabled theatre company Movers, Heartbreak Productions, Playbox Theatre, R J Williamson Shakespeare Company, Phizzical Productions, Creation Theatre, The Castle in Wellingborough and Northampton Theatres.

Site-specific and installation work includes C-Attack in Great Yarmouth (Dende Collective), Special Olympic Village, Streetstyle Sportstyle exhibition, a transformed shopping unit for Leicester Highcross opening weekend and a solo project celebrating the life of Joe Orton.

Art direction for music video includes work for Scouting For Girls, Iglu and Hartley, Leo Ihenacho, Example and Lil' Chris.
www.kateunwin.co.uk

JAMIE VARTAN 107

Jamie has worked extensively as a designer in opera, theatre and dance in the UK and Europe, and has represented the UK at the Prague Quadrennial in 1999 and 2007.

Designs for opera include Ariadne auf Naxos (Salzburg Festspielhaus); The Queen of Spades (La Scala, Milan); Albert Herring and Death in Venice (Salzburg Landestheater); Don Giovanni, Romeo et Juliette (Varna); Manon Lescaut (Teatro Regio, Parma); A Village Romeo and Juliet, Aida and Carmen (Premio Abbiati Award for Best Production 2006, Teatro Lirico di Cagliari, Sardinia); La Statira (Teatro San Carlo, Naples); Der Zwerg (Teatro Comunale, Florence, and Teatro Regio, Turin); La Traviata (Malmö Opera, Sweden); Manon (English Touring Opera); La Vestale (Wexford); May Night (Garsington); Il Pirata and The Saint of Bleecker Street (Opera Marseille); and A Village Romeo and Juliet (Royal Opera House).

Designs for theatre include several productions at the National Theatre of Ireland (The Abbey and Peacock theatres), including The Playboy of the Western World, and Mrs Warren's Profession (nomination for Irish Times Theatre Awards Best Production). He was involved for three years as designer and artist-in-residence with the David Glass Ensemble on The Lost Child Trilogy, with residencies in Vietnam, Indonesia, China, the Philippines and Colombia. The trilogy was later presented at the Young Vic, and he created an installation at the October Gallery, London, based on the work from the overseas residencies.

Design for dance with choreographer Darshan Singh Bhuller includes Requiem for Phoenix Dance Company (Sadlers Wells and UK tour) and Recall (Linbury Studio and UK tour).

JANET VAUGHAN 126

Janet is a visual artist and designer who has designed site-specific and touring film and theatre works, and created installation artworks for unusual and digital spaces. She often works in collaboration with other artists or members of the public on residency-based projects and uses a variety of media to create her work, much of which is concerned with (often temporary) site-specific art for public spaces as part of capital development initiatives or artist-led regeneration of the built environment.

Janet's work can be characterised as creative investigation of people and places, concerned with collecting and re-appropriating memories, artefacts and opinions, making playful connections and concocting plausible fictions as the means of informing and framing her responses to spaces. She is one third of Coventry's acclaimed Talking Birds, and creator of the company's webworks, including [helloland*]; described by The Independent as "innovative and unusual... akin to taking part in a David Lynch movie". www.vornster.co.uk twitter: @vornster

ADRIAN VAUX   86

Adrian studied design at the Slade School. House designer at London's Mermaid Theatre 1964–70. House designer at Leicester Phoenix, and subsequently at the Haymarket, 1971–80. Designed many productions during this time, some of which transferred to the West End, including *My Fair Lady*, *Cause Celèbre* and *Tomfoolery*. House designer at the Old Vic, 1980–2. Credits include *The Merchant of Venice* and *The Relapse*. He began working in Israel in 1986, designing productions for Habimah, Cameri, Haifa and Jerusalem theatres. Association with Sobol began with original productions of Weininger's *Night*, *Ghetto*, *Palestinian Girl*, *Adam*, *Jerusalem Syndrome* and *Nice Toni*. This association led to his working in Germany and United States. Many of these productions raised highly controversial issues, both political and social, such as the great silence surrounding discussions of the Holocaust, and the Israeli/Palestinian conflict.

Recent credits include a US tour of *Miss Saigon*, a US tour of *Oliver!* and, more recently, a UK tour of *Miss Saigon* followed by the Tam Tour of *Miss Saigon* to South East Asia and Australia. All tours were co-produced by Big League, Networks and Cameron Mackintosh respectively. Most recently designed *August, Osage County* for Habima.

MAIRA VAZEOU   86

Maira trained at the Central School of Speech and Drama.

Work includes *The Three Princesses* (Theatre Organisation of Cyprus); *I'm a Minger* (Belgrade Theatre, Coventry); *Chutney* (Greenwich & Docklands International Festival); *Antigone* (Riverside Studios); *Guernica* (National Theatre, Athens); *Velvet Scratch* (Edinburgh, New York and Prague Festivals); *Live Like Pigs* (Embassy Theatre); *Fresh Meat, Canaries Sometimes Sing, Told You So* (Courtyard Theatre); *The Lion of Punjab* (Watermans Theatre); *Ghosts* (Stavros Tou Notou, Athens); *Hand in Glove*, *I Just Broke Up* (White Bear); the educational documentaries *Stonehenge Rediscovery* (National Geographic Documentary), *Schiller* and *Eumenides* (for national Greek and German television).

As assistant designer Maira has worked on *Falstaff*, *Alchina*, *A Midsummers Night's Dream* and *The Marriage of Figaro* (all for English Touring Opera).

FIONA WATT   29

Fiona trained with Motley at the Almeida. She enjoys exploring the relationship between existing architecture and the performance space, unlocking the hidden dynamics within traditional and non-traditional theatre spaces to find the strongest points of exchange between performer and audience.

Selected credits include, for the Traverse, *Outlying Islands* (Fringe First, transferring to Royal Court and World Stages Festival, Toronto); *The Trestle at Pope Lick Creek, Heritage* and *Highland Shorts, The Almond and the Seahorse* (Sherman Cymru); *The Beauty Queen of Leenane* (Best Production, Manchester Evening News Awards); *Boston Marriage* (Bolton Octagon); *Further Than the Furthest Thing* (Byre St. Andrews and tour); *Othello* (Nottingham Playhouse).

Using elements of her scenographic process, and collaborating with artists across a range of disciplines, she has devised a series of projects exploring themes of space, time and identity in the shifting urban landscape surrounding her studio in the massive Thames Gateway regeneration zone, enabling members of the local community to interact with this process of change.

She is creative producer (UK) for Créativité sans Frontières, a transnational, intergenerational community company in association with musicians from Dunkerque, France.

In 2011 she is one of six international artists leading *Six Acts*, a site-specific interaction with the city of Prague for Scenofest at the Prague Quadrennial of Performance Design and Space.

Fiona sits on the management committee for SBTD, the Designers' Committee at Equity and is a visiting/guest lecturer at various institutions in the UK.

www.fionawatt.com

IAN WESTBROOK   127

Ian studied theatre design at Nottingham Trent University. For the Lord Delfont Group Ian designed the Lenny Henry, The Nolan Sisters, Cannon & Ball and Dick Emery shows. After seasons at Nottingham Playhouse, Leicester and Theatre Royal Plymouth, Ian became set designer/artist with the Theatre Royal Norwich and, since 1986, Cromer Pavilion's *Seaside Special* summer shows.

Since 1985 his scenery and prop construction company 3D Creations, in Norfolk, have created well over 450 operas, musicals, plays and events that include Sir Peter Hall's *Blithe Spirit* (Savoy Theatre, London); Michael Flatley's *Feet of Flames* (world tour); *Evita* and *Chicago* (Lebanon's amphitheatre); special fire effects for Chichester Festival and Birmingham Stage Company, and English National Opera, London.

Designing the Broadway musical *See Saw* by Cy Colman and Dorothy Fields; and designs for American illusionist David Blaine.

Rock and pop music arena tours for Iron Maiden (five world tours); Robbie Williams; Pete Waterman; Westlife; Blur; The Spice Girls; Peter Gabriel; and *Thomas the Tank Engine* (Disney TV Corporation); Sony Media; five Royal commissions for HM Queen Elizabeth II at the Sandringham Museum; the UK touring and London West End productions of *Proof, The Horrible Histories* and *Treasure Island* for Birmingham Stage Company.

Ian's stage designs hang at The Victoria & Albert Museum in London. Set location work for *Pirates of the Caribbean* (St Thomas Island). For Qdos Entertainments, Ian designed new pantomime productions of *Peter Pan* and *Cinderella* (Bradford's Alhambra Theatre); and new designs for *Sleeping Beauty* (Birmingham Hippodrome), along with *Cinderella* (King's Theatre, Edinburgh), and *Peter Pan* (Aberdeen). Design and build of two new musicals by Jon Conway for the USA.

NAOMI WILKINSON   126

Recent theatre credits include *Alice* (Sheffield Crucible); *Christ Deliver Us* (Abbey Theatre Dublin); *The Fahrenheit Twins* (Barbican Pit Bite 09); *The Last Witch* (Lyceum Theatre, Edinburgh International Festival 09); *Peer Gynt* (Barbican Bite 09, National Theatre of Scotland, awarded Best Design by the Critics' Awards for Theatre in Scotland 2008); *La Dispute* (Abbey Theatre, Dublin); *Cockroach, The Dogstone, Nobody Will Ever Forgive Us* and *Nasty, Brutish and Short* (Traverse Theatre/National Theatre of Scotland); *On Religion* and *Colder Than Here* (Soho Theatre); *Critical Mass* (Almeida Opera); *A Midsummer Night's Dream* (Dundee Rep, awarded Best Design by the Critics' Awards for Theatre in Scotland, 2007); *Casanova, The Firework-Maker's Daughter, I'm a Fool To Want You, A Little Fantasy, Shoot Me in the Heart, I Can't Wake Up, Happy Birthday Mr Deka D, I Weep at My Piano* (all Told By An Idiot); *Don't Look Back* (dreamthinkspeak Total Theatre Award, Edinburgh, 2005).

Designs for dance include *Just for Show* (DV8 Physical Theatre, National Theatre London and international tour); *Glacier* (Tilted Dance, Queen Elizabeth Hall, South Bank Centre, London); *NQR* (Scottish Dance Theatre, UK tour).

LOUISE ANN WILSON   53

Louise Ann is an artist and scenographer working nationally and internationally to create small- and large-scale site-specific performance, and designs for theatre and opera.

She is the artistic director of the Louise Ann Wilson Company, whose inter-disciplinary, site-specific performances explore the relationship between landscape and human life events and make resonant the life experiences of the people and histories of the locality.

The work is created in collaboration with artists and experts from other disciplines and individuals who have local knowledge's and skills. The company's current work focuses on the rural landscape as a place for performance, and involves audiences walking to experience the work. Productions include *Still Life* (2008) and *Jack Scout* (2010), walking-performance works created and performed with Sap Dance at different locations on Morecambe Bay; and *Fissure* (May 2011), a three day walking-performance (above and below ground) in a Yorkshire dale (commissioned by artevents for the Re-Enchantment & Reclamation Project).

Louise was co-artistic director of wilson + wilson (1997–2008), makers of site-specific theatre whose works include *Mulgrave, News from the Seventh Floor, Mapping the Edge* and *House*.

She has also created site-specific productions for Theatre Rites at the Ruhr Triennale, Germany (scenographer and co-director), one-to-one performances in Europe and India; and has designed sets and costumes for Opera North, The Royal Exchange Manchester, Unicorn Theatre, West Yorkshire Playhouse, English Touring Opera and many other companies.

www.louiseannwilson.com   www.wilsonandwilson.org.uk

ANDREW WOOD   81

Andrew studied theatre design at Nottingham Trent Polytechnic and graduated in 1991. He worked as a freelance designer before joining Contact Theatre in Manchester where, over five years, he filled every position in the design department from assistant to associate director (design). Designs for Contact include *Romeo and Juliet, A Midsummer Night's Dream, The Trial, The Mill on the Floss* and six Young Playwrights' Festivals.

Since returning to freelance work, designs include *Nevilles Island, Skylight* and *Blithe Spirit* (Harrogate Theatre); *Cold, Lockerbie 103*, and the Barramundi and True North Festivals (The Ashton Group Contemporary Theatre, Barrow-in-Furness); the Future Tense, Northern Lines and First Draft Festivals (Live Theatre, Newcastle); *Oleanna* and *Cooking with Elvis* (Hull Truck); *52 Degrees South* (Big Theatre at The Imperial War Museum North); and *To You, Love on the Dole* and *Oh, WoT a Lovely War?* (The Lowry Centre, Salford).

Andrew designed *13.1* for Live Theatre as part of the Great North Run Cultural Programme and continues to work as an associate artist for Storytree in West Cumbria.

For over ten years he worked as a lecturer in performance design at The Arden School of Theatre in Manchester and has worked as a visiting lecturer at the University of Manchester, Manchester Metropolitan University, Liverpool Institute of Performing Arts and Salford University.

ELIZABETH WRIGHT   68

Elizabeth trained at Bristol Old Vic Theatre School and the University of Leeds. In 2009 she completed her PhD, an oral history of British theatre design, at Wimbledon College of Art in collaboration with National Life Stories at the British Library Sound Archive.

She began her theatre design career as a trainee at Theatre by the Lake, Cumbria, where she has designed several seasons of studio plays in repertoire. These include *The Birthday Party* by Harold Pinter, *Frozen* by Briony Lavery, *Blue/Orange* by Joe Penhall, *Ghosts* by Henrik Ibsen, *Tramping Like Mad* by Julie McKiernan, *Wallflowering* by Peta Murray, *Kiss of the Spiderwoman* by Manuel Puig and *Not a Game for Boys* by Simon Block. Most recently she has designed *Shining City* by Conor McPherson, *Silence* by Moira Buffini and *The Glass Menagerie* by Tennessee Williams.

Elizabeth's other design work includes *April In Paris* (Haymarket Theatre, Basingstoke); *Macbeth* and *The Maids* (Edinburgh Fringe Festival); set for *Cider with Rosie* (Bristol New Vic Studio); *The Dwarfs* (New Vic Basement); and costumes for *Our Country's Good* (Redgrave Theatre, Bristol). On the London fringe, Elizabeth has designed *Five Kinds of Silence, The Christian Brothers* and *Hedda Gabler*.

Index

Cyngor Celfyddydau Cymru
Arts Council of Wales

Noddir gan
Lywodraeth Cynulliad Cymru
Sponsored by
Welsh Assembly Government

Supported by
The National Lottery®
through the Arts Council of Wales

Cefnogwyd gan
Y Loteri Genedlaethol
trwy Gyngor Celfyddydau Cymru

THE
LINBURY
TRUST

WHITE LIGHT

ShowTex
AMAZING STAGE FABRICS IN MOTION

www.showtex.com

University of the
Arts London
Wimbledon
* *
* *
* *
*
*

Rose Bruford College
of Theatre & Performance

The School of Design, Management and Technical Arts
at Rose Bruford College is delighted to be supporting
the Society of British Theatre Designers in this
significant Exhibition and Catalogue – Transformation &
Revelation 2011. The UK continues to be at the forefront
of developments in design and scenography for live
performance, as well as delivering excellent opportunities for
training and education in this field.

www.bruford.ac.uk

bucks
new university

ROYAL WELSH COLLEGE
OF MUSIC & DRAMA
COLEG BRENHINOL
CERDD A DRAMA CYMRU

The Royal Welsh College of Music & Drama is proud of
the opportunity to support the Society of British Theatre
Designers' national exhibition, Transformation & Revelation.
The college acknowledges the significant contribution that
the work of British designers has given to the performance
industry across the world and the inspiration provided to the
generation of young designers training at the Royal Welsh
College of Music & Drama and across art and drama schools
throughout the UK.